The Idea of Continental Union

THE IDEA OF CONTINENTAL UNION

Agitation for the Annexation of Canada to the United States 1849-1893

DONALD F. WARNER

Published for
The MISSISSIPPI VALLEY
HISTORICAL ASSOCIATION
by the
UNIVERSITY OF KENTUCKY PRESS

Printed in the United States of America by the
Division of Printing, University of Kentucky
Library of Congress Catalog Card No.
60-8516

Preface

The idea of Canadian-American union has persisted since 1775, and many people have worked to achieve such a goal. This study proposes to describe and analyze their efforts. It is not a definitive work, tracing the annexation movement in meticulous detail and year by year. Though it necessarily deals with the general history of Canada and the United States as background, it will not pretend a reinterpretation of those histories except insofar as the agitation for continental union throws a new light of explanation upon them. Its purpose, then, is to present in short compass an overview of the agitation for political union and its basic characteristics—its origins, areas of concentration, and failures—by studying the three periods of its greatest intensity. Earlier books, dealing primarily with other subjects, have scattered and usually incidental references to annexation. This is the only attempt to focus primarily upon that movement and to carry the story of its career through four and a half decades.

The American attempts to wrest Canada from Great Britain during the Revolution and the War of 1812 receive only passing notice in this study, as does annexation activity during the three decades following the Treaty of Ghent. Shortly after the colonies which now form the provinces of the Dominion achieved a large measure of self-government in the late 1840's, agitation arose in their midst to gain admission to the American Union, to effect a marriage by agreement. That was the real beginning of what is known as the continental union movement. From that point this book carries the story to 1893, when persistent failure and growing Canadian nationalism finally settled the question. The so-called agitation of 1911 is not included because it was almost entirely contrived and insincere, a successful attempt by shrewd Americans to frighten Canadians into rejecting the reciprocity agreement of that year.

The continental union movement has usually been quiescent or carried on clandestinely, but on three occasions it burst forth with such compelling vigor that it seemed to threaten the British connection. For the first period, the late 1840's and early 1850's, previous investigations have been used as the basis for this narrative. In the post-Civil War period and the era of the 1880's and early 1890's, secondary works are less numerous and complete, and the account relies upon original materials. Throughout, most of the emphasis of this study has been centered upon the political union movement in Canada, with the American aspect relegated to a supporting role. There are several reasons for this. First, annexationism was much more prominent in the Dominion than in the Republic. Moreover, barring the use of force, which few advocated, the fate of the agitation would be determined by its acceptance or rejection in Canada. The story of the movements in the United States has been treated to some extent in various works and is fairly well known.

This study is beset with that frustration of the historian, the analysis of human motivation. It might seem easy to determine who was and who was not an annexationist. But this is not so. Public support of annexationism in Canada then, like support of the Communist Party in the United States now, was regarded as treason, or tantamount to it. It was a bold Canadian who proclaimed this sentiment, one willing to face social ostracism and economic boycott. Silent supporters of political union probably outnumbered the assertive ones; on the other hand, many persons were falsely accused of being annexationists. The stigmatic quality of the term made it a handy weapon to use against an enemy, particularly in the sensitive area of political life.

Another and contradictory tendency appears. Some Canadians who boldly espoused annexation spoke from policy, not from conviction. This was because union with the United States has always offered Canadians a potential alternative to continued allegiance to the Empire or the Dominion; a dissatisfied Canada had the option of substituting American for British allegiance. Since the British government was responsive to this possibility, Canadians could—and did—use threats of annexation to secure redress of grievances. But this was a two-edged sword. If Canada could use this menace against the British, provinces or groups could use it against the Dominion. Consequently, the historian must suspect piercing cries for annexation. They may have been sincere, or they may have been an attempt to get something from somebody.

It is thus no easy task to assess the strength of annexationism in Canada. How did the silent multitude feel about the issue? Was politician A working for political union with the United States as politician B so shrilly insisted? Was a group calling for annexation really in earnest, or was it trying to frighten Ottawa? The author has walked gingerly to reach conclusions which are tentative at best. Truly, the words of their mouths did not always echo the meditations of their hearts.

Though the actual strength of the movement might be uncertain, there is no doubt that it was a significant dynamic in the history of Canada. A few examples will illustrate this. The Imperial government granted a responsible ministry to its North American colonies lest they seek it as states in the American Union. The specter of annexation also contributed to the creation of the Dominion, when the separate colonies were federated partly to ward off the danger of their being incorporated one by one into the United States, by military force or by economic pressure. Annexationism has stimulated the growth of Canadian nationalism and helped to check the natural tendency of this feeling to erode the sentimental ties with Great Britain. Economically, as well as politically, the pull to the United States affected the course of Canadian development. It was an important cause of two significant events in the economic history of British North America—the Reciprocity Treaty of 1854 and the adoption of the National Policy, or protective tariff, in 1879.

Even yet, it seems, the conscious or subconscious Canadian fear of the absorptive capacity of the United States is not dead. Many have attributed the surprising defeat of the Liberals in recent federal elections partly to a popular protest against policies which encouraged American investment in, and penetration of, the Dominion's economy. Canadians evidently still believe that closer economic ties might generate centripetal political forces.

The effects of the annexation movement in the history of the United States have been less marked but not negligible. Here they serve as an additional witness of historic acquisitive tendencies and of a continuing fear of European land bases in the Western Hemisphere. The attempts to acquire Canada were an expression of the spirit and philosophy of the Monroe Doctrine, the concept of two worlds.

In conclusion, several problems and arbitrary usages of terminology should be explained. *Annexation, political union,* and *continental union* are employed synonymously throughout, though there is a shade of difference between the first two. Annexation implies the absorption of a lesser by a greater power, while political union connotes the joining of equals. Continental union, applied to Canada and the United States, cavalierly ignores the existence of that part of North America south of the Rio Grande.

American readers are apt to be confused by the changes of Canadian geographic terms, and liberties have been taken for the sake of clarity. Canada, where used prior to 1867, signifies present Ontario and Quebec; where used after Confederation, it includes whatever provinces were in the Dominion at the moment. Since the body of the narrative begins in the late 1840's, Canada East and Canada West will be employed to identify respectively present Quebec and Ontario prior to 1867; the earlier terms of Lower and Upper Canada will not be used. British West and Northwest before July, 1870, designated the area between the western boundary of Ontario and the eastern boundary of British Columbia; after the admission of Manitoba, Northwest includes the region between that province and British Columbia.

Contents

Maps

CHAPTER ONE

The Movement for Continental Union in 1849

The movement to join Canada to the United States actually preceded the Declaration of Independence. In the fall of 1775, with the issue of the siege of Boston swinging uncertainly, eleven hundred battle-experienced soldiers were detached from George Washington's army and sent north (with another force from New York) to add the "Fourteenth Colony" to the rebellion. That these troops were sorely needed in the primary campaign in Massachusetts indicates the importance which Americans attached to the possession of Quebec. They had learned well the lessons of their geography and their brief history. The settlements in the St. Lawrence Valley had been a constant threat to American security in the Anglo-French wars. In the hands of Great Britain, with her seapower, the dark menace of the north had increased. For Quebec was not only a base but a gate which opened into the vitals of the northern colonies. The Richelieu River, flowing into the St. Lawrence, led to Lake Champlain and the Hudson River valley, together constituting a lowland thrust through the Appalachians, whose ramparts elsewhere guarded the American colonies. If this vestibule fell into British hands, the colonies would be split and the Revolution perhaps doomed. Survival could depend upon plugging this vulnerable gap by seizing its northern entry, the St. Lawrence Valley. The invading American forces, however, broke themselves on the defenses of Quebec in 1775-1776 partly because they failed to gain hoped-for support from the French, who were the overwhelming majority of the population of Canada. The latter saw that the weak and undisciplined forces of Continentals had little chance of success. They also resented the unconcealed religious bigotry of the invaders, many of whom were of New England Puritan stock. The Roman Catholic Church led this opposition, preferring to trust its future to the British, who had demonstrated their tolerance in the Quebec Act. The catalog of American errors was completed when their army began to buy its supplies with paper money, which the thrifty French abhorred.[1]

Though the Continental Army failed to gain Canada, the invasion clearly demonstrated a basic cause of the annexation movement. From 1775 to the present, Americans have felt that they cannot suffer Canada to be in the hands of an enemy. The invasion of the northern colonies by John Burgoyne in 1777 gave point to this fear.

To the east, Nova Scotia seemed to offer promise to the Revolutionaries. Three-quarters of its population had come from New England and showed a lively sympathy for the rebellion. Geography and the British navy, however, overruled sentiment and kept Nova Scotia in the Empire. The distances and the wilderness which intervened between the scattered settlements of the colony made it impossible for American sympathizers there to organize an effective force and to attain the unity of plan and of action necessary to military success. Washington refused to send an army north to capture "New England's outpost." He knew that an invasion must go by sea and that the British fleet could intercept supplies and reinforcements sent from the south. The invaders, cut off from succor or retreat and trapped between the Royal Navy and the wilderness and bogs of the interior, would fall an easy prey to the redcoats.

At the peace negotiations the wily Ben Franklin tried to gain

[1] Accounts used for background for the Revolution include John R. Alden, *The American Revolution, 1775-1783* (New York, 1954); Alfred L. Burt, *The Old Province of Quebec* (Minneapolis, 1933); John C. Miller, *Triumph of Freedom, 1775-1783* (Boston, 1948).

by diplomacy what American arms had failed to take. He urged the British ministry to cede Quebec to allay the rancors of war and to avoid future friction. This bold proposal did not convince the British, and Canada remained in the Empire. It is significant to note that the American plenipotentiaries showed little interest in the acquisition of Nova Scotia. Geography made Quebec a potential threat to the new nation, but Nova Scotia gave them little concern.

The conclusion of the Revolution did not end the American fear of Canada as a British knife poised for a thrust against the northern states. Another and immediate danger threatened. The western Indians continued hostilities against American frontiersmen, which convinced the latter that British agents were responsible for their troubles. Economic reasons gave additional impetus to the desire for Canada. Land-hungry American settlers coveted the good soil of British America.

Both a fear of and a desire for Canada motivated the War Hawks of 1812. They believed that it would be a simple matter to seize these colonies, and they had company in their conviction, for many on both sides of the boundary considered annexation inevitable. This belief was especially prevalent in the southwestern section of Canada West, where American-born settlers were numerous. Some of these American Canadians aided the armies of the United States as partisans or as spies, but their support was not as general as American leaders had expected, and its net result was negative. Believing that the inhabitants of Canada West would rise en masse to support them, the American military invaded that province instead of concentrating on their logical objectives, Montreal and Quebec, a blundering strategy which contributed to the ensuing American defeat.[2] This failure to conquer Canada ended the serious attempts at annexation by force.

[2] E. A. Cruikshank, "Disaffection in Upper Canada, 1812-1814," Royal Society of Canada, *Transactions,* 3d ser., VI (1912), 20-65.

Time gradually diluted the hatred caused by the War of 1812 on both sides of the line. Canadians were alert spectators of the growth and prosperity of the Republic, which often seemed to outstrip their own. Economic discontent was joined by political dissatisfaction at the lack of self-government and seemed to foretell an annexation movement. To obviate this threat, the British ministry granted responsible government to the colony in 1847-1848. Ironically, this attempt to preserve the loyalty of Canada nearly coincided with a change in Imperial fiscal policy which precipitated the feared movement for annexation.

The adoption of free trade by the British government in 1846 destroyed the carefully articulated Canadian economic system based upon the "commercial empire of the St. Lawrence." This great river was the natural highway from the eastern seaboard to the interior of the continent. Canadians had dreamed of and worked for commercial domination of that vast area since the earliest settlement of the colony. As long as natural waterways remained the important means of transportation in North America, this hope was justified. The St. Lawrence was the funnel through which the bulk of the trade of the interior—then consisting almost entirely of furs—flowed on its way to Europe. This concept of commercial empire naturally dominated the political thought and action of Canadian leaders. Then the American Revolution interjected a complication and a threat. The political boundary established in 1783 bisected what Canadian merchants regarded as an indivisible economic unit. Those who drew the line expected that the passage of men and goods over it would be unobstructed, but the supplementary treaty providing for this was not negotiated. To preserve the commercial empire and the trade of the western territory of the United States, the British then had to resort to the extralegal means of retaining strategic posts on American soil. Jay's Treaty (1794) provided for the evacuation of these forts but bowed to the overriding concept of the commercial empire by allowing trade across the boundary, thereby preserving for a time the economic dominance of Canada over the Great Lakes region.

Montreal was the capital of this empire of the St. Lawrence. Located at the head of navigation on the river for oceangoing vessels and the natural journey's end of trade from the interior, it was the focal point of the system and would gain immeasurably if its waterway monopolized the trade of the heart of the continent. The merchants of Montreal were aggressive men of boundless vision and with political influence and pretension more in proportion to their wealth than to their numbers. They used this power to cultivate the asset of their location astride the passage to the west, and their fervor to convert others to the belief that the economic future of Canada depended upon the successful exploitation of these commercial advantages. The subsequent campaign for the commercial empire of the St. Lawrence is a rare study in resourcefulness, persistence, and frustration. These merchants, through the North West Company, controlled much of the fur trade of the interior and directed its flow to Montreal until 1821, when the Hudson's Bay Company absorbed their organization and diverted the peltry to its ancient entrepôts, Fort Churchill, York Factory, and Fort Severn.

This redirection of the fur trade hurt the economy of Montreal but did not shatter it as it might have done earlier. The spread of settlement into Canada West after the American Revolution was enlarging and changing the character of the trade of the colonies. Encouraged by Imperial tariff preference, the Canadians were producing surpluses of timber and foodstuffs for markets in the mother country, and the growing stream of this trade naturally flowed with the waters of the St. Lawrence.[3] The new exports were challenging the supremacy

[3] Donald G. Creighton, *The Commercial Empire of the St. Lawrence, 1760-1850* (Toronto, 1937), 89, 116-42.

of furs in Canada's economy long before the amalgamation of 1821. Montreal merchants, specializing in the peltry trade, were diversifying their interests and exerted their influence to persuade the British government to increase and to extend the preferences.

But the ambition of the Montreal merchants was not framed in the narrow confines of increasing and monopolizing the trade of Canada West and Canada East. Their infinite dreams of dominating the international trade of the continent's interior were unfaded. The American states about the Great Lakes, which still seemed to be natural commercial dependencies of the St. Lawrence, had developed into a rich agricultural region. If the merchants of Canada could tap the export and import trade of this area, the dreams of the commercial empire of the St. Lawrence would be richly fulfilled.

But American trade did not gravitate to the commercial orbit of Montreal, and it became apparent that concessions were necessary to lure it there. The colonial merchants, therefore, tried to obtain a measure to admit American raw and semi-manufactured goods (such as flour and meal) into Canada free of duty. The Imperial government feared that such legislation would injure Canadian and British interests. Under advice from the colonial secretary, the Governor General withheld his assent in 1817 to an act which embodied the requests of the merchants.[4] American trade was not barred from Canada, but there were high duties on all important articles.

This unfavorable action dashed the expectations of the Montrealers, and they faced other threats to their hopes. The St. Lawrence was something less than ideal as an artery of trade for heavy cargoes of grain and lumber because of certain rapids-strewn sections. This had been no handicap in the days when the high-value, low-bulk shipments of furs could be carried in canoes which skipped easily through the worst sections of the

[4] Creighton, 192.

river. Heavier cargoes meant much larger vessels of deeper draft not well suited to the difficult stretches of the St. Lawrence. Moreover, the Erie Canal, completed in 1825, immediately became a threatening rival for the trade of the interior. If the merchants of the St. Lawrence system hoped to overcome this competition, they must obtain free admission to Canada for American raw materials and improve the navigation of the river with canals.

Canadians rose to the challenge. The government and private citizens undertook the building of the necessary artificial waterways. The system was not completed until 1848, but it had been sufficiently advanced for some years to test its strength against its American rival.[5] The British government finally cooperated by consenting to admit American goods to Canada duty-free.[6] The St. Lawrence was now doubly armed to enter the economic war with the Erie Canal for the trade of the Great Lakes area. The merchants of Montreal were again confident that their dream of commercial domination was about to be realized.

But this was not to be. The obstacles above Montreal had been removed, but those below the city remained. The new Canadian system now provided a cheaper and faster means of transportation to Montreal than the Erie Canal and the Hudson River did to New York, but trans-Atlantic freight rates were higher from the former than from the latter by an amount which more than offset the initial advantage of the St. Lawrence. Vessels clearing from Montreal must grope through the fog-bound and rock-strewn Gulf of St. Lawrence before reaching the open sea. The risks of such a route greatly exceeded those of a voyage from New York, where the outbound vessel was on the high seas when it left the harbor. Insurance on both ship and

[5] An excellent description of the financing and building of the St. Lawrence canals is found in Gilbert N. Tucker, *The Canadian Commercial Revolution, 1845-1851* (New Haven, 1936), 29-47.

[6] Creighton, *Commercial Empire*, 248.

cargo were consequently higher from Montreal, and port charges for pilotage and wharfage increased the disparity of costs.[7] When Canadians realized this handicap, they laid the blame for it upon the Navigation Acts which gave British vessels the monopoly of shipping from the colony to the mother country.[8] The merchants did not at first agitate against these acts, but accepted them as part of the Imperial fiscal system, which, on the whole, operated to their benefit.

The trade of the west, therefore, tended to use the Erie Canal and New York to secure the cheaper trans-Atlantic rates from that port. The St. Lawrence system fell behind in the race, and the hopes for Montreal's commercial supremacy were still unfulfilled.[9]

The indomitable Canadian merchants doggedly sought to scale these new obstacles. They must secure Imperial legislation which would bring American commerce into the St. Lawrence but protect the agricultural interests of the colonies. The Canada Corn Act of 1843 seemed to bridge this dilemma. It allowed Canadian wheat to enter Great Britain under a duty of one shilling a quarter, with a proportional tariff on flour.[10] American grain imported into Canada upon payment of a three-shilling duty and ground into flour there could enter Great

[7] The St. Lawrence route to Montreal was faster and cheaper by more than £1 a ton. On the other hand, port charges in Montreal were £50 more on a vessel of 700 tons than in New York, and the insurance rate from the latter on a barrel of flour was 6d. less. Tucker, *Commercial Revolution*, 55-62.

[8] The Navigation Acts did contribute to increasing the costs of a voyage from Montreal, but they were only one factor in causing the disparity.

[9] In 1832, a good year, the Lachine Canal carried 91,862 barrels of flour and 293,968 bushels of wheat. Two years later, a bad year, the Erie Canal carried 977,027 barrels of flour and 748,443 bushels of wheat. Creighton, *Commercial Empire*, 251.

[10] The duty on colonial wheat had varied, according to the prices prevailing in the English market, from one to five shillings. The new rate was thus more advantageous than the old.

Britain under the same terms as flour milled from Canadian wheat.[11] The three-shilling duty prevented American wheat from competing with the Canadian product in the latter's home market. The provision which admitted flour ground in Canada from this American wheat to Great Britain as colonial flour normally would give it an advantage over flour shipped from New York and entering under duties levied upon the foreign article.

The merchants of Canada exulted that the passage of this legislation had brought their commercial millenium at last. The magic key of Imperial preference would open the door of a golden future. A wave of optimism swept over the colony and washed away doubt and restraint. To profit from the new order, farmers and millers expanded their production. Capital flowed into the building of mills, warehouses, and wharves in preparation for the anticipated boom in business. Thanks to the psychological effects of the Canada Corn Act, the colony enjoyed a period of exaggerated activity and prosperity.

But these pleasant dreams were followed by rude awakenings. The boom was short lived, for the act of 1843 was not the beginning of a new life but the last gasp of a moribund fiscal system. The Irish famine and the conversion of Sir Robert Peel to free trade gave that system its coup de grace. In 1846 the British Parliament provided that the Corn Laws be lowered immediately and, with their corollary system of Imperial preference, be abolished in 1849.

The news of this action, though foreshadowed, shocked the Canadians. Reaction came swiftly. The assembly of the colony, anticipating the change, begged the Imperial government to soften the blow by obtaining for Canada a reciprocal trade treaty with the United States.[12] The businessmen of Canada

[11] Tucker, *Commercial Revolution,* 89-90.

[12] Charles C. Tansill, *The Canadian Reciprocity Treaty of 1854* (Baltimore, 1922), 17.

protested against the extinction of a fiscal system which had endured for generations, and hinted darkly that a loosening of the commercial bindings of the Empire might weaken its political ties.[13] The merchants predicted that a great depression would afflict their country because its producers and waterway, robbed of Imperial preference, would not compete against their rivals in the United States and Europe. But the British government could not restore the preference without restoring the tariff, and that system had been irretrievably disestablished.

The predicted depression soon appeared. Two years after the repeal of the Corn Laws, the trade of Canada decreased sharply; certain classes of exports showed declines of 50 to 70 percent.[14] Flour mills stood idle, and the new wharves and warehouses were deserted.[15] Montreal received the full force of the blow.[16]

[13] Cephas D. Allin and George M. Jones, *Annexation, Preferential Trade and Reciprocity* (Toronto, 1912), 13-17.

[14] Decline of the three most important exports from Canada:

	1847	*1848*
Oats (bushels)	168,805	49,396
Wheat (bushels)	628,000	235,051
Flour (barrels)	651,030	383,593

United States Congress, *Senate Reports*, 31 Cong., 2 sess., no. 23, p. 330. (American legislative papers hereafter identified as *Congressional, Senate,* or *House.*)

[15] One man, Jacob Keefer, invested $40,000 in a mill near the Welland Canal. Not a barrel of flour was ground in this mill after its completion. Keefer to W. H. Merritt, April 19, 1848, in H. A. Innis and A. R. M. Lower (eds.), *Select Documents in Canadian Economic History, 1783-1885* (Toronto, 1933), 356-57.

[16] Exports from Montreal:

	1847	*1848*
Flour (barrels)	281,009	159,447
Wheat (minots)	561,967	172,207
Peas (bushels)	90,461	45,975
Total value	$3,349,311	$1,545,892

Senate Reports, 31 Cong., 2 sess., no. 23, p. 169.

James Bruce, Earl of Elgin, the Governor General, informed the colonial secretary that three-fourths of the commercial men of that city were bankrupt.[17]

Recent studies indicate that the Canadian depression of 1849 arose from the operation of the general business cycle, exaggerated but not caused by the revolution in Imperial fiscal policy.[18] In the general slump the prices paid for Canadian products in the British and American markets tumbled. Other conditions aggravated the injury. The sudden loss of Imperial preference also operated indirectly to produce deflation by puncturing the balloon of speculation which had overexpanded credit in Canada and made eventual collapse inevitable. The Congress of the United States added to Canada's troubles. It had passed an act, which became effective in 1846, permitting Canadian goods to traverse American soil duty-free in bond. Much trade was thereby diverted from Montreal to New York.[19]

The repeal of Imperial preference particularly galled Canadians because it removed the advantageous features of the old Imperial system but allowed the disadvantages to remain when it left the Navigation Acts standing. As mentioned above, Canadians blamed the higher trans-Atlantic freight rates prevailing from Montreal upon these acts and now demanded their abrogation. The slowness of the British government to comply strained the loyalty of the colony.

Whatever actually produced the depression from 1847 to 1850, the Canadians single-mindedly laid the blame upon the repeal of Imperial preference. The apparent responsibility of the

[17] *The Elgin-Grey Papers, 1846-1852*, ed. by Arthur Doughty (Ottawa, 1937), I, 349.

[18] Creighton, *Commercial Empire*, 361-62; Tucker, *Commercial Revolution*, 214-15.

[19] In 1850, for example, 723,487 bushels of Canadian wheat and 283,018 barrels of Canadian flour, valued at $1,538,042, were received in bond at New York. *Senate Reports*, 31 Cong., 2 sess., no. 23, p. 702.

mother country for their plight angered them and produced an overwhelming psychological effect on the merchants of Montreal. These men had struggled for years with fanatic zeal to make Montreal the commercial capital of central North America. The construction of the Erie Canal, a shrewd blow, had only spurred them to greater efforts. Their unfaltering persistence in the face of adversity had obtained the improvement of the St. Lawrence and forced a grudging British government to pass the Canada Corn Act of 1843. Now, at last, the merchants had felt that the combination was right; the St. Lawrence canals and the Imperial tariff preference must focus the trade of the Great Lakes region upon Montreal. Then what happened? Just as they were sitting down to the magnificent feast which they had labored so long and arduously to prepare, the British government whisked it away. Their loyalty vanished with it.

Rosy hopes of prosperity faded and a black future lowered over Canada and over Montreal in particular. Not only was the hope of future commercial mastership shattered, but the foundations of the existing economic life of the colony were undermined. The loss of the preferential advantage in the British market would shrink the export of Canadian produce, and agriculture might sink to a subsistence level. Montreal would decay into a sleepy provincial town, its inhabitants able only to dream of a vigorous past and of a glittering future which was once almost within their grasp.

The only apparent preventive against such senile rot was to find, in the United States, a market to replace that of Britain. The free admission of Canadian produce into the neighboring Republic might preserve colonial agriculture and crowd the St. Lawrence waterway with new trade. The Canadian and British governments, therefore, sought to negotiate a reciprocity treaty with the government in Washington. The Mexican War blocked congressional action on this subject in 1846; in 1848, the

Grinnell bill for reciprocal trade passed the House but bogged down in the Senate.[20]

The failure of these attempts to obtain reciprocity and the gaunt specter of economic disaster made the merchants and businessmen of Montreal desperate. But they had never supinely accepted defeat in the past, and they did not propose to do so now. If the American market could not be gained by a treaty, they could enter it through a political union with the Republic. They could disarm the explosive charge of disloyalty by pointing out that it was Britain herself who had first weakened the bonds of the Empire by casting the colony off economically.

This argument appeared to be sound politically as well as economically. The mother country had given the colonies responsible government in the conviction that their departure from the Empire was imminent. Public men in Britain had pronounced that the greatest tragedy of Imperial history, the American Revolution, must never be repeated. If the colonies wished to leave, they should be suffered to depart in peace, as friends not as enemies. Thus the severance of fiscal and commercial bonds between the homeland and British North America was, like the granting of responsible government, another step in the direction of Canadian independence or annexation to the United States. Many in Britain were ready to welcome either move.[21]

Here were the primal overt signs of the annexation movement. It should be mentioned that some local as well as Imperial factors had also been working for some time to bring Canada into union with the United States. One such factor was the Irish element in the colony's population. Some of these sons

[20] Tansill, *Reciprocity*, 17-22. Joseph Grinnell, author of the bill, was a Whig from Massachusetts with strong commercial interests.

[21] E. L. Woodward, *The Age of Reform, 1815-1870* (Oxford, 1938), 350-52; Robert L. Schuyler, "The Rise of Anti-Imperialism in England," *Political Science Quarterly*, XXXVII (September, 1922), 440-71.

of Erin were republicans, while others were less anxious to become American citizens than to strike a blow at the oppressor of their native land. It should be noted, however, that these Irish elements were relatively unimportant in number and in political influence.[22]

The Parti Rouge was more significant. This was a French-Canadian political faction led by Louis Joseph Papineau, the rebel of 1837, who had recently returned from exile in the United States a full-blown—and blowing—republican. His program was concise: republicanism, anticlericalism, and nationalité, the last defined as the defense of the French language, laws, culture, and religion against the infringements of British intolerance. He constantly extolled the advantages of annexation to the wealthy Republic, an activity in which his followers and supporting press joined, and often surpassed, him.[23] The Parti Rouge was noisy but, in reality, only a minority of the French Canadians and concentrated in the urban centers. Its success in returning Papineau to the assembly in 1847 made it appear more powerful than it was, and gave concern to the opponents of annexation.

But the most dangerous political malcontents in Canada were not the Irish or the French but the English minority in Montreal, most of whom were Tories heretofore surcharged with loyalty. That party had controlled the government of the colony so long that it regarded its incumbency as part of the natural order. However, the new Governor General, Lord Elgin, believed that responsible government was necessary. When the Reform Party won a substantial majority in the assembly of 1848, he

[22] Elgin, however, believed that the Irish were generally restless and gave some credit to absurd rumors that they would revolt in prelude to a projected American invasion. Elgin to Henry, Earl Grey, July 18, 1848, *Elgin-Grey Papers,* I, 209-10.

[23] Papineau carried his annexation proclivities into an election address which he issued in 1847. *Elgin-Grey Papers,* I, 103-15.

formed an administration of its leaders and dethroned the Tories.

This blasphemy was a blow for all Tories, but it was most painful to the merchants of Montreal. Because they were relatively few in number, these English Canadians lived in dread of domination by the French, from whom they differed in language, religion, and culture; indeed, John Lambton, Earl of Durham had earlier written that this minority was determined to remain English even if at the expense of ceasing to be British. The election of 1848 had evidently put the habitants in the saddle, for every constituency predominantly French had returned a Reform member. Thus, for the Montreal English, political defeat joined economic frustration as twin signposts of the future, pointing south. Annexation to the United States seemed to offer their only salvation.[24]

At the beginning of 1849, many Canadians thus desired union with the United States, but they hesitated to take definite steps to obtain it. Political and economic disaster had eroded their ties of loyalty, but some emotional disturbance was needed to break through the barriers of training and environment and galvanize them into decisive action to snap the Imperial bonds.

The Rebellion Losses Bill touched off the necessary explosion. This act appropriated £100,000 to be paid those who had suffered property damage or loss in the outbreaks of 1837. Innocent in appearance, it was packed with dynamite. Many who claimed this compensation had been rebels and at the time when their property was destroyed were bearing arms against their government and their Queen. This was no secret, and Louis Lafontaine, leader of the French wing of the Reform Party, boldly insisted that compensation be paid even to the convicted insurgent leaders who had been deported. It was no

[24] The best description of the situation in Montreal is found in Tucker, *Commercial Revolution*, 178-79.

wonder that the Tories raged at the bill as an appropriation levied upon loyalists for the reward of traitors and—unkindest cut of all—French-Canadian traitors.[25]

Fear as well as anger inspired English opposition to this measure, for its passage was an evil portent. French-Canadian politicians made notorious the fact that they would use their majority to reward their friends and to punish their enemies. This practice could become a frontal attack upon the interests of the minority in Canada East. The English in Montreal were certain that, barring a drastic change, their wealth and influence would be ground out between the upper millstone of French domination and the nether millstone of economic depression. So the Tories opposed the bill with the fierceness born of desperation.[26] Despite their efforts within and outside the assembly, it passed by the decisive margin of forty-seven votes to eighteen. Defeated here, the opposition retreated to their last barricade, demanding that Lord Elgin veto the hated bill. To their consternation, he approved it, April 25, 1849.

This rebuff unhinged the reason of the English minority. The British government had now doubly forfeited their loyalty by plunging Canada into a depression and by delivering the English of Canada East into the hands of their enemies the French. Hysteria seized them. Spurred on and joined by their leaders, the minority in Montreal became an unreasoning mob, exploding into violence. Crowds which gathered in the streets and pelted the Governor General with stones and rotten eggs when he ventured forth in his carriage, then invaded and fired the Parliament building, gutted the home of Francis Hincks, a Reform leader, and looted Lafontaine's residence. For several days the turbulent Tories ran amuck until action had drained their violence.

[25] Creighton, *Commercial Empire*, 375-76.
[26] Elgin to Grey, March 1, 1849, *Elgin-Grey Papers*, I, 299-300.

Returning calm did not bring reviving loyalty. In cold reason the Tories now moved to obtain political union. Leaders of the various annexationist factions—French, Irish, and English—repressed their mutual antipathies and sought alliance. During the summer of 1849 they amalgamated their forces and issued a manifesto, an apologia for their movement. This document appeared in the Montreal *Gazette* of October 11, 1849.[27]

The Montreal Annexation Manifesto perfectly typifies the political union movement in nineteenth century Canada. Its authors based their case entirely upon narrow economic self-interest. From the first to the last line of the manifesto, they advocated political union to improve Canada's financial situation. The preamble of the document recited the history of the "increasing depression" in the "material interests" of the colony, and traced its misfortunes to the repeal of Imperial preference. Merchants, producers, and farmers alike suffered the effects of depression. Real estate found no market, securities depreciated, and banks foundered. The canal system, built at great expense, was idle and had failed in its purpose to make Montreal the entrepôt of the west. In short, Canada was "in decay," a "humiliating contrast" to the United States.

It was obvious, continued the manifesto, that heroic remedy was necessary to relieve this distress. Measures had been suggested to ameliorate the situation, but they were either unattainable or mild correctives for a serious disease. Some had suggested that Great Britain revive her tariff and the preference, but her commitment to free trade was final. The alternative proposal of a Canadian tariff might ease the depression for the moment by creating a colonial manufacturing interest, but this industry would starve on the lean diet of its local market.

[27] A copy of the manifesto is printed in *Elgin-Grey Papers*, IV, 1487-94. The analysis of and quotations from the manifesto given below are taken from this copy.

Independence for the colony offered no hope of permanent improvement because the new nation would be splintered by particularism and by cultural and religious differences. Reciprocity with the United States in natural products seemed impossible to obtain; if it came, it might prove to be only a temporary and partial relief.

Having shucked off the husks of inadequate proposals, the authors of the manifesto arrived at the kernel of solution. The only complete and sovereign remedy for Canada's ills was, to quote again, "a friendly and peaceful separation from British connection and a union upon equitable terms with the great North American Confederacy of sovereign states." The results of annexation would be breathtaking. American capital would pour into the colony, real estate values would double, trade and commerce would expand, the St. Lawrence waterway would swarm with ships, and a new industrial growth, soundly based on the swelling American market, would enrich impoverished Canada.

Anticipating the accusation of treason, the authors of the manifesto defended themselves against it in advance. They pointed out that public men in the mother country were daily urging the colony to depart from the Empire. Annexation would be a boon, not a blow, to Great Britain. It would relieve her of the expense of maintaining and defending Canada, ease her frictions with the United States, and, by enriching the Canadians, enlarge the North American market for British goods.

The manifesto ended with an appeal. If its reader felt that the action proposed was "laudable and right," he was invited to discard old affiliations and to join in the new cause with "that earnest and cordial co-operation in such lawful prudent and judicial means as may best conduct us to our common destiny."

This was a calculated document. There is in it no trace of

great principle or sentiment, no call to enthrone democracy in British North America, no slightest suggestion of affection for the Americans whom its authors proposed to join in the brotherhood of common citizenship. It is not the liberty bell but the cash-register bell which resounds in it. The political unionists might love Great Britain, as they earnestly protested, but they loved the American dollar more. Annexation was a business proposition.

The "dollars and cents" approach seems to have been a popular one, for the English minority and the Parti Rouge in Montreal greeted the manifesto with enthusiasm, and more than a thousand citizens signed it. Many of these people were, or became, famous figures in Canada and lived to regret their hasty signatures.[28] Encouraged by this reception, the annexationists formed a permanent society and started a recruiting campaign. Their plan was simple: the Montreal Annexation Association would correspond with sympathizers in a given district and distribute its pamphlets through them. When the situation ripened, local annexationists would form their own organization, tightly linked to the mother society, and assume local propagation of the faith, aided by money, literature, and speakers from Montreal. It was hoped that eventually each of these branches would become strong enough to present candidates for election to the assembly. Control of the legislature would clear the way for the next step.

This campaign met with varied results, mostly unfavorable. In Canada East, aside from Montreal, it made headway only in the predominantly English-speaking Eastern Townships, where the American origin of many in the population made them

[28] Among these signers were Jacob De Witt and Benjamin Holmes, members of the assembly; J. J. C. Abbott, later Sir John and Prime Minister of the Dominion; Luther Holton; A. A. Dorion; and John Rose, later Sir John and first Canadian high commissioner in London.

receptive.[29] Moreover, the Townships had not escaped the blight of the depression in Montreal, upon which they were partly dependent economically. They produced large surpluses and suffered from the tumbling prices in their nearest market. These ills gave additional pain because the Townships bordered upon the United States and their inhabitants were aware of the greater demand and higher prices across the line.

The agents of the Montreal association, finding a cordial reception in the Townships, soon organized five branches in Sherbrooke County alone. The entire press and most of the prominent men of that area aided them.[30] The loyal inhabitants held their peace, fearing that counterdemonstrations would merely betray their own numerical weakness. Soon the initial burst of enthusiasm subsided, and sober second thought and improving economic conditions in the Townships led many who had welcomed the movement loudly to depart it quietly.

The leaders of the association were unaware of this silent desertion until March, 1850, when a byelection was held in Sherbrooke County, which had been the strongest annexationist center. Expecting an overwhelming victory, members of the organization were shocked when their candidate was returned by the thin margin of thirty-four votes.[31]

The Montreal association also dispatched its emissaries to the city of Quebec, but here only the English inhabitants received their overtures. This group, mostly Tory merchants, had suffered the same vexations as their brethren in Montreal—political defeat, economic depression, and a boding sense of the dangers

[29] The Eastern Townships comprised the area south and west of Montreal, lying between the St. Lawrence and the American border.

[30] A. T. Galt, later a minister of finance and then representing Sherbrooke County, advocated annexation as "the only cure for our manifold ills." Oscar D. Skelton, *The Life and Times of Sir Alexander Tilloch Galt* (Toronto, 1920), 153.

[31] Skelton, 155; Allin and Jones, *Annexation*, 291-96.

of their minority position. These malcontents organized a branch society, solicited the support of the French majority, and, with amazing optimism, offered one of its members in a local byelection. The Reform candidate defeated the annexationist handily, thanks to the French vote.[32] This result hinted that annexation was not acceptable to the folk which constituted half the population of United Canada, a conclusion demonstrated by the failure of the Montreal association to win converts in the rural and French regions of Canada East. A few parishes where the Parti Rouge was strong furnished the exceptions to this rule.[33]

Canada West was also cool to the evangelism of the Montreal Annexation Association. The only hope here was to convince the inhabitants that the mother country was anxious to be rid of her colonies and favored the union of Canada to the United States. The uncooperative British government spoiled this argument by a denunciation of the agitation.[34] Branches of the association were established in a few places such as Toronto, Hamilton, Kingston, and Prescott, but the members of these organizations were painfully shy, conducting their activities

[32] The division of the vote was as follows:

	Chabot (Reform)	*Legare (Annexationist)*
French	1,679	609
English	308	588
Irish	125	217
Scottish	6	12

Before the election, it was assumed that the Parti Rouge controlled the French vote in the city. *Elgin-Grey Papers,* II, 597-99.

[33] Five parishes in Rouville County voted in favor of annexation, and in the neighboring county, Charles Laberge, the local leader of the Rouge, succeeded in organizing a branch association at St. Athanase (Iberville). Laberge to A. A. Dorion and Robert McKay, January 7, 1850, in Arthur Penny, "The Annexation Movement of 1849," *Canadian Historical Review,* V (September, 1924), 236-61.

[34] Gray to Elgin, January 9, 1850, *Elgin-Grey Papers,* II, 594-95.

clandestinely and with the support of only three newspapers.[35] The districts bordering Michigan were anxious for annexation because they wanted duty-free access to American markets, but there is no evidence that the association proselyted in this area. The annexation movement in the west gradually merged with the movement for Canadian independence.[36]

Why did the campaign of the Montreal Annexation Association to gain popular support fail so dismally? A number of factors were responsible, and the economic situation was the most important. The depression which bred the agitation was primarily commercial and did not bite deeply into the rural districts where most of Canada's population lived. Except for those who sold to local city markets, the farmers escaped most of the economic pressures which drove the merchants to desperation. The people of the rural areas regarded annexationists with aversion as mercenary traitors, prepared to sell their heritage for Yankee gold.

A second fundamental cause for the failure of the movement was the opposition of most of the French Canadians. Nationalité was the reason for their stand. The preservation of their language, religion, and customs has been the guiding principle of French-Canadian polity since 1760. In Canada they possessed constitutional guarantees of their peculiar institutions which they would lack in the United States. Annexation would also jeopardize their favorable political situation. The election of

[35] Allin and Jones, *Annexation*, 235, 239; H. B. Willson to R. McKay, December 19, 1849, A. L. Taylor to McKay and A. A. Dorion, January 9, 1850, in Penny, "Annexation Movement," 245-48, 257. The annexationist papers were Kingston *Argus*, Prescott *Telegraph*, and Toronto *Independent*. The last of these was founded to agitate for Canadian independence, but its editor, H. B. Willson, was virtually forced into supporting the annexation movement. He constantly appealed to Montreal for financial aid until lack of funds forced the discontinuation of his paper. Willson to McKay, November 23, 1849, in Penny, "Annexation Movement," 238-39.

[36] Allin and Jones, *Annexation*, does not discuss this movement fully. For the independence agitation, see *Elgin-Grey Papers*, II, 633-34.

1848 had put the French and their allies of Canada West in power. If Canada joined the United States, the French would become a numerically and politically insignificant fraction of the American population.

The Quebec hierarchy of the Roman Catholic Church, the guardian of nationalité and the fountainhead of French-Canadian opinion, had especial reasons for detesting annexation. They were convinced that republicanism and anticlericalism were indissolubly wedded. Papineau buttressed this belief by his constant iteration that the American government would not tolerate ecclesiastical prerogatives and would unseat the church from the privileged position it now enjoyed in Quebec.[37]

If they had much to lose by annexation in other respects, the French had little to gain from it economically. Most of them were farmers. The general rural hostility toward union with the United States was most pronounced in the French countryside, for the habitants were more self-sufficient than the English-speaking settlers. The promise of access to the American market and trade which annexation would bring had no allure for the French farmer, who had little to buy or to sell.[38] So the

[37] Elgin made no official attempt to persuade the hierarchy to condemn annexation, although Papineau's press accused him of doing so. Individual members of the clergy denounced the agitation, probably as the result of strong hints from their ecclesiastical superiors. See Quebec *Journal*, undated, enclosed in Elgin to Grey, December 10, 1849, *Elgin-Grey Papers*, II, 554-56. It is interesting to note—and impossible to explain—the inconsistencies in Papineau's policy, for he ardently supported nationalité and at the same time worked for annexation which might gravely endanger French institutions and privileges.

[38] The following export figures for wheat illustrate the fact that the French Canadians were not as dependent on agricultural surpluses as were the farmers of Canada West:

	Canada East	*Canada West*
1842	942,835 bushels	3,221,991 bushels
1851	3,045,600 bushels	12,674,503 bushels

Henry Y. Hind, *Eighty Years Progress of British North America* (Toronto, 1864), 52.

persistence and ingenuity of even the Montreal merchants could not overcome the peasant stubborness with which the habitant repulsed their most seductive propaganda. Thus the Montreal association won little support from the two most numerous classes in the colony—the farmers of Canada West and the French of Canada East. Neither political defeat nor economic depression was gnawing at their loyalty to the Empire.

Several minor factors aided in the frustration of the annexationists. One was an active counteroffensive by the loyal elements in the colony. The Canadian and British governments and the Reform Party had ignored the disloyal agitation prior to the passage of the Rebellion Losses Bill, fearing to dignify the movement by recognizing its existence and hoping that it would wither unattended. The violent outburst in the fall of 1849, however, forced them to act.

Lord Elgin began the open opposition to the advocates of political union by removing the seat of government from Montreal to Toronto. The Governor General thought to punish the unseemly conduct of the former city and to flatter the inhabitants of Canada West and cement their connection with the Empire. He also intended to remove the assembly from the dangerous atmosphere of Montreal, where the minds of the loyal, but naive, might be infected by the virus of treason. By December, 1849, Elgin was congratulating himself that his move had preserved the loyalty of the west and localized the plague to Montreal and its environs.[39]

The Reform Party soon joined the Governor General in smiting the disloyal. They had good reason to do so. The leaders of the agitation came primarily from the ranks of their

[39] Elgin to Grey, October 25, December 2, 1849, *Elgin-Grey Papers,* II, 525, 552. The annexationists also testified to the effectiveness of this move. Many political unionists in Toronto, delighted because their city had been made the capital, refused to aid the association. H. B. Willson to John Redpath, December 26, 1849, in Penny, "Annexation Movement," 251.

bitter rivals the Tories. It was useful to be able to brand their political opponents with the stigma of treason. Beyond this, the Reform Party had much to lose by union with the Republic. The recent election had given power and patronage into their receptive hands. If Canada became part of the United States, their likely fate was submergence as an insignificant fraction of one of the great parties there. It should be noted, too, that the two groups in Canada most resistant to annexationism, the French Canadians of Canada East and the agrarian population of the west, were also the backbone of the Reform Party. Therefore, Robert Baldwin, leader in Canada West, moved to check the slight inroads which the movement had made in his ranks. In an open letter he pronounced ex cathedra upon the agitation: "All should know . . . that I can look upon only those who are for the continuation of that connexion [with Great Britain] as political friends—those who are against it as political opponents."[40] Thus, in one sentence, he read the annexationists out of his party.

Baldwin also prevailed upon his cabinet to punish the political unionists within its reach. At least one of their papers had unwisely challenged the government with the taunt that a number of civil servants had signed the manifesto.[41] Thereupon, by cabinet order, the provincial secretary sharply demanded an explanation from each holder of public office or honor whose name appeared on the document. Those who did not disavow their connection with the movement were summarily dismissed.[42]

The British government, as already suggested, added its weight to the growing pressures upon the annexationists. Henry, Earl Grey officially informed Elgin that the Queen was "determined to exert all the authority which belongs to her for the purpose

[40] Robert Baldwin to Peter Perry, October 4, 1849, enclosed in Elgin to Grey, October 11, 1849, *Elgin-Grey Papers,* II, 520-21.

[41] This paper was the Montreal *Gazette. Elgin-Grey Papers,* II, 537.

[42] Allin and Jones, *Annexation,* 152.

of maintaining the connection of Canada with this country" and instructed the Governor General "to resist to the utmost of your power, any attempt to bring about the separation of Canada from the British Empire."[43] Lord John Russell bolstered Grey's pronouncement by declaring that "the Crown could give nothing but a decided negative" to any proposals for the annexation of Canada to the United States.[44] This unequivocal stand by the Imperial authorities confuted the annexationist contention that their agitation was really loyal because the home government was anxious to be rid of the colonies.

But perhaps the worst disappointment to the annexationists came from the indifference to the proposition in the United States, presumed beneficiary of the movement. This unexpected attitude was a sharp contrast to the aggressive American activities of 1775 and 1812. Except New York and Vermont, which had profitable economic connections with Canada, even the northern and western sections of the Republic gave little notice to the annexation movement.[45] These states apparently felt they had nothing material to gain from the acquisition of the colony; indeed, it was possible that they would lose, for many American producers of raw materials feared Canadian competition. The depression, rioting, and general unrest in the colony added nothing to its attractiveness. Moreover, the Republic was gorged with new territory as a result of the Mexican War. These acquisitions were causing political indigestion which any further additions would complicate. The United States, convulsed over the question of the status of slavery in the recent annexations, had little attention to spare for developments in Canada. It

[43] Grey to Elgin, January 9, 1850, *Elgin-Grey Papers,* II, 595.

[44] Allin and Jones, *Annexation,* 278-80.

[45] For illustrations of American press opinion, see Allin and Jones, 376-80, 383; New York *Commercial Advertiser,* April 5, 1849, quoted in *Elgin-Grey Papers,* I, 331. Very few American papers expressed a desire for annexation.

would be dangerous to intensify the threatening situation by throwing additional territory into the hopper. This reluctance was probably wise, though at least some from the South were ready to accept the annexation of Canada unless it appeared to be a plot hatched by abolitionists to add to the free states.[46]

In short, the desire for annexation in the United States was localized to a few border areas, and was weak and wavering even there.[47] The American government reflected the opinion of the great majority of its citizens when it refrained from giving aid or encouragement to the Canadian advocates of political union.[48]

Though the campaign of the Montreal Annexation Association made little progress through this thicket of obstacles, it persisted in its efforts and carried the fight into the Canadian assembly in 1850. Here its measures were supported by seven members, two of whom had been elected on the annexation issue.[49] Their efforts met with unvarying failure, however, and

[46] Southern opposition to annexation seems to have been somewhat exaggerated in earlier accounts. Several newspapers, representative of southern opinion and examined by the author, contained no adverse comment on the proposition, and *De Bow's Review*, IX (October, 1850), 397-412, counseled its readers to support annexation unless it appeared to have abolitionist origins.

[47] Buffalo Express, undated, quoted in *Elgin-Grey Papers*, I, 431-32.

[48] Secretary of State John M. Clayton sent a special agent to Canada to gather information on annexation and on commerce. This man, Israel D. Andrews, did not attempt to aid or encourage the annexationists in the colony. Department of State, Special Agents, XVI (National Archives, Washington). See especially the dispatches of June 28, July 31, August 29, October 30, December 6, 1849.

[49] J. S. Sanborn (Sherbrooke) and Papineau (Montmorency) were the two elected on annexationist platforms, the others being converted to that cause after they were elected. They were Jacob De Witt and Benjamin Holmes, Reform members from Montreal and signers of the manifesto; John McConnell, a representative from the Eastern Townships, who issued an annexation address; Colonel John Prince from Sandwich, Canada West, a persistent advocate of political union or independence; and Malcolm Cameron. Allin and Jones, *Annexation*, 334.

they finally abandoned the hopeless struggle. Popular support of the movement disintegrated, and by the autumn of 1850 even the pessimistic Governor General admitted that "there never was before in Canada such contentment."[50]

The sudden and complete eclipse of the agitation was the natural result of economic and political developments in the colony and Empire. The ascent to normality began late in 1849 as Canadians accommodated themselves to the new economic and Imperial order, and the depression was practically gone within a year. The revival of trade and business in Canada was almost miraculous. Agricultural production soared above the average of both 1849 and 1850. The harvesting of bumper crops fortunately coincided with a revived, and even an increased, demand for foodstuffs and raw materials in the markets of Great Britain and the United States. The gold rushes in California and Australia gradually increased the supply of money and the prices paid for Canadian grain, flour, and lumber. American buyers appeared in the colonial marts and made large purchases for export.[51] A further cause for renewed prosperity and reviving loyalty was the action taken by the Imperial government to repeal the Navigation Acts and sweep away the disadvantages of the old fiscal system. Trade increased greatly, and the commercial men of Canada, sublimating the dark memories of 1847 to 1849, settled down contentedly to enjoy the new prosperity.[52] Their minds accompanied their incomes back

[50] Elgin to Grey, October 6, 1850, *Elgin-Grey Papers,* II, 720-21. The annexationists joined either the extreme wing of the Reform Party (Clear Grits) or the agitation for independence.

[51] Innis and Lower, *Select Documents,* 260.

[52] Statistics of Montreal and Canadian exports:

	Montreal	*Canada*
1849	$1,700,960	$ 6,829,987
1851	2,503,916	12,706,022

Senate Documents, 32 Cong., 1 sess., no. 112, pp. 19, 426.

to normal. These happy developments showed that the annexationist campaign of 1849-1850 had been an attempt to sell Canada short on a rising market.

The memory of the three-year nightmare which Canada's economic distress had given to Lord Elgin marred that gentleman's enjoyment of the golden age after 1850. Dazzling prosperity did not blind him to the fact that joy and cash surpluses are fleeting and the unctuous loyalist of today might throw rotten eggs and hatch treason tomorrow, as he did yesterday. The Governor General's unhappy experiences taught him that the recurrent wrinkles in the Canadian economy must be ironed out to prevent future depressions with accompanying annexation movements. The only certain means to this end seemed to be a reciprocity in raw products with the United States to insure a steady market and trade for Canada. Undeterred by the failures of 1846 and 1848, he persuaded the home government to send Sir Henry Bulwer to Washington in 1849 with instructions to obtain the desired agreement, preferably by concurrent legislation in the United States and the several British North American colonies. To tempt the Yankees, several concessions could be dangled before them. The governments of the Maritime Colonies agreed that Bulwer might offer the right to use their inshore fisheries, and the Canadian government would add the use of the St. Lawrence by American shipping, on equal terms with British, as an additional bonus.

Bulwer made these offers in 1850 and 1851, but he was thwarted by an informal congressional alliance between the protectionists of the North and some southerners who feared that reciprocity might lead to annexation. In 1852, however, the situation began to change, and American opposition and indifference started to fade. In that year, the Imperial government dispatched nineteen cruisers to the fishing grounds with instructions to seize any American vessels poaching on British territorial waters.[53] Pressure from New England fishing interests compelled Washington to send a squadron to protect the "rights" of its nationals to fish. The danger of a collision between the two naval forces alarmed the American government and convinced it that agreement must be reached on outstanding issues. The reciprocity proposals then became an obvious solution for the emergency. Since further recourse to concurrent legislation seemed bootless, William L. Marcy, the American secretary of state, and John G. Crampton, British minister in Washington, proceeded to negotiate a treaty. In 1853 they produced a draft agreement providing for reciprocal free trade in raw materials between the United States and the colonies, for the admission of American ships to the St. Lawrence on terms of equality with Canadian ships, and for American use of the inshore fisheries of British North America.

Before final action could be taken, it was necessary to prepare colonial opinion for the acceptance of the treaty, particularly in the Maritime Colonies, whose inhabitants feared that their fisheries were being traded for a Canadian song. To help in overcoming their resistance, the American government sent a special agent, Israel D. Andrews, to the area. His persuasive powers and the silent eloquence of an ample secret service fund proved effective in paving the way for acceptance of the treaty in the colonies by the sea. At Andrews' suggestion, Lord Elgin appeared in Washington May 26, 1854, empowered to conclude the treaty. The urbane Governor General coordinated his social and diplomatic talents, washing away the opposition of skeptical but thirsty senators with a freshet of conversation and champagne. The treaty passed the Senate on August 2, 1854, by a good margin, and the President signed it three days later. Elgin

[53] Americans had been fishing within the three-mile limit in open violation of the law. There was some difference of opinion in measuring the limit; Americans claimed that it followed the sinuosities of the coast, while the British insisted on measuring it from the headlands.

could now return to England confident that he had laid the ghost of annexation by removing the possibility of future depressions.[54]

The history of the annexation agitation of the 1840's points to conclusions which should be reiterated. A prosperous United States set dangerous temptations before any class of Canadians who were in economic distress. His appreciation of this fact led Elgin to persist through vexatious disappointments until he had achieved reciprocity, even after the annexation movement had subsided. His alarm had validity. The allure of annexation was economic, not sentimental. But this was also its weakness, limiting its appeal in Canada to those who were, or believed themselves to be, in extremities, and to those who were close to the United States and could contrast the conditions in the two countries. Thus the sentiment for annexation was strongest from 1848 to 1850 among the merchants and in the areas adjoining the Republic.

On the other hand, it was equally evident that large and influential groups in Canada would resist political union stubbornly. The French Canadians treasured their nationalité above all else and opposed annexation because it would be fatal to it. Privileged institutions would clutch their British allegiance as the guarantee of their prerogatives; thus both the Roman Catholic Church and the party in power had much to lose and nothing to gain by annexation.

A final and important barrier to annexation was the cool indifference or the hostility of most Americans to the proposition. They had no desire to add an area which offered little

[54] The treaty gave Americans the right to take fish in the territorial waters of the colonies as well as the use of the St. Lawrence and its canals. There was to be reciprocal free trade in all important raw materials, such as wheat, lumber, fish, wool, cotton, coal, meal, meat, and flour. The treaty was terminable on twelve months' notice by either party after its minimum term had expired. The description of the negotiations is based on Tansill, *Reciprocity*, 30-81.

prospect of material benefit and might even entail loss, for the Canadian producers could be formidable competitors.

Thus the annexation movement of 1848-1850 had a tottering foundation and determined enemies. Failing to undermine the loyalty of the great majority of Canadians, it was as ephemeral as the depression which had produced it.

CHAPTER TWO

Reciprocity, Annexation, Confederation 1854-1867

Ironically, the reciprocity which Elgin deemed the salvation of British North America eventually threatened to become its nemesis. This inversion of intent was not soon apparent, for the ten years which followed the ratification of the treaty of 1854 were a period of golden contentment. The prosperity of these colonies, like that of other young economies, depended upon their exportation of raw materials. In 1853 the exports from British North America to the United States were valued at $6,527,559. By 1857 they had grown to $22,008,916, and during the remaining life of the treaty, sales of colonial products to the Republic averaged around $25,000,000.[1]

This phenomenal growth of trade flowed from the confluence of several factors, of which the Reciprocity Treaty of 1854 was only one. The development of a "commerce of convenience" helped to increase Canadian-American trade. For example, Canada West purchased its coal from nearby Pennsylvania, while New England bought its fuel from Nova Scotia. This type of trade was developing prior to 1854; the treaty stimulated it, but did not cause it.

The reexport trade was likewise responsible for much of the increase in commerce. As already noted, the trans-Atlantic freight rates from New York were notably cheaper than those from Montreal, and Canadians naturally used the American entrepôt whenever they could. Like the trade of convenience, this tendency appeared before reciprocity and, under the American drawback system, had steadily gained from 1845 to 1853.

The Civil War in the United States created an extraordinary demand for foodstuffs, timber, and horses from the colonies, and would have done so without reciprocity. The growth of American industry and the multiplication of transportation facilities between the two countries also brought a greater exchange of commodities across the border even when relatively high duties prevailed.[2]

Canadian-American trade was thus swelling under the spur of a number of causes which were independent of the treaty of 1854. The role of that agreement was to enhance these forces, to clear the channels of manmade snags, and to permit the passage of goods to occur naturally.

At the time, however, the people of British North America were oblivious of these forces and credited the growth of their commerce with the United States to the treaty. Perhaps inevitably, they invested reciprocity with ever greater importance until many of them came to believe that it was the foundation of their economy and the guarantee of their livelihood. In short, the treaty of 1854 occupied the place in public esteem formerly held by the dream of the commercial empire of the St. Lawrence and the reality of Imperial preference.

The intent of Lord Elgin was thus twisted and turned in upon itself. He had expected reciprocity to dispel the dangers of annexation. Instead, the faith of the colonists in the treaty had led them to believe that they were economically in thrall to free access to the American market. If the treaty ended and a depression ensued, Canadians might again urge annexation to get free trade. It was, under these circumstances, inconceivable that the government of any of the colonies would kill the goose which kept laying such agreeably golden eggs. Its lifespan depended entirely upon the American attitude.

[1] Trade statistics in *Senate Executive Documents,* 53 Cong., 2 sess., no. 106.

[2] Donald C. Masters, *The Reciprocity Treaty of 1854* (London, 1937), 191-202.

Though the United States as a whole found the treaty satisfactory, various interests and elements began to amalgamate into a formidable opposition to it. The commercial men of New York were certain that the treaty was diverting western trade into the St. Lawrence system. Mine operators in the Middle States feared the spreading importation of Nova Scotian coal, which had already gripped the New England market. Some farming and lumbering groups believed that Canadian competition had become injurious.

The opposition of American manufacturers to the treaty was the most serious of all. They had accepted it reluctantly, for it violated their dogma of protection. The proponents of reciprocity had persuaded them to give it a trial on the ground that the agreement would enrich the Canadians and enable them to buy more American manufactures, though these articles were not on the free list. Results belied expectations. The largest sale of such goods in Canada occurred in 1854, the year before the treaty went into effect; their exports to the colonies declined thereafter.[3] Open opposition of the industrialists to the treaty replaced their grudging toleration. The agreement had not been the expected boon, and it was a dangerous entering wedge for free trade.

The industrialist was a formidable enemy. His economic importance was growing at a fast rate, and his political influence had a parallel acceleration as the Republicans embraced protection partly as a heritage from the Whigs and partly as a shrewd identification with the coming economic interest. Members of the party in Congress who spoke for the manufacturers constantly voiced their opposition to reciprocity and were ready to use any opportunity to kill the agreement of 1854.

Their first chance to strike a blow came in 1858. Fiscal necessity and pressure from Canadian industrialists forced the colonial government to raise the tariff from 15 to 20 or 25 percent

[3] Masters, 73-74, 205.

on products which comprised the bulk of manufactured imports from the United States.[4] Though the treaty of 1854 did not include such commodities, the American enemies of reciprocity denounced the action as a violation of the spirit of the treaty and of the unwritten law that neither party would increase tariff rates during the life of the agreement. They launched a Senate investigation to determine whether the United States should give notice of the abrogation of the treaty as soon as it was legally possible to do so.[5] Israel T. Hatch, an economist and merchant of Buffalo, asserted in a report that Canada had violated both the terms and the spirit of the treaty, which he believed should be terminated.[6]

Though such clamor reduced the popularity of the treaty, its friends still had the votes to preserve it.[7] The South was committed to a low tariff and fought hard to maintain this example of free trade. The West, as a whole, also supported it. The opening of the St. Lawrence route was a valuable asset to them, for they used the threat of cheap Canadian transportation to secure lower rates on American canals and railroads and to reduce the delays occasioned by overcrowding of those facilities. Certain interests which benefited from the treaty also defended it. Most commercial men of the border states were reaping rich profits from the increasing trade between the two countries. The fishermen of New England could now make their catch in the territorial waters of the colonies and run into their harbors for supplies and repairs without hindrance or vexing regulations. Even a few of the manufacturers, principally those of New England, favored the treaty because it enabled them to import raw materials from the colonies duty-free.

These friendly interests were able to fend off the onslaughts on the treaty, and it seemed safe to assume that the agreement

[4] Masters, 113-17.
[5] *Senate Journal,* 35 Cong., 2 sess., 209, 292-93.
[6] *House Executive Documents,* 36 Cong., 1 sess., no. 96, II.
[7] *House Exec. Doc.* 96, I.

would continue to exist after 1866 in the warm climate of friendly Anglo- and Canadian-American relations. But the Civil War rapidly cooled this genial atmosphere. Shortly after the firing on Fort Sumter the North began to exhibit toward Great Britain an antipathy which expanded as the conflict continued. Americans simmered at the recognition of southern belligerency by the British government. The Trent affair and the outspoken sympathy of the governing classes in Great Britain for the rebels added fuel, and the building of commerce raiders, particularly the *Alabama,* fanned the flame into a dangerous blaze. To many northerners, Great Britain was an enemy equal to the Confederacy.[8]

As usual, American antipathy toward Great Britain comprehended everything British, including the neighboring colonies. This was natural, for Canada was contiguous and vulnerable, and Britain distant and unassailable. The War of 1812 had given warning that the United States would avenge wrongs suffered at the hands of the mother country by striking at the exposed flank of her Empire.

Nor was the animosity of Americans toward British North America entirely a vicarious expression of wrath against Great Britain. In American eyes the neutrality record of the colonies was not spotless. Halifax and St. John were notorious centers for blockade running.[9] Some members of the governing classes in all the colonies aped their English counterparts in loud eagerness for Confederate victory. Though this group did not represent colonial opinion, its prominence guaranteed it an audience in the United States. Far more serious were the incidents which occurred on the border. The Confederate government sent two commissioners, C. C. Clay and Jacob Thompson, to Canada in 1864. Here they discharged with virtuosity their

[8] For difficulties with Great Britain, and particularly the *Alabama* affair, see Allan Nevins, *Hamilton Fish: The Inner History of the Grant Administration* (New York, 1936), 142-47.

[9] Masters, *Reciprocity,* 133.

instructions to harass the North from their neutral vantage, perhaps in hope of provoking an American attack upon Canada and embroiling Great Britain in the war. The agents organized riots in northern cities, commissioned privateers to attack American commerce on the Great Lakes, and plotted armed incursions into the United States. On one occasion a group of Confederates slipped away from Canada to release southern prisoners held on an island in Lake Erie. They failed to reach their objective, but succeeded in scuttling two American ships. The St. Albans raid was more spectacular. A band of Confederates filtered across the border and burst into the Vermont town on October 19, 1864. They lent a quasi-wildwest touch by shooting up the town, robbing the bank, and appropriating horses as "contraband" to aid their escape. Canadian authorities promptly seized the Confederates on their return from this foray, but a local court, overtaken by finicky and unwelcome precision, did Canadian-American relations untold harm by releasing the prisoners on a technicality.[10]

It is understandable that American wrath should explode over unpunished forays from the privileged sanctuary of a friendly neutral. Several thousand troops were stationed at the border to prevent further incursions, and the officer in charge, General John A. Dix, ordered his men to pursue raiders across the border in spite of the danger of collisions with the British soldiers in Canada.[11] Senator Zachariah Chandler of Michigan, notoriously anti-British, loudly demanded that the government station an army on the border and a fleet upon the Great Lakes. Though this was not done, such pressures and the gust of public anger forced William H. Seward, American secretary of state, to bow to the storm. In October, 1864, he instructed the American minister, C. F. Adams, to notify the British government that

[10] James M. Callahan, *American Foreign Policy in Canadian Relations* (New York, 1937), 280, 282-83.

[11] Joe Patterson Smith, *Republican Expansionists of the Early Reconstruction Era* (Chicago, 1933), 14-15.

the United States would terminate the Rush-Bagot agreement in twelve months. When public anger had subsided, the notice was withdrawn, March, 1865.

It was to be expected that such alert opportunists as the foes of reciprocity would exploit this revulsion of American opinion toward Canada. They returned to their assaults upon the treaty of 1854, shrewdly arguing that it would be folly further to enrich a country which was the virtual ally of the Confederacy. The friends of reciprocity fought hard, but the odds against them had grown when the withdrawal of the southern members of Congress shattered the free trade bloc. With a supreme effort they beat back an assault in May, 1864, mustering a small majority against a House measure to abrogate the treaty. By December of the same year the temper of Congress was malign, for the St. Albans raid had occurred in the meanwhile. After a debate which bristled with hostility toward Canada, the House passed a resolution requesting the President to give notice of abrogation.[12] Though they had used the St. Albans affair as ammunition in the House, the protectionists discarded it in the Senate, where they already had a majority. Here their theme was the desperate need for more revenue to prosecute the war: abrogation of the treaty would restore the tariff on trade with Canada. They also pointed out that the treaty was indirectly preventing the assessment of excise taxes upon the articles on the free list. Such a levy would increase the costs of American producers and give the advantage to their Canadian competitors while free trade prevailed. The debate was a solemn sham enacted for the benefit of public opinion, for the protectionists always had the votes to achieve their aim. When the resolution for abrogation was allowed to come to a vote, it passed thirty-three to eight. Seward, on March 17, 1865, gave the required twelve months' notice for termination.[13] Thus the six-year strug-

[12] *Congressional Globe,* 38 Cong., 2 sess., 31 *et passim.*
[13] Callahan, *Canadian Relations,* 284.

gle between the forces of free trade and the forces of protection ended in victory for the latter. The Reciprocity Treaty of 1854 became another casualty of the Civil War.

The abrogation of reciprocity was not a complete surprise to realistic Canadians, who recognized that its continuation depended upon a protectionist and Anglophobe Congress; but it was nevertheless a blow to them.[14] However, they still had a year in which to find means to fend off disaster, for the treaty would remain in effect until March, 1866. The colonists saw two possible solutions for this problem: Canada might offer Congress better terms to renew the treaty, or the colonial governments might construct an alternate market by hastening the completion of confederation. At the moment, the former alternative seemed to offer the better chance of realization before the year of grace expired.

Canadian hopes for a new treaty were not unrealistic. Some of the congressmen who had voted for abrogation declared that they were not opposed to the principle of reciprocity but to the terms of the treaty of 1854, which had favored Canada.[15] An amended treaty, adding manufactures to the free list, might win their votes and dissolve the hostility of American idustrialists. Moreover, many Americans who had supported reciprocity were not disheartened by abrogation and were taking steps to revive the agreement.[16] Midwesterners feared that their loss of the use of the St. Lawrence would expose them to higher rates and lower standards of service because the operators of American railroads and canals would be freed from Canadian competition. Seward, a reliable barometer in Canadian-American

[14] In 1864 some Canadians were worrying about the danger of the termination of the treaty in 1866. Charles Stanley, Viscount Monck to Henry Pelham, Duke of Newcastle, March 15, 1864, G 465, Despatches to the Colonial Secretary, 1864 (Public Archives of Canada, Ottawa).

[15] Masters, *Reciprocity*, 153-54.

[16] *Congressional Globe*, 38 Cong., 2 sess., 71.

affairs, registered these pressures and cautiously warmed a bit. He informed the British chargé at Washington that when the war was over, the American government would "cheerfuly" enter negotiations to determine whether "a just, fair and equitable reciprocity in trade can be established between the United States and Canada." He warned that the unsatisfactory terms of the earlier agreement must be revised in any new treaty.[17]

The British and Canadian governments leaped to seize this implied invitation and informed Seward that they were ready to open negotiations for a new treaty. The wary secretary, with one eye on the protectionists of his own country, chilled their ardor by saying that public opinion in the United States was not yet ready for such action. He carefully sidestepped further responsibility by suggesting that the Canadians take up the question with the proper committees of Congress before submitting definite proposals to the Department of State.

Despite Seward's coolness to the advances which he had encouraged, the colonists continued their efforts to renew reciprocity.[18] In July, 1865, the Canadian cabinet appointed A. T. Galt and W. P. Howland as agents to secure a new treaty. They hastened to Washington and interviewed both Seward and Hugh McCulloch, secretary of the treasury. Their reception was disheartening, and the Canadians returned to Ottawa to report to their government in December, 1865.[19]

Persistence was one of the virtues of these emissaries, who returned to Washington to approach Congress when it convened. They conferred with the House Committee on Ways and Means and offered to make almost any concession to save the life of the expiring treaty. As a result of these meetings, the

[17] Seward to J. H. Burnley, March 9, 1865, Diplomatic Notes, Great Britain, LXXVII (National Archives, Washington).

[18] Smith believes that Seward never intended to renew reciprocity negotiations. Smith, *Republican Expansionists*, 48-49.

[19] Sir John A. Macdonald Papers, Reciprocity, 1865-1866 (Public Archives of Canada, Ottawa).

committee promised to submit the project of a new treaty to the House. By its terms, the inshore fisheries must be reopened to American use. In return, the colonies would receive the munificent free list of millstones, grindstones, gypsum, and rags. The Canadian delegates had no choice but to reject this mocking proposal.[20]

While the Canadian government was conducting these abortive attempts to preserve the old treaty or to negotiate a new one, American friends of reciprocity busied themselves to the same purpose. They sought to create public pressures which would force Congress to act favorably. The boards of trade in cities near the border and in the colonies were urged to send delegates to a convention in Detroit in July, 1865, to publicize the advantages of reciprocity and to devise means to force Washington to renew the abrogated agreement. About four hundred and fifty delegates attended the meeting, representing cities from Bangor, Maine, to St. Paul, Minnesota, and eighteen commercial organizations in British North America. The conference unanimously adopted a resolution urging the negotiation of a new reciprocity treaty, but despite the influence represented in this convention, Congress ignored the request.[21] The protectionists would not easily abandon the spoils of their hard-earned victory in 1865.

When it became evident that the treaty of 1854 was gone beyond recall, a new annexation flurry blew up. Many businessmen in British North America felt, as their predecessors had in 1849, that the economic foundation of their country had been destroyed and that depression would beset them until they could restore free trade with the United States. Since all hope of reciprocity was closed, annexation was the only remaining gate to this free trade, and some Canadians were ready to enter it.

[20] Macdonald Papers, Reciprocity, 1865-1866.

[21] Reports of the conference in New York *Times*, July 13, 14, 15, 17, 1865; New York *Daily Tribune*, July 14, 15, 18, 1865.

This new movement, which lacked the vigor and organization of its predecessor, was strongest in the larger cities, such as Montreal and Toronto, which had the most to lose from a decline of commerce. American consuls in these centers informed Washington that local business leaders were publicly urging annexation to continue prosperity. In Montreal, even the loyal press admitted that the movement was strong and growing in both parties. Many were reported as saying that union with the United States was Canada's inevitable destiny and "the sooner it is brought about the better for the peace and prosperity of the province."[22]

In Canada West, proximity to the United States promoted the movement in the Niagara Peninsula and adjacent areas. Here it was serious enough to earn the dignity of formal denunciation, and the threat of the law was invoked on those careless of their loyalty. The grand jury of Victoria County in their presentment at assizes vigorously deplored "the views of some wily politicians who are . . . setting forth the financial depression of the country and recommending as a panacea annexation to the United States." If necessary, the people of the area would use force of arms to frustrate such purposes and preserve the British connection.[23] Unabashed by this warning, newspapers and individuals continued the agitation. The St. Catherines *Post* and the Galt *Reporter* were bold for political union, as were papers in Kincardine and St. Mary's. Others did not openly favor the change but discussed it freely while complaining bitterly of current conditions. A local politician stated: "Speaking of annexation, who is there whether Whig, Tory or Radical that does not acknowledge this . . . to be our inevitable destiny. For my part, I say . . . that this would be for the material benefit

[22] D. Thurston to Seward, March 31, 1865, Consular Despatches to the Department of State, Toronto, I, 9 (National Archives, Washington); John Potter to Seward, undated but obviously 1865, Consular Despatches, Montreal, VI.

[23] Niagara *Mail*, June 7, 1865.

of Canada. Therefore I say 'Let it come.' "[24] The St. Catherines *Post* declared that "a majority of our people would unhesitatingly adopt any fair and honest terms of union" with the United States.[25] It would appear that the audience for such pronouncements was, as in Montreal, among the merchants and Tories; the farmers seemed to pay little attention to the movement.[26]

The loyal press fought back, patiently trying to persuade the annexationists of the economic and other disadvantages of joining the United States or, alternately, scolding them angrily for their sedition.[27] Unfortunately for these journals, the heat of their righteous indignation was somewhat cooled by an untimely article in the London *Times* which stated that the British government should not object to the extension of American territory to Mexico or Canada if "it is done honestly and with the consent of the people concerned." Indeed, concluded the Thunderer crushingly, it was "not . . . considered a matter of great moment to England." This sentiment was gleefully quoted by the annexationists to prove that they were not traitors, and grumpily reproached by the loyal, who felt deserted in their thankless task of trying to preserve a connection seemingly unwanted by the mother country itself.[28]

The annexation tremor of 1865, however, lacked the vigor and endurance of its predecessor, and soon died out. Several weaknesses hastened its rapid demise. For one thing, it grew from anticipated rather than actual effects of the abrogation of reci-

[24] Letter quoted in Niagara *Mail,* August 21, 1865, and taken from St. Catherines *Post* of the same date. The writer was unidentified except for the notation that he was a politician currently seeking election.

[25] St. Catherines *Post,* undated, quoted in Niagara *Mail,* December 27, 1865.

[26] Thurston to Seward, February 23, March 29, 1865, Consular Despatches, Toronto, I, 7, 20; New York *Daily Tribune,* July 8, August 4, 1865.

[27] Niagara *Mail,* October 4, 18, 1865.

[28] London *Times,* undated, quoted in Niagara *Mail,* December 27, 1865.

procity, since the treaty would remain in effect until 1866. In reality, Canada was enjoying considerable prosperity. The advocates of political union argued that this was bottomed on free trade with the United States and was not likely to survive it, but their logic was not irresistible and attracted relatively little support.[29] It is true that many Canadians held the melancholy conviction that absorption by the United States was probably their ultimate destiny, but they were not anxious to hasten the process. Their loyalty to colony and Empire had a tenacious quality which would yield only to compelling necessity. A merely potential "depression" lacked such compulsion.

If there was no desperation to drive Canadians into the United States, neither was there attraction to lure them in. The Republic was moderately prosperous, but other factors balanced this. The country had just emerged, exhausted, from the Civil War with its heritage of enormous debt, heavy taxes, and such perplexing problems as reconstruction, reconciliation, and the future of the freedmen. Canadians shrank from sharing these burdens.[30]

Beyond this, the attitude and utterances of many Americans goaded the majority of colonists into resentment which engendered an angry reaction to any suggestions of political union. During the Civil War, some newspapers and public men in the United States suggested the invasion and conquest of Canada to avenge the unneutral acts of Britain; they even proposed to combine the Union and Confederate armies for this agreeable purpose.[31] Others favored economic coercion as a cheaper and kindlier means to the same end. If the United States barred

[29] Isaac Buchanan, *The Relations of the Industry of Canada with the Mother Country and the United States* (Montreal, 1864), 19-20.

[30] Niagara *Mail*, October 18, 1865. This article features statistics which indicate that economically the Canadian was in a more favorable condition than the American.

[31] Albany (New York) *Atlas and Argus*, undated, quoted in the New York *Times*, January 9, 1865. The Richmond *Enquirer*, a leading Confederate paper, was also advocating this idea.

imports from the colony, it must seek annexation to escape ruin.[32] The Radical Republicans, striving to gain control of the government, were particularly articulate on this theme. Alarmed at the general condemnation of the abrogation of reciprocity among American commercial interests, they pointed out that the termination of reciprocity would force Canada into the United States and restore permanently the trade which American merchants feared lost. In short, the Radicals had no real desire for acquiring Canada, but used the proposition as bait to attract votes.

This was not apparent to Canadians, who naturally took these sinister suggestions seriously, and with fear and resentment.[33] Their desire to stay in the Empire was hardened by American threats, whether of armed invasion or of economic coercion. Several events showed that colonists and British officials alike had become ultrasensitive to and furious at the slightest suggestion of annexation.

In March, 1865, for example, Robert Walker, a former senator from Mississippi and a supporter of the Union during the Civil War, visited Canada. The baseless rumor at once spread that the American government had sent him there to stimulate the movement for political union. One newspaper reported that he was liberally supplied with cash to grease the path, for the United States was willing to pay $100,000,000 to gain Canada. Denials issued by the amazed Walker and by Seward were received with cold disbelief in Canada.[34]

Another episode which was magnified into a serious threat to Canada had a broader touch of the ridiculous. Sir Fredrick

[32] Smith, *Republican Expansionists,* 33.

[33] Most American papers were hostile to the idea of annexation by coercion of any sort. For example, see Cincinnati *Commercial,* July 19, 1865; New York *Times,* July 22, 1865.

[34] J. H. Burnley to John Earl Russell, March 24, 1865, Foreign Office, Great Britain, Series 5: 1017 (Library of Congress photostats, Washington; hereafter cited as F. O. 5). Walker's mission in Canada was to treat with the Confederate commissioners there.

Bruce, British minister at Washington, became excited over an advertisement in the Brooklyn *Eagle* calling for volunteers to join an expedition which had the notably flexible goal of conquering either Canada or Mexico. Bruce reported this episode to London and earnestly protested to Seward against any contemplated aggression by Brooklyn.[35]

These incidents inflated Canadian wrath, which finally exploded in July, 1865, as a result of an episode connected with the Detroit commercial convention mentioned above. A number of Americans present were annexationists, but they recognized Canadian sensibilities on the subject and forbore to mention it.[36] Unfortunately, there was a militant bull in this shop of delicate china. He was John Potter, ebullient American consul general at Montreal, who was attending the meeting at Seward's suggestion. Other Americans tried to prevent him from exercising his lungs in a public address to the assembly, but he would not be totally silenced. At a private meeting with his countrymen, Potter entertained with samples of his best spread-eagle oratory. Some Canadians tip-toed into the room during the speech, bringing a reporter with them. The following day a local paper printed a verbatim account of the Potter effusions, and the Canadian press was quick to copy it. Colonial readers were interested to learn that the consul general accredited to their country opposed the renewal of the treaty of 1854 because he wished to force them into annexation: "I believe that in two years from the abrogation of the Reciprocity Treaty the people of Canada themselves will apply for admission to the United States." When several of the Canadians present cried "No! No!" Potter firmly reiterated his statement.[37]

[35] Sir Fredrick Bruce to Russell, May 16, 1865, F. O. 5: 1017; Bruce to Seward, May 19, 1865, Diplomatic Notes, Great Britain, LXXXVIII, Sir Fredrick Bruce.

[36] H. H. Emmons to Seward, August 4, 1865, Miscellaneous Letters to the Department of State, 1865, August, I (National Archives, Washington).

[37] New York *Times*, July 21, 1865.

This was too much. Canadians had vainly fumed at American press references to economic pressures, but the same proposal from an American official stationed in Canada was intolerable and the angry colonials could not allow it to pass. They drew up a petition asking their government to investigate Potter's conduct and stating that it was the common belief in Montreal that he "has been engaged in subverting our government . . . [and] . . . with others has by meetings and otherwise taken active measures to promote the annexation of the Province of Canada to the United States of America."[38] Colonial officials with difficulty dissuaded the people of Montreal from holding meetings to demand Potter's recall. The temper in Canada now made annexation a forbidden word there. Its advocates, who had been increasing in number and in the candor of their remarks, were driven to cover and to silence before the blast of public indignation. Most Americans viewed these incidents with much amazement and some amusement. The press urged Canadians to shed their fears, for the United States had no desire to acquire Canada by any means. With a touch of hauteur the New York *Times* remarked that "we should not, in fact, know that such a thing [annexation] was ever thought of by anyone if we did not from time to time learn of it from the Canadian papers."[39]

Though American indifference to and Canadian wrath at annexation killed the ephemeral movement of 1865, this did not convince the Imperial and colonial governments that Canadian loyalty would be impregnable before the assults of a commercial depression. As already noted, there seemed to be two means to avert this eventuality: renewal of the treaty of 1854 or the completion of confederation. Since the attempts to restore reciprocity had proved abortive, the union of British North America remained as the main hope of continuing prosperity.

[38] New York *Times*, July 21, 1865.
[39] New York *Times*, July 22, 1865.

This concept was born at the time of the American Revolution and kept alive by continuing fear that the United States would gobble up the weak and isolated colonies. But the various plans proposed for union had miscarried because the Imperial government had been inimical, fearing that union of their provinces would hasten their independence and, probably, their absorption by the American Republic. Changing conditions dissolved the indifference and the hostility to federation in the middle of the nineteenth century. The Union Act of 1840 joined Canada East and Canada West but failed to endow them with a stable administration. The government staggered from one constitutional crisis to another. The problem of the British West also demanded attention and solution. American settlers were filtering into the fringes of this vast empire, and decisive action might soon be necessary to prevent an encore of the Oregon story.

The Civil War was probably the greatest catalyst in precipitating confederation. As seen above, Americans were bitterly hostile to Britain and to Canada, and some had not scrupled to urge that the colony be seized to replace the departed southern states.[40] The *Trent* crisis showed the British government that war was possible, and their North American colonies were ill prepared to fight it. The Imperial cabinet had hastened to reinforce Canada and warned the colonials to prepare to defend themselves. Their slowness to respond and the lack of cooperation between them dismayed the home authorities, as did the inadequacy of transportation between the Maritime Colonies and Canada. The Imperial troops dispatched during the *Trent* emergency had reached Canada only with the greatest difficulty, which might well prove fatal in the event of actual hostilities. Obviously, British America was utterly unprepared to meet a real crisis.

[40] For the press campaign favoring the conquest of Canada, see Lester B. Shippee, *Canadian-American Relations, 1849-1873* (New Haven, 1939), 183-89.

The conclusion of the war did not end the threat. Certain American papers inquired, "Whom do we fight next?" and answered their own question by urging that American armies be turned upon Canada.[41] At the same time, the increasing urgency of American notes to Napoleon III suggested that the United States might undertake the pleasing task of expelling European powers bodily from their American holdings. These portents were not erased by Seward's official assurances that the United States "did not contemplate war with Great Britain whether for Canada or any other object," nor by the mustering out of the American army.[42] The colonists remembered that this same Seward had publicly promised in 1860 that all British North America would soon become part of the United States. The American army had dissolved, but it could easily be reassembled if the government decided to attack Canada.

The Fenian raids in particular seemed to discount pacific assurances from the United States. The Fenian Brotherhood, a secret organization of Irish republicans, boasted 100,000 members in the United States, many of them veterans of the Civil War. They planned to invade Canada less to annex it than to create a diversion of British troops to North America to aid a simultaneous revolt in Ireland. Many Americans wished them well, seeing their activities as a just retribution of an angry God upon those who had harbored the St. Albans raiders. The society was thus encouraged to launch attacks from New York and Vermont in June, 1866.[43] Though these invasions failed, it was evident that colonial defenses might be overset by an incursion in real force. Canadians must shore up their ramparts by union with the other colonies.

[41] Smith, *Republican Expansionists*, 29, 33.

[42] Seward to C. F. Adams, March 10, 1865, Diplomatic Instructions, Great Britain, XX (National Archives, Washington).

[43] Callahan, *Canadian Relations*, 291; Shippee, *Canadian-American Relations*, 213-39.

The need for defense did not obscure other pressing reasons for confederation. The problem of the British West, the need for railroads which no single colony could afford to build, and the end of the Reciprocity Treaty all suggested the necessity of joint efforts.

At the beginning of the Civil War, the assembly of Nova Scotia asked the home government to state its attitude toward the union of British North America. The colonial secretary replied that the cabinet would give serious consideration to any such proposal from the colonies. The governments of the other provinces, however, considered the suggestion premature.[44]

But growing fear of American military force or economic pressure rapidly ripened their desire for closer unity. In the waning summer of 1864, the governments of Nova Scotia, New Brunswick, and Prince Edward Island called a conference at Charlottetown to consider the formation of a Maritime federation. A delegation from Canada appeared before this meeting and convinced it that the wider latitude of a union of all British North American colonies was possible and necessary. The conference adjourned to meet again in Quebec the following month, October, and construct the framework of federation.[45]

During the interval between the two sessions, the Canadian government prepared a set of resolutions which it proposed as the constitution of the new union. The Quebec Conference adopted these, with some modifications, and then dissolved, the delegates returning to their respective colonies to fight for the acceptance of the seventy-two resolutions.[46] Necessity whipped them to haste.[47] Reciprocity would end in March, 1866, and

[44] Reginald G. Trotter, *Canadian Federation, Its Origins and Achievements* (Toronto, 1924), 39-42.

[45] Trotter, 86-90, 92-99. [46] Trotter, 108-16.

[47] Lord Monck, the Governor General, was constantly spurring them on. Monck to the Executive Council of Canada, June 6, 1866, G 180 B, 94, Secret and Confidential Despatches, 1856-1866 (Public Archives of Canada, Ottawa).

federation must soon be completed if it were to play any part in warding off the dreaded depression which seemed certain to follow. Moreover, the imminent end of the Civil War would soon free the American army for hostile adventures against the colonies. Since delay might mean the difference between annexation and federation, the supporters of union urged a speedy acceptance of the Quebec Resolutions.

They met with success in Canada. The most serious objections to confederation in the Canadian legislature came from the French members. The Quebec proposals set them upon the horns of a dilemma. They would be a minority in the new federation, with the dangers attendant upon that position. On the other hand, if the choice lay between confederation and annexation, the defense of nationalité demanded the former as the lesser evil. So the resolutions passed the Canadian legislature with much debate but little difficulty.

Hostility in the Maritimes, however, doomed the drive for a speedy completion of confederation. Their people had initiated the movement for union and expected that leadership would be the reward of authorship. Instead, it was painfully apparent that Canada would assume the dominant position in the federation and the Maritimes would be a minority with particular interests which might be subverted by the majority.[48] A psychological factor complicated the situation: particularism was a salient characteristic of political thinking in Nova Scotia, New Brunswick, and Prince Edward Island. The people of these colonies lived in their own world, geographically separated from the St. Lawrence Valley and with little desire to be politically coupled to it; they lived by and from the sea and tended to look out upon it and not toward the heart of the continent.

[48] These provinces were afraid that Canada would not consent to providing an adequate protection for their fisheries. Moreover, the total population of Nova Scotia, New Brunswick, and Prince Edward Island was not equal to that of either Ontario or Quebec.

Moreover, confederation would strike them in the pocketbook. The Maritimes had been wedded to free trade, for they depended upon lumbering and fishing for their livelihood and had to import much of what they consumed. Canada, on the other hand, dreamed of industrialization and would surely girdle the new union with its tariff wall.[49] Nova Scotia particularly disliked the financial terms which would compel her to surrender most of her sources of revenue to the central government, receiving in return an annual per capita subvention of eighty cents. Such a bargain would beggar them. The income of the provincial government, which had been $1,500,000 in 1865, would shrink to $750,000 under confederation. Besides, the province would have to contribute $640,000 annually to the upkeep of the new government, leaving little to support such necessaries as education and public works.[50]

These were the reasons sufficient to impel the people of the Maritimes to resist adoption of the Quebec Resolutions. The governments of Newfoundland and Prince Edward Island rejected the scheme out of hand, but they were small and peripheral colonies whose adherence was not considered essential.[51] It was quite otherwise with Nova Scotia and New Brunswick; the completion of the union depended upon their acceptance. When S. L. Tilley, the confederationist premier of New Brunswick dissolved his assembly and held an election on the question of confederation, he was roundly beaten.[52] Dr. Charles Tupper, leader of the Nova Scotian government and likewise a con-

[49] The Canadian tariff averaged 20 percent; that of Nova Scotia, levied principally on luxuries, averaged 10 percent. Joseph Howe Papers, 26, pt. I, Miscellaneous Papers on Confederation, 152-54 (Public Archives of Canada, Ottawa).

[50] Yarmouth *Tribune*, June 27, 1866.

[51] Trotter, *Federation*, 125.

[52] The returns showed twelve of the assembly for union, twenty-six opposed, and one doubtful. St. Andrews *New Brunswick Standard*, March 22, 1865.

federationist, learned wisdom from this example and did not make an issue of union in his colony. But the damage was done. New Brunswick was the geographic pivot of the proposed federation, and its rejection of the scheme seemed a fatal wound.

Fortunately, this was the darkness before dawn, and other forces were soon at work moving the recalcitrant province. The British government put its overwhelming pressure upon New Brunswick to accept the Quebec Resolutions. Lieutenant Governor Sir Arthur H. Gordon, who had sympathized with the anti-confederationists, was a hasty convert to the "true faith" upon receipt of a sharp admonition from the colonial secretary.[53] The voting public lacked such clarifying revelations, but found the same conclusion in other experiences. They were deeply disappointed by the failure of attempts to renew reciprocity, upon which they had counted heavily. Talk of annexation in the United States, in Canada, and in New Brunswick itself gave them concern, and the Fenian raids frightened them.[54] The chastened Gordon virtually forced a new election on his anti-confederationist government in 1866, and the results of the previous year were reversed. Nova Scotia also found the ways of righteousness, though through an iniquitous bypath. The wily Tupper, who had declined to challenge the federation question by making it an election issue, coaxed from his assembly a resolution providing for the renewal of negotiations for union. Using this as a virtual carte blanche, he dispatched a delegation

[53] For a complete discussion of the change in New Brunswick, see George Wilson, "New Brunswick's Entrance into Confederation," *Canadian Historical Review*, IX (March, 1928), 4-24.

[54] The American consul at St. John reported that a quarter of the people of the province favored annexation. James Howard to Seward, May 14, 1866, Consular Despatches, St. John, VI, 159.

Curiously, the Fenian raids seem to have promoted the cause of annexation as well as the cause of confederation, for many Canadians who felt that their country was defenseless were ready for "peace at any price." Monck to Henry Herbert, Earl of Carnarvon, September 28, 1866, G 180 B, Secret and Confidential Despatches, 1856-1866.

to London, where they joined representatives of the other two colonies. The upshot was the enactment of confederation by the British Parliament in the form of the British North America Act.

The anticonfederationists fumed and sputtered at this trick which Tupper had played upon them, and none more than their leader, Joseph Howe, a great and yet a pathetic figure in the history of British North America. He had had his day of glory when he led, and won, the struggle for responsible government in his colony. His interminable journeyings and campaigns throughout Nova Scotia had added to the fame which this victory had given him. There was scarcely an inhabitant of that province who had not seen and heard the gregarious "Joe" and shaken his hand—or been kissed by him if the subject were female, young, and pretty. Yet Howe's stature had diminished by 1860. He had never duplicated his great triumph, and he had cheapened himself by his constant petitions to the British government for office. Charles Tupper, less flamboyant but a stumper of rare and rude power, was coming to dominate Nova Scotia. Howe needed again to lead a popular cause to restore his ancient glory. It is understandable that he should seek to retrieve fame by opposing confederation, for most Nova Scotians would follow him in this. Jealousy also dressed him for the role; it is legend in Nova Scotia that when asked why he opposed union, Howe candidly replied that he refused "to play second fiddle to that damned Tupper." There were more honorable reasons. Howe sincerely believed that the terms of the Quebec Resolutions were a bad bargain for his province, and he resented the trick by which Tupper had sent a delegation to London.

The "antis," as the opponents of union were called, fought to block confederation in the British Parliament. They formed the League of the Maritime Provinces and sent Howe and others to London under instructions to point out to the Colonial Office that there were "propositions . . . made . . . in the Congress of the United States [which is] publicly entering the field in compe-

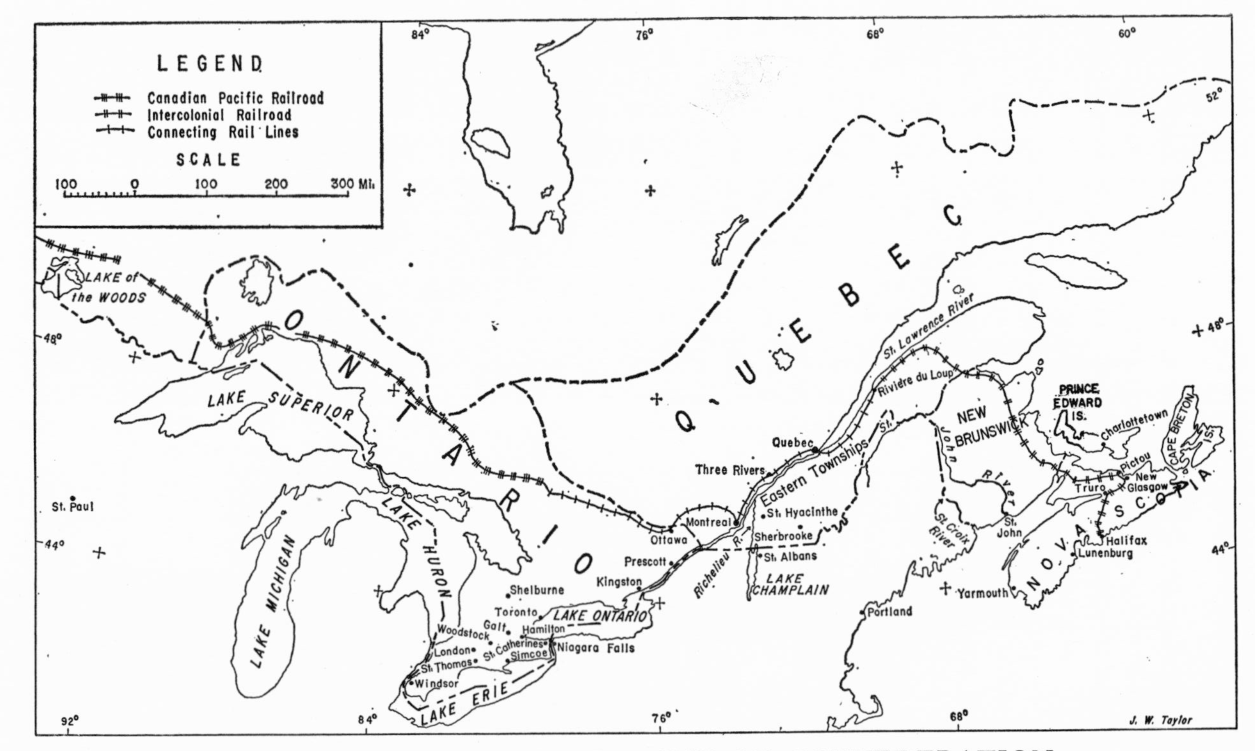

EASTERN CANADA AT THE TIME OF CONFEDERATION

tition with Canada for the possession of the Provinces."[55] Howe was also to hint that if the Imperial government accepted the federation scheme, there would be "changes which none of us desire to contemplate and all of us deplore."[56]

The Nova Scotian delegation was obviously shaking an annexation stick at the British. Howe continued in the same vein by pointing out to the Imperial government the "range of temptation" which political union with the United States offered to the people of the Maritimes: they would have free trade with a market of 34,000,000 people, access to American capital, and the benefit of American fishing bounties.[57] But the Colonial Office was unmoved by intimidation and gave Howe and his delegation no encouragement. He then sought to influence the public and political climate by showering the newspapers and leading men with pamphlets stating Nova Scotia's case.[58]

Persuasion was no more successful than threats. The British were inexorably committed to confederation, and talk of annexation entrenched their convictions. Despite the efforts of John Bright and a few others whom Howe had converted, the government pushed the British North America Act through Parliament after a debate less lively than that on a dog tax bill which followed.

But the British had no more succeeded in convincing Howe and his party in Nova Scotia of the sapiency of Imperial policy than he had convinced them of its folly. These opponents of confederation would be heard again, and in unmistakable tones.

The eight years from 1860 to 1867 constitute a significant era in Canadian history because the Dominion of Canada came into being then. The threat of annexation was an important im-

[55] This is an obvious reference to the Banks bill, described in the next chapter.

[56] Instructions to Howe from the League of the Maritime Provinces, Howe Papers, IV, Letters to Howe, 1864-1873.

[57] British Parliament, *Accounts and Papers, 1867*, XLVIII, 14-15.

[58] Howe Papers, IV, 159-86.

mediate cause of this development. Though the colonial agitation to join the United States was weak, loyalists feared that the impending depression and American hostility would harry the colonies into joining the United States.

This fear of American aggression was groundless. The Civil War period illustrates the general American indifference to the acquisition of Canada and the peaceful intent of most of the annexationists in the United States. The Republic had provocation to invade the colonies and an effective instrument in an immense and war-hardened army; the conquest of Canada would have been rapid and certain. But the American government disbanded its troops without seriously considering an excursion into British America. The principal authority on this movement indicates that most Americans who blatantly called for the conquest of Canada were insincere; their outcries were to win votes, not territory.[59]

The history of the period also reiterates the connection between Canadian-American trade and the annexation question. The colonial movement for annexation produced reciprocity, and the death of reciprocity revived annexation. A large number of Canadians were becoming convinced that their real prosperity demanded permanent free trade with the United States, whatever the political basis.

As in 1849, the mother country reacted to the impact of annexationism. Some British might be indifferent to the fate of the colonies, but those who formulated foreign and colonial policy were determined to prevent their accession to the United States. The Republic was a brawny young giant, a dangerous rival whose strength must be circumscribed. Confederation would, so the authorities in London fondly hoped, prevent annexation and keep the power of the United States in leash. The union was consummated more to keep the colonies out of the

[59] Smith, *Republican Expansionists,* last chapter.

Republic than to keep them in the Empire, for British statesmen believed that the new Dominion would soon become independent. Federation would better enable the provinces to stand on their own feet and would bolster their resistance to the pull from the south. But the success of the union hinged upon the answers it offered to crucial questions. Would it be able to reconcile the anticonfederationists, especially in the Maritime Provinces? Would it prevent the dreaded depression? Would it kill the annexation movement?

CHAPTER THREE

Annexation in the Postconfederation Period

The Dominion of Canada, which came into existence on July 1, 1867, was established in part to save the colonies of British North America from the United States. Nevertheless, it failed for the time to solve the old problems which had suggested annexation, and it raised new difficulties which pointed in the same direction.

Canada was more a name than a nation on that first Dominion Day and for some time thereafter. Between the settled areas of the Maritime Provinces on the east and Ontario and Quebec on the west, nature had thrust a gap of wilderness which man had not bridged. Communication between Montreal and Halifax, always slow and difficult, was almost impossible at times. The Grand Trunk Railway, threading its way parallel to the St. Lawrence, stopped abruptly two hundred and eighty miles east of Montreal at Rivière du Loup. In the Maritimes, Nova Scotia had constructed a railroad covering the sixty-one miles between Halifax and Truro. Some two hundred miles of almost unsettled country lay between these railheads. No private corporation could afford to link them, and some years would pass before the government did so. In 1867 the only means of communication between the Maritimes and the old colony of Canada were the St. Lawrence River and a few wretched post roads. Winter choked these channels, and even in summer, communication between Truro and Rivière du Loup was aggravatingly slow and uncertain. Mail, passengers, and freight going from Montreal or Quebec to the Maritimes usually sought the dependable route through the United States, via Portland, Maine.[1]

Geography and lack of transportation thus wedged the provinces apart and tended to nullify their political union. Since the grain of the continent runs generally north and south, each section of Canada was linked to the neighboring section of the United States rather than to the nearest part of Canada. Thus the Maritimes looked to New England, and Ontario and Quebec to New York and the Middle West. These convenient and practical trade lines were invisible ropes, exerting a gentle and inexorable southward pull upon the new federation.

Geography was not Canada's only handicap. The pattern of settlement accentuated the danger of gravitation to the south. The Dominion was a nation stretched thin over a great length and lacking in depth. Horace Greeley aptly described it as an "eel-skin of settled country."[2]

Political factors also impeded the integration of the new country. The British North America Act had combined the colonies in law but not in spirit. There was no love for the Dominion in the hearts of its citizens, but rather a love of each for his own province. Particularism excluded nationalism from their political thought. It is not surprising that many of the colonists looked upon the newly constructed country as an artificial creation from which they could expect nothing and to which they owed nothing.

In one respect, it is even possible that the formation of the Dominion had weakened the resistance to political union with the United States. The allegiance to the mother country had formerly been direct; after 1867, it became indirect, because Canada claimed the first loyalty of its citizens and was interposed between them and Great Britain.

But the cause of Canada was far from hopeless. Significant

[1] Trotter, *Federation,* 148.
[2] New York *Daily Tribune,* June 28, 1865.

forces were working toward unity. In its gropings for nationhood the Dominion was moving with the great currents of history. The period after confederation was an age of nationalism in western civilization and would soon reach a first climax in the emergence of Germany and Italy. Canadians could not be impervious to the sweeping tides of their civilization and, earlier or later, must be caught up in them and carried forward to their national destiny.

Closer to them than this general movement was the policy of the British government, which had earlier resolved, as seen above, that its North American colonies must and could be saved from the United States. Gently but unswervingly, Britain had pressed them together in federation and would now do what was possible to consummate the union she had willed. In this she would have the eager assistance of many Canadians who saw the unloved but utilitarian union as their best hope of escaping the United States. Foremost was the Dominion's first Prime Minister, Sir John A. Macdonald, a principal architect of confederation who labored for it with the fanatic zeal characteristic of the latter-day convert. Sir John was irretrievably committed to the conviction that Canada's greatest danger lay in her growing dependence upon the United States. Guided by instinct and by intellect, he formulated a bifurcated policy for the salvation of his country: it must be united within, politically, economically, and spiritually; without, it must maintain an alliance with Great Britain to fend off a union with the United States.

Preeminently practical, a Canadian Alexander Hamilton, Macdonald hoped to use economic self-interest as the cement of federation, and set about constructing a viable Canadian national economy. This necessitated long and difficult steps. Canada must soon attain the size and diversity to make such a plan practical. She too would have her expansion, her West, her window on the Pacific. Then her economy must develop the processing as well as the production of raw materials; in short, industrialization would be essential. The Dominion must be interlaced with a network of transportation facilities so that her dispersed sections could exchange their complementary products. In this fashion, Canada might shake off her dangerous dependence on the nation to the south.

This monumental task would add new dimension and tension to Canadian politics and polity. During the ensuing decades, three concepts were to entwine in a tangle of conflict and accommodation. First would be Macdonald's new policy, which to a considerable extent would contradict the old principle of political and economic dependence on the mother country, weakened but not destroyed by Britain's fiscal revolution of the 1840's. His task would be complicated by the rise in England of a movement to renew and tighten the bonds of the Empire in a federation, even at the expense of free trade dogma. The Canadian leader was in a delicate position. He needed a British alliance, and Canadian producers needed the British market. He could not endanger his policy and his economy, nor risk suspicion of treason, by a brusque rejection of British advances. Neither could he fight annexation to the United States by reannexation to Great Britain.

Equally difficult was the task of resisting, yet accommodating, the persistent idea of a continental economy, a concept which had already passed through two major phases and was still a powerful force. As described above, it took root and grew vigorously during the days of the fur trade and reached a first important climax in the dream of the commercial empire of the St. Lawrence. As that dream grew dim and faded, many Canadians accepted a variation on the continental theme by advocating the freest possible trade with the United States. The patron saint of this creed was the revered Lord Elgin. His Reciprocity Treaty was still immensely popular with nearly all Canadians, who looked back longing upon its years, now clothed in the shimmering vagueness of a Golden Age. It would be long before any Canadian statesman would dare to slam the door on reciprocity. Yet Macdonald feared that it could mean the death of an independent Canadian economy and, ultimately, a Canadian nation. Again, he must steer carefully because the Dominion needed access to the American, as well as the British, market.

In respect to the concept of continental economy, the Liberals were to be formidable obstacles to Macdonald's plans. It was the valid purpose of the opposition party to criticize his offerings and to present alternatives so that the Canadian people might have choices in the mart of national options. Macdonald's concept of a national economy, by natural democratic processes, drove the Liberals to support a continental economy. To his argument that closer connections with the United States were dangerous to Canada, they cogently countered the Elgin thesis that freer trade relations were the safest course, for they brought the economic benefits of annexation without the necessity of political change. And perhaps they were right!

Thus for some years a war would ensue between three ideas: closer Empire ties, continental economy, and the creation of a national Canadian economy. All three were primarily concerned to negate a fourth concept, political union with the United States. From this confused conflict of ideas, no unadulterated policy would emerge. Macdonald the realist knew the uses and necessity of compromise while keeping his ultimate goal clearly before him. Yet he could not break with Britain, and he could not drop a curtain between Canada and the United States; he needed the goodwill and the markets of both. He must pick his way with the care of a man on an icy walk, moving rapidly when the way was open, but usually slowly and circumspectly. He must keep the Canadian people abreast of him in their support, and give them at least a glimpse of his vision of the future to sustain them through the dislocations, hardships, and costs inevitably accompanying a change in the national economy, however slow. He could not know that these natural difficulties would be exacerbated by the ravages of a great and testing depression. If he would construct a national economy as a fort against American acquisitiveness, he must persist through such troubles, though there would be some Canadians, perhaps many, to whom immediate cost and hardship were more significant than ultimate goals—and some who would question the validity of the goals themselves.[3]

These were the challenges which lay before Macdonald and his party. But before he could enter upon, or even plan, broader strategy, he must first master the crisis of opposition to confederation which arose in Canada, in areas he hoped to add to the Dominion, and even in the United States.

Some Americans had been watching, sullenly and even fearfully, the unfolding movement for federation to the north. An old resentment reawoke. The united colonies would be a British sword of Damocles dangling precariously over the head of the Republic. Monarchy was pushing into North America, continent sacredly dedicated to republicanism. Encased between Maximilian to the south and a new British kingdom to the north, the United States would have to resume the long-unaccustomed posture of defense. It was natural that some efforts would be made in the Republic to check the development of this menace. Individual annexationists petitioned the Department of State to protest against the projected union of the colonies.[4] Several states bordering on British North America also gave anxious official attention to the prospects of confederation. The governor of Maine, in his annual message to his legislature, described his

[3] The story of the political struggle, included as background for the annexation movement, is best followed in the excellent biography by Donald G. Creighton, *John A. Macdonald: The Old Chieftain* (Boston, 1956).

[4] Miscellaneous Letters to the Department of State, 1867, February, pt. I, June, pt. II.

visions of a plot. The union of British America, he said "along with the French Empire in Mexico [is] a part of a great conspiracy against Liberty on this youthful continent." He urged Americans sternly to oppose these moves to take advantage of their internal involvements.[5] In New York a group of French Canadians resident in the United States took note of this warning and urged their legislature to be alert to the threatening developments. A resolution was introduced in Albany denouncing the formation of a nonrepublican government in North America. Washington was urged to protest against such an action.[6]

These alarums sounded in the outer marches were heard in the national capital. In 1866, General Nathaniel P. Banks, representative from Massachusetts and chairman of the Foreign Affairs Committee, introduced a bill calling for the annexation of the British provinces to the United States. It provided for the admission of all the colonies and the purchase of the Hudson's Bay Company's lands for $10,000,000. The American government would assume public lands and state-owned bonds and the right to levy taxes and, in return, would take over provincial debts to the total of $85,700,000 and give an annual subsidy of $1,646,000 to the new states. In addition, the United States would connect Canada with the Maritimes by rail and spend $50,000,000 to complete and improve the colonial canal system.[7] Banks' bill never came to a vote. In February of the following year, Congressman Henry J. Raymond, editor of the New York *Times*, submitted a resolution asking the President

[5] St. Andrews *New Brunswick Standard*, January 16, 1867.

[6] Quebec *Morning Chronicle*, May 2, 1867; *Montreal Pays*, March 12, 1867.

[7] This bill was suggested to Banks by the Minnesota annexationist and Treasury agent, James W. Taylor, an expert on Canada. *House Executive Documents*, 39 Cong., 1 sess., no. 128. See also Fred H. Harrington, *Fighting Politician: Major General N. P. Banks* (Philadelphia, 1948), 178-79.

whether the government of the United States had remonstrated against colonial union or had given its consent to it. The House Committee on Foreign Affairs could not act upon this resolution prior to adjournment.[8] Banks then returned to the fray in March, 1867, with a joint resolution asserting that the United States was an interested party to any proposals for colonial union. The establishment of a government based upon monarchical principles "cannot be considered otherwise than as in contravention of the traditions and principles of this [American] government."[9] The Banks resolution passed the House almost without debate but was not considered by the Senate. Nor did Americans heed a similar measure by the untiring Raymond, reiterating the fear that the construction of a powerful monarchy to the north would constitute a threat to the peace and safety of the United States. When objection was raised to the resolution, it was carried over and not heard from again.

It was patent that these protests were lone voices crying in a wilderness, and that most Americans were indifferent to their clamors. Indeed, some actually favored the confederation of the colonies as a step toward the Americanization of British America, or even toward annexation.[10]

The opposition to the union in the United States was mild compared to the distaste with which many in Canada regarded their new country and government. This antagonism, with its accompanying danger to the British connection, was present in Quebec and Ontario, but reached its greatest pitch in Nova Scotia. Here the anticonfederationist leader Howe had warned that his province might seek annexation to the United States if the Imperial government insisted on forcing it into the union. Nova Scotians showed no signs of accepting the Dominion as a

[8] *Congressional Globe*, 39 Cong., 2 sess., 1617, 1646.
[9] *Congressional Globe*, 40 Cong., 1 sess., 392.
[10] New York *Daily Tribune*, February 17, 1865; New York *Times*, May 11, June 18, 1867.

fait accompli even after July 1, 1867, when their province became part of the federation. They stubbornly asserted that they would not remain in the union; the equally obstinate British government refused to heed their demands for release from it. A crisis was mounting and a small annexation movement had already made its appearance in the disaffected province.[11] Confederation was inducing what it had been designed to prevent, rather than acting as an antidote to it.

The British North America Act thus brought protest south of the line and political disaffection north of it. This discontent became more acute when confederation failed to fulfill its economic promise to insure the continuation of prosperity despite the abrogation of reciprocity. The export trade of the colonies had reached a peak in 1866, when $48,528,628 worth of produce was shipped from the colonies to the United States, much of it hustled across the border to escape the American tariff which would rise when the Reciprocity Treaty terminated in March. The following year saw a slump in commerce, business, and certain types of production. Exports to the Republic declined nearly 50 percent to $25,044,005, and Canadian goods paid over three and a quarter millions in duties. The merchants and commercial cities in all the provinces felt the blow, and its impact was greatest in the Maritimes, whose staple exports of fish, coal, and lumber were subject to a high tariff.[12]

This economic distress caused greater discontent because it

[11] There were many instances of annexationist activities in Nova Scotia. C. D. Randall to Macdonald, January 7, February 25, 1868, Macdonald Papers, Nova Scotia Affairs, III; Yarmouth *Herald*, July 18, 1867. Much of the annexationist materials described in this section on Nova Scotia has previously appeared in the author's article, "The Post-Confederation Annexation Movement in Nova Scotia," *Canadian Historical Review*, XXVIII (June, 1947), 156-65. I wish to express thanks to the editor, John T. Saywell, for permission to use the material in this study.

[12] Trade statistics in *Senate Executive Documents*, 53 Cong., 2 sess., no. 106; Masters, *Reciprocity*, 185, 252; New York *Times*, April 12, 1869.

seemed in contrast to conditions in the United States. A speculative frenzy swept the Republic after the war, with the expansion of railroads and industry. Money and credit were plentiful, inducing speculation and unsound enterprise. The Canadians, like the Americans themselves, were blinded by the glittering prosperity and did not notice the tottering foundations of this boom. They envied their neighbors and hankered to share the good times. Bitterly they denounced those who had pushed confederation with the argument that it would create a new interprovincial trade to replace the international trade lost in 1866. When this failed to materialize, they were more certain than ever that free trade with the United States was essential to Canadian prosperity; and annexation seemed the only means left to gain free trade.[13]

As usual, adversity wore several aspects. In 1867 and 1868 the bank and inshore fisheries were failures, leaving thousands of families in the Maritimes to struggle against hunger and privation. Pleas for help swamped local merchants who were accustomed to extend credit to those temporarily in need. The distress from this misfortune visited its full force upon southern Nova Scotia, but neither New Brunswick nor Quebec escaped it.[14] Unable to obtain employment at home, many Canadian fishermen shipped on American vessels, and then returned with their pockets and minds stuffed with arguments for annexation to the United States.

The fiscal policy of the new federal government did nothing to lighten the burdens. Despite protests from Nova Scotia and New Brunswick, the higher duties of the old colony of Canada replaced their revenue tariffs. This increased the price of necessities at a time when incomes were decreasing. A further

[13] Confederation was followed by a slight increase in interprovincial trade, but it fell off again by $300,000 in 1868. New Glasgow (Nova Scotia) *Eastern Chronicle*, November 25, 1869.

[14] Yarmouth *Tribune*, May 22, December 11, 1867, January 5, 1869.

adjustment of the tariff was said to have cost the Maritimes $356,000 a year; even the lieutenant governor and the confederationists in Nova Scotia condemned such measures which worked hardship on their province.[15]

The local governments also fell into financial straits after confederation. The public revenues in the Maritimes had derived largely from their tariff receipts. The British North America Act transferred this tax source to the central government, compensating the provinces by annual subsidies which proved quite inadequate for local needs. The governments of Nova Scotia and New Brunswick, after futile scraping and pinching to match income and outgo, yielded to the unpopular necessity of levying additional taxation on the hard-pressed population.[16]

This catalog of grievances will indicate why confederation did not appear to be a panacea for the ills of British North America and why many refused to accept it as final. The increased burdens incident to the union brought hardships to those least willing to make sacrifices for the new government. A commercial depression afflicted cities from Halifax to Sarnia and, supplemented by local economic grievances, produced a dangerous discontent. These difficulties which beset the Dominion in its crucial years recall the critical period through which the United States passed before its existence as a nation was assured.

It is not surprising that the resentment and protest was most acute in Nova Scotia. As already noted, the people of that province had carried their opposition to union to the Crown, only to be spurned. When Joe Howe returned from his fruitless mission to London, he found his province tottering on the brink

[15] St. John *Morning Freeman*, September 7, 1868; Lieutenant Governor Hastings Doyle to Macdonald, December 31, 1867, P. S. Hamilton to Macdonald, February 24, 1868, Macdonald Papers, Nova Scotia Affairs, I.

[16] St. John *Morning Freeman*, September 7, 1868.

of disloyalty. He had set a dangerous precedent and course when, in his correspondence with the Colonial Office, he had listed the temptations which annexation offered to his people. The antis of Nova Scotia continued in this direction. Newspapers and public speakers vied with each other in skipping along the verge of treason. Although many of their hints of annexation were attempts to frighten the British government into permitting the secession of the province, some of them were sincere.[17]

This incipient annexation movement, however, soon received a check. Most of the antis still looked upon political union with the United States as a last resort and hoped to relieve their distress by other means. These soon seemed to offer. At the first provincial election under the new Dominion, the opponents of confederation achieved a smashing victory. Thirty-six of the thirty-eight members of the provincial assembly were antis, and Tupper was the only unionist among the nineteen members of the federal House of Commons returned from Nova Scotia. This was no victory for annexation. The repealers were confident that their startling success would compel the British government to heed their wishes, and the majority of Nova Scotians still believed that their problems could be solved within the Empire by a return to the status of a separate and self-governing colony. They could restore their old revenue tariff, the income of their government would rise, and no Canadian majority could trample their interests. They also believed that the United States would renew the treaty of 1854 with Nova Scotia alone. This questionable conclusion arose from the dubious assumption that Americans regarded the Canadian economy as competitive

[17] Some annexationists were even appealing to the Department of State for assistance in their projects. J. B. Cossitt to Seward, June 20, 1867, Stephen Howard to Seward, March 26, 1867, A. McLean to Seward, June 29, 1867, Miscellaneous Letters to the Department of State, 1867, March II, and June, II.

with their own, but the Nova Scotian economy as its complement. So the anti triumph in the election of 1867 convinced Nova Scotians that annexation was unnecessary; they would soon escape the Dominion and return to reciprocity and prosperity.

Since secession from Canada was the key which would unlock the door to this pleasant future, the repealers sought to gain it. The provincial assembly passed resolutions requesting the British government to release Nova Scotia from the Dominion, sent Howe to London bearing this appeal, and awaited confidently for news of their deliverance from the Canadian yoke.

Howe did not share their optimism. His previous mission had taught him that the home government was committed to confederation as the only preventive for annexation.[18] If Nova Scotia seceded, New Brunswick would probably follow, and the Dominion would collapse. The Governor General, Lord Monck, had reached the same conclusion. He pressed the colonial secretary to refuse Howe's request graciously but firmly; if the union broke up, wrote Monck, "I have no hesitation in expressing my opinion . . . that the maintenance of British power or the existence of British institutions in America will soon become impossible."[19] This advice from the man on the spot fortified the determination of the British government to deny the repeal of confederation. As further insurance, the Dominion government sent Charles Tupper to London to counteract the eloquence of his anti rival.

The colonial secretary proved to be courteous in hearing the complaints of Nova Scotia but adamant in refusing to permit

[18] Though outwardly confident, Howe had written gloomy letters to his friends before departing for London. Archbishop T. L. Connolly to Macdonald, October 26, 1867, Macdonald Papers, Nova Scotia Affairs, III; Howe to A. Musgrave, January 17, 1868, Howe Papers, XXXVII, Howe Letter Book.

[19] Monck to Richard Campbell Grenville, Duke of Buckingham, February 13, 1868, G 573 A, Secret and Confidential Despatches, 1867-1869.

its secession. Early in June, 1868, he informed Monck that the Imperial government could not consider any request for secession; all provincial grievances must and could be redressed within the framework of the Dominion.[20]

The publication of this dispatch, frustrating their highest hopes, was a terrible shock to the antis. They rained sorrowful and angry denunciations down upon the Canadian and Imperial governments. Many went beyond philippics and vowed that their loyalty was gone. A member of the Dominion Parliament and a former chief justice of Nova Scotia were enthusiastically applauded when they spoke for political union with the United States at a meeting in New Glasgow.[21] Other town meetings became forums on annexation.[22] The leading paper in the province, the Halifax *Morning Chronicle,* asserted that "with 30,000,000 of freemen alongside of us, Britain and Canada well know that they cannot crush Nova Scotia, or force it into a hateful connection."[23] The annexation movement in the province, it was obvious, was waxing as repealers joined its ranks.

This sedition was a startling contrast with the past. Nova Scotia had been a devoted colony. The Loyalists who flooded into it after the American Revolution brought with them love of mother country and antipathy to the United States. The Nova Scotians considered themselves a chosen people, and their demonstrations of attachment to the Crown seemed to outdo those of the English themselves. Extreme devotion was followed by immoderate reaction. Nova Scotians were overcome with anger when Britain repaid their loyalty by ruthlessly pushing

[20] Buckingham to Monck, June 4, 1868, Macdonald Papers, Nova Scotia Affairs, III. Attempts by John Bright to set up a royal commission of inquiry were defeated, a good sign that Howe's cause was hopeless. Creighton, *Macdonald,* 17.

[21] Yarmouth *Herald,* August 13, 1868.

[22] Connolly to Macdonald, September 16, 1868, Macdonald Papers, Nova Scotia Affairs, III.

[23] Halifax *Morning Chronicle,* July 11, 1868.

them into the unwanted union. To be told that confederation was a *fait accompli* and they must make the best of it was unendurable.

This disloyal talk frightened Howe, who realized that the situation was becoming dangerous. Before his second mission to London, he had been uneasy over the doctrines held by some of his followers and knew that unceasing efforts would be necessary to restrain those who would make a "bear garden" of the province; one paper even demanded that the provincial government announce its secession from the Dominion by seizing the customhouses, public buildings, and railroads.[24] In London, Howe had listened to "that damned Tupper" urge him to leave the repeal movement before he was smudged with its disloyal tendencies.[25] Now he must have remembered Tupper's warning, for it was clear that, like Frankenstein, he had created a monster which was slipping from his control.

Instead of deserting the anti movement, Howe determined to discipline it. Calling a meeting of its leaders soon after his return from London, he lectured them sternly for their seditious utterances and bluntly warned them that he would oppose any violent action, "which I know can only end in failure and disgrace." If Nova Scotians took overt steps toward annexation, they would be "sure to be resisted with the whole power of the empire and to fail after our country was a desert unless the United States came to our aid, of which there is no prospect."[26]

This plain speaking had effect. The meeting resolved to follow the suggestion of its leader to seek secession only by "lawful

[24] Connolly to Macdonald, October 26, 1867, Macdonald Papers, Nova Scotia Affairs, III; Yarmouth *Tribune*, April 18, 1868. Interestingly, this paper was one of the first to desert the anti movement.

[25] Lord Monck to Sir Charles Tupper, April 26, 1868, Sir Charles Tupper Papers, Miscellaneous, I (Public Archives of Canada, Ottawa).

[26] Howe to Ned Macdonald, July 18, 1868, Howe to John Livingston, August 12, 1868, Howe Papers, XXXVIII, Howe Letter Book.

and constitutional means."[27] In turn, Howe expressed a confidence, which he knew unwarranted, that success awaited them.

The conversion of many to "lawful and constitutional means" was superficial and transitory. Soon they were again using violent language, advocating treasonable action, and hinting that American aid and annexation would be forthcoming. One member of the provincial government, Attorney General Martin Wilkins, declared in the assembly that Nova Scotia would establish its own tariff and enforce it in defiance of the Dominion government. If the colony were too weak to do this herself, "she would appeal to other people to assist her," a pointed reference to American intervention. Wilkins later added that "the political system of any other civilized country would be better" than that provided by the British North America Act.[28]

This continued agitation, in defiance of Howe's commands, indicated that the antis were split into two factions, though they pretended unity. One group followed their leader and his desire to adhere to lawful means. Like Howe, they wearied of the hopeless fight and began to think of accepting confederation if they could secure terms which would not violate their consistency. On the other hand stood the intransigents. They included the provincial cabinet, which had gained power by agitation and feared to lose it by quiet, and the leading editor of the province, William Annand of the Halifax *Morning Chronicle*.[29] These extremists planned to send a final appeal to London. If it failed to secure permission for secession, the provincial government would seize the federal revenue offices and proclaim annexation to the United States, certain that Great Britain would not try to restrain them by force. This group

[27] Resolution printed in St. John *Morning Freeman*, August 11, 1868.

[28] Hastings Doyle to Macdonald, September 4, 5, 1868, Macdonald Papers, Nova Scotia Affairs, I.

[29] Macdonald to Howe, November 4, 1868, Macdonald Papers, Nova Scotia Affairs, II.

feigned admiration for Howe while secretly circulating all manner of rumors designed to discredit him.[30]

Howe soon realized that his efforts to smother disloyalty in the League of the Maritime Provinces had failed and that it would be futile to repeat them. The repeal movement was in a cul-de-sac, and he must either abandon opposition to confederation or attempt to bring Nova Scotia into the American union. To Howe, the former was distasteful, the latter abhorrent. So the time had come for moderate antis to give up their irretrievable cause and join a war against those extremists who were entering forbidden paths. As a shrewd politician, Howe had privately kept the door open for this exit from the repeal movement. In July he had informed Tilley, still the confederationist leader in New Brunswick, that he might accept the Dominion if the federal government would make its terms more palatable. Tilley immediately urged Macdonald to come to Halifax and confer with Howe.[31] Sir John grasped this opportunity to exploit the dilemma of his opponent. He went to Nova Scotia in August and addressed a repeal convention, stating his determination to oppose secession and his willingness to redress provincial grievances. The speech was as genial as its author and made a favorable impression on the moderates.[32] They decided, however, to make a final effort to check the extremists in their ranks before yielding.

Nevertheless, Howe continued to negotiate privately with Macdonald. Persistent rumors that he was preparing to capitu-

[30] J. McCully to Macdonald, September 22, 1868, Howe to Macdonald, October 29, November 16, 1868, Macdonald Papers, Nova Scotia Affairs, II.

[31] Sir Leonard Tilley to Macdonald, July 17, 1868, Macdonald Papers, Nova Scotia Affairs, II. Tupper had also informed Macdonald that Howe would listen to reason. Creighton, *Macdonald*, 17-18.

[32] Macdonald to Lord Monck, September 4, 1868, Macdonald Papers, Nova Scotia Affairs, III.

late to the confederationists forced him to issue a letter of mild denial in which, again, he took the occasion to point out the folly of annexation agitation.[33] Its proponents were playing carelessly with fire, for their policy led to the risk of an Anglo-American war which would be ruinous to all. Howe added that he was responsible for the direction of the anti movement and was conscious of the fact that in all previous constitutional struggles in the province no life had been lost and not a single pane of glass shattered.[34]

In view of his seemingly inexorable commitment to repeal, it is understandable that the whole province was thrown into confusion when Howe suddenly announced his withdrawal from the anti ranks. He justified his action by stating that he had hoped to the end for redress from Britain, but even friendly John Bright could give him no assurance there. He had then tried to revive the project of Maritime federation, but emissaries reported from New Brunswick and Prince Edward Island that this cause was dead. With all doors closed and the repeal movement becoming merely a screen for annexationism, the time had come to face the facts and the future. Confederation was here and nothing could be done about it: "I will not deceive them [the repealers] by vain hopes or conceal the truth from fear of their displeasure." Those who wished to continue the agitation, resist the Dominion, or seek annexation could do so: "For these pastimes, I have neither inclination nor leisure."[35] Speaking thus, the great anti leader left the fold.

This action stunned most of the extremists and all of the

[33] New York *Times*, October 12, 1868.

[34] Quebec *Morning Chronicle*, November 2, 1868. These rumors were based on truth, for Macdonald and Howe had reached a tentative agreement during the former's visit to Nova Scotia. Creighton, *Macdonald*, 22-23.

[35] St. Andrews *Standard*, November 11, 1868; Sarnia *Observor and Lambton Advertiser*, November 27, 1868.

moderates.[36] Some of the latter followed Howe out of the movement, but others refused to do so because his action was ill conceived and ill timed. It came without warning, for he had denied his intent to desert repeal up to the very eve of doing so. Many of the moderates were angry because he had neither counseled with them nor warned them so that they could gradually and gracefully ease themselves out. They felt compelled to remain in the movement for the sake of consistency. Howe's autocratic action cost him many followers and tended to defeat the purpose of his move. He had to admit that he had probably carried only his own county with him out of the anti group.[37]

The extremists in the repeal movement were furious. That portion of the English language fit to print was inadequate to express the feelings of most of these antis about their former leader. His announced intention of fighting annexationism seemed to reinforce their desire for union with the United States.

They soon had an opportunity to discredit this renegade. When Howe withdrew from the repeal movement, he also resigned his seat in the federal Parliament and sought reelection as a confederationist to vindicate his action. The repealers yearned to inflict a crushing defeat on him. Thus the campaign in his constituency of Hants prior to the balloting in March, 1869, was vigorous and vicious, as each side spared neither money nor vocabulary. The repealers and annexationists opened

[36] Apparently some of the extremists had done their best to goad Howe into this action, hoping to rid the movement of him and his moderating influence. Howe to William Murray, December 1, 1868, Howe to Rose, December 7, 1868, Howe Papers, XXXVIII, Howe Letter Book.

[37] A survey indicated that about half the antis in Queens and Lunenburg counties went with Howe, but other areas were almost unaffected. R. Huntington to Howe, December 24, 1868, Howe Papers, IV, Letters to Howe, 1864-1873. Many confederationists, including the lieutenant governor, were greatly displeased with Howe's tactics. Howe to Macdonald, November 16, 1868, Hastings Doyle to Macdonald, February 25, 1869, Macdonald Papers, Nova Scotia Affairs, I, II.

their well-supplied war chests, while on the other side, Macdonald sent large sums to Howe and made some four hundred appointments to aid him in his "Holy War."[38] The Imperial government also intruded by informing the Governor General that its door was closed to further repeal resolutions or delegations; redress for Nova Scotia could be found only in Ottawa.[39] Finally, the Canadian government announced that it was ready to give better terms to Nova Scotia by taking over an additional million dollars of its debt and increasing its annual subsidy.[40]

This concerted effort and Howe's popularity in his district brought him a narrow victory. But his triumph was incomplete, for it did not result in the expected decline of the support for repeal and annexation.

The dust raised in Hants obscured the significance of two other byelections held at about the same time. One was in Yarmouth, at the southern tip of the province, and the other in Richmond, a county on Cape Breton Island. In the latter, a candidate reputed to be an annexationist was returned after a canvass which aroused little outside interest. The campaign in Yarmouth was more closely watched and contested. The confederationists were anxious to carry this constituency, which was a citadel of annexationism. They raised a large campaign fund, they induced Macdonald to appropriate $2,000 to survey a railroad route from Annapolis to Yarmouth, and they informed the local voters that the road would be built if Nova Scotia remained in the Dominion. But the tantalizing odor of the pork barrel did not tempt the appetite of the annexationists. They nomi-

[38] Macdonald to Howe, January 12, March 8, 16, 1869, Howe Papers, IV, Letters to Howe, 1864-1873. It was notorious that at least 130 votes were for sale in the constituency and both sides vigorously bid for them. Hastings Doyle to Macdonald, March 5, 30, 1869, Macdonald Papers, Nova Scotia Affairs, I.

[39] George Leveson-Gower, Earl Granville to Sir John Young, January 12, 1869, printed in Yarmouth *Tribune*, February 9, 1869.

[40] Young to Granville, February 11, 1869, G 573 A, Secret and Confidential Despatches, 1867-1869.

nated Frank Killam, a merchant and one of the wealthiest men in the province. Both banks and every man of means in Yarmouth supported him and annexation.[41] The confederationists lost hope of defeating him at the polls and planned instead to "work on him" after his election.[42] The returns indicated the wisdom of this decision; Killam received two-thirds of the votes in Yarmouth County and a majority in every district in the constituency.[43]

Thus the elections in Yarmouth and Richmond offset the results in Hants. Moreover, they demonstrated that the annexation agitation was strong and had been growing since the British government refused the second petition for repeal. The movement might appear to be insincere, an attempt to frighten the Imperial government into consenting to secession. This is less than a half-truth. The advocates of annexation were, at first, reacting in blind fury and in the hope that the quality of their recklessness would alarm the British ministry into allowing secession. Though their wrath soon cooled, their loyalty to the Empire was not rekindled. Nova Scotians began to view their political future unimpassionedly. Stripping away sentiment, they concluded that only union with the United States would alleviate their distress, an opinion which the provincial press began to reflect in the summer of 1868.[44] Desire to join the Republic no longer sprang from warm anger but from cold self-interest.

The movement grew steadily. Howe, who knew the political sentiment of the province better than any other man, warned

[41] J. McClellan to Macdonald, February 23, 1869, Macdonald Papers, Nova Scotia Affairs, III.

[42] Howe to Macdonald, March 30, 1869, Howe Papers, XXXVIII, Howe Letter Book; Young to Granville, April 8, 1869, G 573 A, Secret and Confidential Despatches, 1867-1869.

[43] St. John *Morning Freeman*, April 22, 1869. The vote in Yarmouth was 1,220 for Killam and 598 for the confederationist candidate.

[44] Halifax *Morning Chronicle*, September 16, 1868; New Glasgow *Eastern Chronicle*, January 9, 1869; M. M. Jackson to Seward, August 29, 1868, Consular Despatches, Halifax, XI.

Macdonald that "a clean, unfettered vote of the people might take it [Nova Scotia] into the American Union." He later added that there were "whole districts where the sentiment of loyalty is dead."[45] The extreme antis were now largely annexationists, and the repeal league worked to increase the sentiment in favor of joining the United States.[46] Well-known and respected men of all classes openly supported the agitation.

The strength of the movement was soon apparent. At a meeting of the League of the Maritime Provinces held in June, 1869, the annexationists in its ranks gained control of this anti organization and changed its purpose to coincide with theirs. Their manifesto of justification for this action had a familiar ring: "Our only hope of commercial prosperity, material development and permanent peace lies in closer relations with the United States. Therefore, be it resolved that every legitimate means should be used by members of this convention to sever our connection with Canada and to bring about a union on fair and equitable terms with the American Republic."[47] The convention invited all believers to form branches of the reconstituted league. During the summer of 1869, meetings were held in many parts of the province for this purpose.

The support of annexation centered in well-defined areas. One was the southern third of the province, comprising the counties of Yarmouth, Lunenburg, Queens, and Digby. This region was the center of the fishing industry, which wanted free access to American markets and an influx of American capital to discover and develop additional natural resources.[48] Yarmouth

[45] Howe to Macdonald, October 29, November 16, 1868, Macdonald Papers, Nova Scotia Affairs, II.

[46] Halifax *Citizen*, March 13, 1869.

[47] Manifesto printed in St. John *Morning Freeman*, June 24, 1869; Quebec *Morning Chronicle*, June 19, 1869.

[48] See accounts of annexation meetings reported in Yarmouth *Herald*, April 15, 1869, February 3, April 14, 21, 26, 30, 1870. Among the towns at which such gatherings took place were Yarmouth, Wolfville, Digby, Argyle, Bridgeport, Rockville, Burnside, and Brooklyn.

was particularly anxious for union with the Republic. Of all the towns in the province, it lay closest to the United States and was virtually a commercial suburb of Boston.[49] Proximity to the Republic also stimulated political union in other commercial centers of southern Nova Scotia such as Digby, Lunenburg, and Shelburne.

The northeastern mainland portion of the province and the adjacent counties of Cape Breton Island also had numerous annexationists. The coal industry dominated this region and wanted duty-free entry into the United States; such a privilege, mine operators estimated, would increase their annual sales in that market from 200,000 to 11,000,000 tons.[50] Nearly all of the owners and managers of the mines were Americans, but the workers, good Nova Scotians, were also annexationists, for the end of reciprocity had thrown thousands of them out of employment. Conditions in the coal regions were wretched, in contrast to the prosperous years from 1854 to 1866.[51] The discontent in such towns as Pictou and New Glasgow made them strongly annexationist. In Halifax, the leading commercial city, the numerous advocates of political union came from the distressed trading and shipping industries.[52] Their salvation lay, they believed, in participation in the American coastal trade, open only to citizens of the United States.

In all, the annexationists apparently preponderated in seven or eight of the eighteen counties in Nova Scotia and comprised perhaps a third of its population. More important was the fact that the movement was strongest among the economic elite of the province: the merchants, fishermen, coal operators and

[49] Yarmouth *Tribune*, July 20, 1869.

[50] The American duty of $1.25 a ton was a serious handicap to sale in the United States. Boston *Daily Advertiser*, October 14, 1868; New Glasgow *Eastern Chronicle*, November 25, 1869.

[51] Boston *Daily Advertiser*, October 17, 1868.

[52] Young to Granville, April 8, 1869, G 573 A, Secret and Confidential Despatches, 1867-1869.

miners, and allied interests. Those who depended upon commerce for their livelihood—ship captains, sailors, and commission men—also supported annexation, which would move trade out of the doldrums.[53] These monied interests invested freely in the movement.[54]

Heartened by the encouragement and support of such influential groups, the anti cabinet of Nova Scotia, which had gained office through audacious agitation, tried to keep it by the same means. They blustered and threatened, defying the whole Empire to hold them within its bonds. But though they roared as lions, they acted as rabbits. This was particularly true of their real leader, Attorney General Martin Wilkins, who, in a pinch, reacted to the inhibitions imposed upon him by poverty, a large brood, and an overmastering desire to mount the bench. The lieutenant governor, Hastings Doyle, was a British general of the "no nonsense" breed. He soon assayed his cabinet as resolute in speech and flabby in act, and he took rare delight in bullying them and in calling their bluffs. If a cabinet member uttered a particularly swashbuckling speech, Hastings Doyle would promptly force him to retreat and retract; he constantly challenged the government either to accept confederation or to implement their disloyal threats by action.[55] Humiliation at the hands of this gruff soldier became almost daily fare for the cabinet of Nova Scotia.

The annexation movement was bound to suffer from ineffectual leaders who became the laughingstock of the province. This, and other reasons to be examined later, led to the decline of the agitation in the fall of 1870 and its disappearance in 1872. The tide first began to ebb in the coal regions. The mine operators deserted the movement in December, 1869, and it

[53] This analysis from Young to Granville, April 8, 1869.

[54] J. McClellan to Macdonald, February 23, 1869, Macdonald Papers, Nova Scotia Affairs, III.

[55] Hastings Doyle to Macdonald, June 25, 1869, Macdonald Papers, Nova Scotia Affairs, I.

soon collapsed in that area.[56] The annexationists of southern Nova Scotia had sterner stuff. When the provincial government, which had fathered the movement, tried to commit infanticide by urging its followers to cease their agitation, the annexation league fought back. In March, 1870, it issued another manifesto reiterating that political union was "absolutely necessary to a permanent freedom of commerce with the United States." The coal and fishing industries were, according to this document, desperate for American markets and the entire province needed an infusion of American capital.[57] The league concluded with a promise to form a political party to contest future elections, but its brave words were soon belied by its disappearance.

Annexation meetings continued to occur in the southern part of the province through 1870 with decreasing frequency, and ceased altogether in December. Even the Yarmouth *Herald*, most intransigent of the papers, declared that the time was not yet ripe for union with the United States.[58] The surrender of this journal may be taken to mark the decease of the postconfederation annexation movement in Nova Scotia.

The agitations for political union in the other three provinces were much weaker than that in Nova Scotia, but were otherwise similar to it and may be more briefly described. Again the causes were primarily the distress occasioned by the depression of 1867 and the continuing opposition to confederation on the part of a considerable minority.

In New Brunswick the antis had temporarily lapsed into inactivity after their defeat at the polls in 1865. The pinch of

[56] The last annexation meeting in the northeastern part of the province apparently occurred early in February, 1870, at Merigomish. Yarmouth *Tribune*, February 9, 1870.

[57] R. Haliburton to W. B. Vail, January 18, 1870, Macdonald Papers, Nova Scotia Affairs, III. The manifesto was dated at Halifax, March 21, 1870, and signed by R. Wilson, secretary of the league. It was printed in Yarmouth *Herald*, March 31, 1870.

[58] Yarmouth *Herald*, December 5, 1870.

depression, however, revived the comatose local repeal league in 1868, and it succeeded in electing its candidate, John W. Cudlip, to the provincial legislature in a byelection in St. John.[59] Despite this and other similar successes, the league made no attempt to win political control of the province or to cooperate with its counterpart in Nova Scotia.[60] When the failure of Howe's second mission to England blighted the hopes of secession for New Brunswick as well as for Nova Scotia, many of the antis gravitated into the annexation movement.[61]

These developments gave the ambitious Cudlip aspirations to become the Moses who would lead the children of New Brunswick into their Promised Land. On March 17, 1869, he arose in the assembly to recite the well-worn tale of provincial woes: trade was declining, producers were losing money, and bankruptcy was the common refuge of businessmen. At the end of the lugubrious catalog, Cudlip electrified his auditors by stating that "it becomes worthy of consideration whether we should not, as a province, seek to carry out what our people are doing individually and ask the United States to admit us into the Union on fair and equitable terms." "We are compelled to look for a more extended market," he continued, "and however averse it may be to our long-cherished predilections and associations that the tie which has so long bound us to the Mother Country should be severed, we are forced to the conclusion that . . . the nature of our productions and the geographical position of our country point to the United States of America as our natural market and that can be best and most surely secured by a union with the United States." The resolution concluded

[59] Quebec *Morning Chronicle,* April 8, 1868.

[60] Howe to Livingston, August 1, 1868, Howe Papers, XXXVIII, Howe Letter Book.

[61] St. John *Morning Freeman,* January 18, 1868; St. Andrews *Standard,* February 17, 1869; D. B. Warner to Seward, December 2, 1868, Consular Despatches, St. John, VII, 92.

with a stipulation that a committee of three be appointed to explore possible means of securing annexation.[62]

The motion failed of a second, but it succeeded in creating a sensation, and annexation became the topic of public discussion. The St. John press agreed that Cudlip "was leading where many were disposed to follow." As yet, advocates of political union were in the minority, but "Unless our trade is revived . . . and employment at good wages is afforded the working classes, the minority may soon become the majority."[63] These papers spoke for the dominant mercantile interest of the city, and economic considerations were not only their principal, but their sole, theme. The *Morning Freeman* was perfectly candid on this point: "the loyalty of the pocket is the only true loyalty of the present day and all other is sham."[64]

In Quebec also, hostility to confederation evolved by frustration and by the distress of depression into annexationism. Here the opposition to the Dominion and the desire to join the United States arose from two self-conscious minorities, one on the provincial and the other on the national plane. The first was the English-speaking group in Quebec. With their fellows to the west, they had outnumbered the French in the united colony of Canada, but with Quebec again a separate province, they would become a permanent and hopeless minority whose rights and institutions were in jeopardy. Annexation was preferable to this hateful prospect.

Curiously, political union also gained some French support for a similar reason. In the Dominion as a whole, these people

[62] Yarmouth *Herald*, March 25, 1869; New York *Times*, April 10, 1869.

[63] St. John *Morning Freeman*, March 20, 1869; St. John *Globe*, March 18, 1869, enclosed in D. B. Warner to E. B. Washburne, March 19, 1869, Consular Despatches, St. John, VII, 105.

[64] St. John *Morning Freeman*, July 8, 1869; Sir John Young, Baron Lisgar to Macdonald, September 7, 1869, Macdonald Papers, Governor-Generals' Correspondence, III, Lord Lisgar; D. B. Warner to Seward, December 8, 1869, Consular Despatches, St. John, VII, 92.

would be a minority as their English neighbors were in Quebec. Though the local hierarchy of the Roman Catholic Church threw its powerful weight behind confederation as the surest bulwark against annexation and the soundest defense for nationalité, a considerable number of the laity, particularly from the Parti Rouge, bitterly dissented. They held numerous meetings throughout the province and railed at the plan as an attack upon their religion, language, and culture, which would be slowly but steadily chipped away by the majority.[65] The dissidents were unimpressed by the argument that the choice was between Canadian or American union. They replied that only annexationism would profit from attempts to harry a reluctant Quebec into the Dominion.[66]

This prophecy seemed validated when the agitation for political union increased after the Imperial government answered the demands of the anticonfederationists everywhere with obdurate silence. French resistance to the union, with its annexation overtones, was also inspirited by the support of other groups. One was a small but vocal Irish group in Quebec, and a second, the growing colony of American-born businessmen in the province.[67] Uniquely, the latter had a sentimental motivation for their desire, but economic considerations were also present. These Americans were largely engaged in lumbering and quarrying, and appreciated the importance of access to the markets of their native land.[68]

[65] For examples of French hostility, see Montreal *Pays,* January 2, 7, 14, February 11, March 14, 1865, June 4, 1867, July 21, 1868. Also Quebec *Canadien,* undated, quoted in *Montreal Pays,* July 29, 1865; Quebec *Evènement,* undated, quoted in Montreal *Pays,* August 6, 1868, May 4, 1871.

[66] Quebec *Canadien,* undated, quoted in Montreal *Pays,* March 6, 1866.

[67] Quebec *Morning Chronicle,* January 14, 15, 16, 17, 1867.

[68] W. Averell to Seward, June 27, 1868, Consular Despatches, Montreal, IX, 108; Charles Robinson to Seward, December 14, 1868, Consular Despatches, Quebec, III, 30.

Their Irish and American neighbors, however, had less effect on the attitudes of the French Canadians than the opinions of their numerous brethren emigrated to the United States. Though conservatives and the church in Quebec might denounce the departed as traitors who had deserted nationalité and religion for the American fleshpot, the average habitant watched with interest, tinged with envy, as former countrymen achieved success in their adopted land.[69] This gregarious people formed numerous clubs and societies in American cities from coast to coast. They frequently discussed and approved annexation on the premise that all French Canadians, freed of the social fetters and exploitive features of a semifeudal colonial society, would blossom and prosper, even as the emigrants had done. Since all French could not go to the United States, annexation would bring the United States to them.[70]

This potpourri of national support for annexation in Quebec did not promise close integration in the movement, but it did foretell considerable activity. The first moves came from a few secondary Liberal and Rouge leaders who apparently hoped to use popular discontent and political union to repair their tattered political fortunes.[71] To promote their campaign, these annexationists repeatedly approached Seward both directly and through the American consul general requesting sums ranging from a modest five thousand to an ambitious hundred thousand dollars.[72] In return, they promised to deliver the Dominion to the

[69] Montreal *Pays*, December 5, 1865.

[70] Accounts of such societies and their endorsements of annexation were numerous in the press of the day. For typical samples, see Montreal *Pays*, December 2, 5, 1865, March 29, 1866, January 19, 1871; Quebec *Morning Chronicle*, October 15, 1868; St. Andrews *Standard*, July 5, 1871.

[71] The Rouge had elected only ten members to Parliament and six of sixty in the local assembly. Quebec *Morning Chronicle*, September 17, 1867.

[72] W. Averell to Seward, December (?), 1866, L. A. Dessaules to Averell, January 24, 1868, enclosed in Averell to Seward, February 17,

United States when they had gained power. One prominent Montreal Liberal even proposed to submit a plan for the conquest of Canada, adding confidently, "I know all the weak points."[73] But Seward ignored both pleas and plans.

This rebuff of silence did not dishearten the political unionists, nor did the pastoral letters issued by Roman Catholic bishops of St. Hyacinthe, Trois Rivières, and Quebec, who sternly forbade parishioners to participate in this movement which would bring "the certain destruction of French-Canadian nationality."[74] Undeterred by this thunder from the pulpit, the Quebec annexationists carried on a vigorous and public agitation. They wrote letters to the papers, held public meetings in both Montreal and Quebec, formed an annexation league similar to the one organized in 1849-1850, and made several unsuccessful attempts to hold an international political union convention at Niagara Falls, New York, in company with American sympathizers.[75] By March, 1870, the American consul general informed his superiors that there were more annexationists than ever before in the province, all convinced that Canada must soon have free access to American markets or be overwhelmed by economic disaster.[76]

The brisk agitations in Nova Scotia, New Brunswick, and

1868, Consular Despatches, Montreal, VII. Dessaules was a politician, economist, and journalist, president of the Institut Canadien and editor of Monteral *Pays*. He had been an annexationist in 1849, as befitted the nephew of Louis Joseph Papineau.

[73] Fredrich Driscoll to Seward, September 12, 1867, Miscellaneous Letters to the Department of State, 1867, September, I.

[74] Quebec *Morning Chronicle*, June 25, 1867.

[75] St. Catherines *Daily Journal*, September 12, 1868; Quebec *Morning Chronicle*, August 24, 31, September 7, 14, 20, 1869; Yarmouth *Herald*, September 23, 1869, June 30, 1870; A. Watson to Hamilton Fish, May 19, 1869, Miscellaneous Letters to the Department of State, 1869, May, II.

[76] W. Dart to J. C. B. Davis, March 17, 1870, Consular Despatches, Montreal, X, 56.

Quebec had a much weaker counterpart in Ontario. This province had little of the bitter opposition to confederation, which had been one of the roots of the continental union movement elsewhere. Moreover, the small but lively group of annexationists there had been driven to cover in 1865, as already noted, by the angry reaction to American threats and the incredible speech of Consul General Potter on commercial coercion. Though the depression also visited Ontario after 1866, relatively few dared to suggest annexation as a counter to it except a number of commercial men and shipowners and some inhabitants of the border areas.[77]

There were some marked similarities between the annexation movements in the four provinces. Economic distress and the fear that it would continue were the root from which they all grew and drew nourishment. Opposition to confederation was an aggravating force except in Ontario. The personnel of the several movements came from the same interest groups. Everywhere, merchants and others dependent on commerce were the core of the agitation. They had suffered most from the depression and would gain most from the free trade with the United States which annexation would bring. Producers who looked to the American market also gravitated into the movement. They included the fishermen of the Maritime Provinces, lumbermen of New Brunswick, and farmers and quarriers of the Eastern Townships of Quebec.[78] Behind these merchants and producers were their financial backers, whose prosperity fluctuated with that of their debtors.

[77] New York *Times*, December 29, 1866; F. Blake to H. Pratt, April 14, 1868, Consular Despatches, Fort Erie, I; F. Hanse to Fish, October 1, 1869, March 21, 1870, Consular Despatches, Kingston, I, III. The movement in Kingston was led by an Anglican clergyman, the Reverend J. Allen, and was said to include the mayor and other prominent men in the town.

[78] Yarmouth *Herald*, April 1, July 8, 1869; St. John *Morning Freeman*, August 8, 1869.

The movement also assumed a definite geographic pattern. Its citadels were the commercial centers such as Yarmouth, Halifax, St. John, Montreal, and Toronto. The strength of the movement everywhere was also proportional to nearness to the United States. The boldest and most numerous annexationists were found in southern Nova Scotia, the St. Croix and St. John valleys in New Brunswick, the Eastern Townships of Quebec, and the southeastern and southwestern corners of Ontario.[79] In such places, firsthand comparisons of the economic conditions on both sides of the line were easily made. Disparity made the political boundary appear to be the barrier to prosperity.

The annexation agitations in New Brunswick, Quebec, and Ontario were also similar in the mode of their exit, for all three were absorbed into the movement for Canadian independence after 1870. This interest in a free Canada was stimulated by the Fenian raids. Canadians were incensed because Britain was denuding the central provinces of troops, leaving them exposed to those who attacked them precisely because they were part of the Empire.[80] Independence would end this connection and its accompanying danger. Moreover, it would soften the attitude of the United States toward Canada and, perhaps, lead to a renewal of reciprocity.

The proponents of political union promptly joined this new movement—and not from simple fickleness nor the fact that independence was more respectable than annexation. Their support was sincere, for many people did not believe that Canada could stand alone; freedom from Britain would not be a terminal but a stage on the road to union with the United States. The loyal press of Quebec and Ontario had reason to denounce this agitation for independence as a screen for annexation when

[79] St. Catherines *Evening Journal,* April 22, May 26, 27, 1867; S. Pace to Fish, August 21, 1869, Consular Despatches, Sarnia, I, 15.

[80] C. P. Stacey, "Britain's Withdrawal from North America 1864-1871," *Canadian Historical Review,* XXXVI (September, 1955), 185-98.

avowed political unionists now called loudly for a free Canada and the American consul general held a seat in the inner council of the independence group. Perhaps because of such accusations, the new movement was short-lived, and the annexation agitation expired with it in 1871.[81]

What limited the agitation for political union and what caused its collapse? One of its weaknesses was the fact that it was national in extent, but local in organization. There was little interprovincial communication and no interprovincial organization. It was not a unified movement, but a series of independent, though coincident, stirrings.

More important was the nature of the depression which had been the principal cause of the agitation. It was commercial, not agricultural, and it soon passed away. Most Canadians were farmers who produced for the European market and were relatively insensitive to the pain of declining trade with the United States. Even the merchants did not suffer long. Exports to the United States dropped from their peak in 1866 to their nadir in 1867, then began to rise. By 1870 they were over sixteen million dollars greater than they had been in 1867; the annual trade of the provinces was well above the average attained during the years of reciprocity.[82] Like the traveler in Aesop's fable, the commercial men shed the garment of annexation under the warm rays of prosperity.

Provincial economic grievances had also melted away by 1872. The fishing grounds compensated for the failures of 1867 and 1868 by yielding bounteously from 1869 to 1873, and the Treaty of Washington brought a new day for the Maritime Provinces

[81] Quebec *Morning Chronicle,* June 8, 1869; W. Dart to Fish, September 14, 1869, Consular Despatches, Montreal, IX, 26; Montreal *Pays,* December 9, 1870.

[82] *Senate Executive Documents,* 53 Cong., 2 sess., no. 106; Canada *Year Book, 1936,* pp. 125-26. The latter volume contains historical surveys and statistics of the important industries and occupations in Canada, as well as studies of prices and production.

by admitting Canadian fish to the United States duty-free in exchange for American use of the territorial waters. As exports of coal from Nova Scotia also increased, so did employment and wages, and the mining district emerged from its dark days.[83]

Reciprocity was again prescribed as an antidote to annexation. Macdonald encouraged the belief that a revival of the treaty of 1854 was possible if the agitation for political union disappeared.[84] He pointed out that Congress would never ratify such a treaty if it meant the end of annexationism, so that agitation must die before reciprocity could be reborn. This tangled rationalization was used to considerable effect.[85]

A further inhibition upon Canadian desire to join the United States was a byproduct of the Civil War—the enormous debt incurred by the American government. Since the annexationists harped on the single string of economic reasons, loyalists could meet them on the same theme with a poser: if annexation came, would not the taxes required to retire this debt outweigh Canadian gains from higher prices, wider markets, and increased trade?[86] There was no convincing answer, and Canadian political unionists urged the American government to promise to excuse any British territory entering the Republic from paying a share of the debt. These efforts were unsuccessful, of course, and

[83] St. John *Morning Freeman*, November 13, 1869.

[84] Macdonald sent an agent to Washington to lobby for reciprocity. This man, who was paid to get results, was optimistic in his reports. Macdonald undoubtedly took them with a grain of salt, but they were useful in persuading Canadians that reciprocity was possible and were given the widest possible publicity. Macdonald Papers, Secret Service, I, George W. Brega.

[85] R. Haliburton to Macdonald, December 24, 1869, Macdonald Papers, Nova Scotia Affairs, III. The coal operators admitted that they still believed in ultimate annexation to the United States but were suppressing the movement in their area in hopes of clearing the way for reciprocity.

[86] Yarmouth *Tribune*, July 7, 1868; Halifax *British Colonist*, undated, quoted in Yarmouth *Tribune*, May 25, 1869; Niagara *Mail*, October 18, 1865.

some Canadians with annexationist proclivities were discouraged by the thought of this staggering debt.[87]

But it would be unjust to suggest that material considerations alone preserved Canada's ties with the Empire. The loyalty of most of her people remained an unbreachable bulwark. Annexation was economic in appeal, and man does not live by bread alone. To suggest that Canadians would peddle their loyalty for cash was a crude and intolerable proposal to most of them. Few of them loved the United States or respected its government and culture.[88] American activities and diplomacy increased their antipathy toward the Republic. Canadians considered the Fenian raids, for example, a repulsive pressure sanctioned by Washington in an effort to coerce Canada into annexation. The negotiations over the *Alabama* had the same flavor when such dignitaries as Senator Charles Sumner inferred that British America should be ceded to satisfy these American claims. Canadian antipathy reached its peak over the negotiations of 1871 at Washington, when the United States used its claims to force open the inshore fisheries of the Dominion but refused to consider the damages caused by the Fenian raids, Canada's equivalent of the *Alabama*. Outraged Canadian opinion after this episode found suggestions of annexation detestable.

In Quebec the loyalty of the majority of the French Canadians again lay as an unyielding dam in the course of the annexationists. The habitants were still convinced that union with the United States would destroy their nationalité, which Canada safeguarded constitutionally. For this reason, the natural leaders

[87] The number of Canadian annexationists who made this suggestion to Washington indicates the importance of the issue in their minds. Reverend J. Allen to S. Hanse, March 19, 1870, enclosed in Hanse to Fish, March 21, 1870, Consular Despatches, Kingston, III; E. Kimball to Thurston, March 31, 1865, Consular Despatches, Toronto, I; A. McLean to Seward, June 9, 1867, Miscellaneous Letters to the Department of State, 1867, June, II.

[88] Quebec *Morning Chronicle*, April 25, August 1, 1867.

of this people, the Roman Catholic clergy, set their faces implacably against annexation. The advocates of continental union lacked their favorite weapon for breaching this wall of opposition because the French, predominantly agrarian, were almost impervious to the distress of commercial decline.

The attitude of the Imperial government tested the resolution of all annexationists and intimidated the fainthearted. The courteous but stern response of the colonial secretaries to the repeal delegations from Nova Scotia created the impression that British troops would smash any forcible attempts to secede from Canada and to join the United States. Overt actions would fail unless help came from the United States, a delusive hope. With few exceptions, the American people were indifferent to the acquisition or opposed to taking positive steps to achieve it. The press bluntly warned Canadian annexationists that they were on their own: "We beg the people of Nova Scotia not to appeal to us for assistance against England. . . . We don't think the quarrel is one that is worthwhile to go to war about—certainly it is not worthwhile for us to go to war about it."[89]

Some American journals scolded the Canadians for their shortcomings and warned them to mend their ways before seeking membership in the American Union.[90] Others which were warmer to the idea of annexation put the burden of the initiative on the people of the Dominion. A Maine newspaper commenting upon the fear of "intensely loyal" Canadians that they would be forced to join the United States reassured them: "We beg them to dismiss their terrors. There is no one in this country who desires to annex one of their provinces unless the mass of the population desire it. Should they, in obedience to a natural law of centripetal force, gravitate to us, we will welcome them

[89] New York *Times,* September 5, 1868. The *Times,* June 25, 1869, added that the only justification for annexation would be to gain the coal and fish resources of the Dominion.

[90] Boston *Daily Advertiser,* December 30, 1869; Boston *Zion's Herald,* undated, quoted in Yarmouth *Tribune,* November 24, 1869.

cordially . . . but until they are ready to come to us, we have not the slightest disposition to interfere in or to influence their affairs."[91]

Congress was also cool to the acquisition of Canada. The few members who raised the question ran into a wall of indifference. Senator Samuel C. Pomeroy presented an annexation petition from Canada to his colleagues and proposed that the President should negotiate with Great Britain for that purpose if he deemed it advisable. The Senate ordered his resolution printed but gave it no further attention.[92] Representative Luke Poland, Republican of Vermont, introduced a similar measure which met an identical fate.[93]

The executive department showed a greater, if inconsistent, interest. President Andrew Johnson, busy fighting the Radical Republicans, almost completely ignored British America. Seward did little more. Long known as an archannexationist, this secretary of state had either lost his appetite for Canada or was too deeply involved in Alaskan and West Indian adventures to give more than occasional and casual attention to the Dominion.

The inauguration of Ulysses S. Grant temporarily changed the mood in Washington. Both the President and his secretary of state, Hamilton Fish, were expansionists.[94] The powerful Charles Sumner, a leader of the Senate Radicals and chairman of the Committee on Foreign Relations, completed a triumvirate eager to acquire Canada. Sumner was aware that many in England wished to shed their Empire because they felt that its defense and administration burdened the British taxpayer with-

[91] Portland *Press,* undated, quoted in Quebec *Morning Chronicle,* April 6, 1869.

[92] *Senate Miscellaneous Documents,* 41 Cong., 2 sess., no. 14.

[93] *Congressional Globe,* 41 Cong., 2 sess., 4601.

[94] Shippee, *Canadian-American Relations,* cites many instances of the expansionist tendencies of the Grant administration. Grant opposed reciprocity, fearing it would kill the annexation movement in Canada. Don Piatt to G. Brega, March 31, 1870, Macdonald Papers, Secret Service, I, George W. Brega.

out compensatory return.[95] The senator from Massachusetts obligingly evolved a plan which would relieve them of their millstone and work to the mutual benefit of Great Britain and the United States. He implied that the British government should cede Canada to the United States in payment for the indirect claims arising from the *Alabama*.[96] Fish readily picked up this idea and carried it to Edward Thornton, British minister at Washington. The secretary added that Canada was rampant with unrest and disloyalty, indicating that its citizens longed to snip their ties with Great Britain.[97] Thornton listened politely and remarked that Britain would release Canada when convinced that the Canadians wished it. To date, his government had no evidence of this; to the contrary, Canadians were happy with their lot and resented any suggestions of change, whether from England, from the United States, or from their fellow colonists. Some of the British people and political leaders were beginning to turn away from the anti-imperialism of the "Little England" faction, and his government was unlikely to strengthen the rival United States by doubling its area at the cost of the British Empire. Knowing this, Thornton could well refer to Fish's tentative suggestions of annexation as "delusive hopes."[98]

Important segments of American opinion also opposed using the *Alabama* claims as a lever to pry Canada out of the Empire. Influential papers denounced the plan, and eighteen congressmen impatiently wrote to Fish urging him to discard his delu-

[95] Robert L. Schuyler, "The Climax of Anti-Imperialism in England," *Political Science Quarterly*, XXXVI (December, 1921), 537-38; New York *Times*, August 21, 1869.

[96] Sumner argued that England's unneutral actions had prolonged the Civil War, costing the United States a modest $2,500,000,000, an indirect claim which must somehow be paid. Charles Sumner, *Charles Sumner, His Complete Works* (Boston, 1900), XVII, 53-93.

[97] Young to Granville, January 22, 1870, G 573 A, Secret and Confidential Despatches, 1870; Nevins, *Hamilton Fish*, 296-300, 385-86.

[98] Edward Thornton to George W. F. Villiers, Earl of Clarendon, 4, January 3, 1870, F. O. 5: 1191.

sions and get on with the practical business of negotiating a new reciprocity agreement with the Dominion.[99] Such opposition daunted the secretary, and he abandoned his hopes of intertwining the *Alabama* and expansion. This flurry was the only attempt by the American government to exploit the annexation movement in Canada.

The relatively few Americans who hankered to expand northward may be divided into two groups. One might be called the political expansionists—those who thought that the United States should absorb all the area north of the Rio Grande and who dreaded the construction of a strong British nation in North America as a perpetual threat to their Republic. This lot was not numerous and generally had its habitat in the states along the border. The same area harbored nearly all of the other group—the economic expansionists who were anxious to annex the trade, markets, and resources of the Dominion. States which had well-worn trade routes to Canada or which produced articles in demand there were naturally interested in annexation.

The annexation movement in Canada had collapsed by 1871, but it could revive unless fundamental problems were settled. A spirit of Canadian nationalism was essential to reinforce the loyalty to the Empire which might become weaker as it became indirect. The Dominion must attain a viable national economy to down the politically dangerous belief that its prosperity depended upon free trade with the United States. Railroads must span the country and rivet it together with their steel bands, lest the thin line of settlement buckle from the pull to the south. East-west lines of trade and communication were needed to challenge and to master the natural and mature north-south lines. It seemed likely that the flag would follow trade; the question remained, which trade and which flag?

[99] New York *Times*, April 13, 22, 1869; Brega to Macdonald, November 10, 1870, encloses a copy of this letter. Macdonald Papers, Secret Service, I, George W. Brega.

CHAPTER FOUR

The Union Movements in the West 1866-1871

In the east, confederation was operating to revive the specter of annexation which it was designed to destroy. Now the same apparition appeared in the west, beyond the outposts of the new Dominion. Here, too, it stimulated a national union movement and so hastened the expansion of Canada from sea to sea.[1]

Most annexationists in the United States felt that all of British America would one day be part of the Republic, but it was that part lying between the Rockies and Lake Superior whose American destiny seemed most manifest. Here nature had rolled the plains, furrowed the valleys, and piled the mountains on a north-south axis. Here the soil, the climate, and the socioeconomic potentials on both sides of the forty-ninth parallel were so identical that the thin political line seemed a mockery. American expansionists believed that nature and her forces would avenge this frustration of her great purpose, blot out the boundary, and make one nation of those living on both sides of it. They were willing to serve as catalytic agents for this natural process, and the period after confederation seemed propitious.

The roots of the story lie deeply embedded in the past. In 1670, by careless charter, Charles II of England bestowed upon the Hudson's Bay Company the vast empire which drained into Hudson Bay and Hudson Strait. The company was interested only in peltry and did not develop its domain. In the 1860's the only real settlement was Fort Garry, at the junction of the Assiniboine and Red rivers. At first this colony was a closed corporation under the company which controlled its economy and its tenuous link with the world, the arduous water route to Hudson Bay. Gradually, this grip relaxed. The rise of St. Paul at the head of navigation on the Mississippi made it the entrepôt for the trade of the Northwest and the commercial capital of that politically divided area. Long processions of Red River carts creaked and shrilled their ungreased way across the rolling and lake-dotted prairie between Fort Garry and the capital of Minnesota. Steamboats twisted their way up the tortuous Red River of the North, and stagecoaches lumbered from St. Paul toward British America.[2] These easier approaches supplanted the trade line through the bay, and the company's hold on the economic affairs of the colony slipped. Moreover, the government broke down when it tried to prevent the colonists from setting up a private trade in furs via the cart trail and in violation of its charter monopoly. In attempting to smother this activity, government officials merely succeeded in fanning a blaze which they could not put out. Their strongest efforts only advertised their futility. The government of the colony was broken beyond repair. What would replace it?

Westward from Fort Garry and beyond the ramparts of the Rockies there had been little settlement until the middle of the nineteenth century, when, alarmed by the Oregon crisis, the

[1] General accounts of the background of Red River history and of the Riel Rebellion used here include: Alexander Begg, *History of the North-West* (Toronto, 1894-1895); George F. G. Stanley, *The Birth of Western Canada: A History of the Riel Rebellions* (London, 1936); Arthur S. Morton, *A History of the Canadian West to 1870-1871* (London, 1939); Robert E. Lamb, *Thunder in the North* (New York, 1957); and William L. Morton, *Manitoba: A History* (Toronto, 1957). Much of the material on annexation originally appeared in an article by the author entitled "Drang Nach Norden: The United States and the Riel Rebellion," *Mississippi Valley Historical Review*, XXXIX (March, 1953), 693-712, and is used here with the consent of the editor, William C. Binkley.

[2] New York *Times*, December 28, 1869; Morton, *Manitoba*, 101.

British government gave Vancouver Island to the Hudson's Bay Company to colonize. But this contained only a handful of people, and the mainland had no white population until 1858, when the discovery of gold in the Fraser River valley brought a rush of fortune seekers, destroyed the company's trading monopoly, and necessitated some new provision for government on the Pacific coast. The Imperial government then created the crown colony of British Columbia on the mainland, bought back Vancouver Island, and forced its governor to sever his connections with the company. The "golden days" soon passed away, succeeded by hard times. The two governments sank into debt and were united in 1866 under the name of British Columbia.

The United States was casting its shadow over this vast region from Lake Superior to Vancouver Island. The rapid advance of the American frontier, emphasized by the admission of Minnesota and Oregon, constituted a serious threat to the British West. Here the expansive drives of the Republic and of the Dominion would lock and grapple for this empire.

Obviously, the future of the entire area depended upon the fate of Fort Garry and the Red River settlement. If these became part of the United States, the Canadian approach to the entire West was irretrievably blocked and a vast new area would fall into the receptive hands of the Republic. The danger of such a development loomed ever larger through the 1860's. The economic ties of the Red River with the south grew steadily as those with the British territories withered. American settlers followed the Red River cart trail and clustered around Fort Garry, where, dynamic, restless, and aggressive, they became the yeast of political ferment. Thus the first fingers of the tide of the American frontier had crawled north of the forty-ninth parallel, perhaps soon to be followed by a flood which would wash away British authority. Painfully aware of the similarity between this situation and that which had existed earlier in Oregon when the same British company played King Canute to the same irresistible force, Imperial officials hastened their efforts to save the Northwest.

The most logical means to forestall American occupation of the Northwest was purchase of the region by Canada. Moreover, if Canada were to become a great nation, it must have room to expand, a West comparable to that of its neighbor.[3] Already the surplus population of Ontario was spilling into Michigan, squeezed out of Canada by the cramping Laurentian Shield. As Canadians saw their frontier escaping over the line, they became anxious to obtain the Northwest.[4] The Imperial government also hoped that Canada would take over the empire of the company and the lonely British colony on the Pacific littoral. A British parliamentary committee recommended in 1857 that Canada should be allowed to annex those lands in the company's possession which would be suitable for settlement.[5] In the same year the inhabitants of the Red River district petitioned to be joined to Canada.[6] The Canadian government was more eager to acquire the Northwest than to pay for it. They pretended that the ancient charter of the company was invalid and that Canada had inherited the sounder claim of New France to this territory. The company warmly denied this contention and refused to submit the validity of its charter to the scrutiny of the Privy Council as Canada suggested. This acrimonious quibbling delayed changes which conditions in the Northwest made daily more imperative.

In the 1860's the looming threat of the United States made such bickering too expensive a luxury longer to be tolerated. The swelling stream of American traders and settlers moving into the territory and the breakdown of its government there

[3] Halifax *British Colonist*, December 14, 1867.

[4] Trotter, *Federation*, 222-23.

[5] Stanley, *Western Canada*, 21-22; Trotter, *Federation*, 234-43.

[6] Correspondence on the petition and a copy of the petition in British Parliament, *Accounts and Papers, 1870*, L, no. 207.

made the Hudson's Bay Company desirous to peddle its lands for what it could get before the United States took them gratis. It spurred Canadian interest by considering an offer from an Anglo-American syndicate which wished to acquire the Northwest and to organize and settle it "on the American plan."[7] This sly suggestion fulfilled its purpose. Both the Canadian and British governments grew extremely anxious, and their hope of acquiring the Northwest for Canada and of providing it with proper communications to the east hastened confederation, for obviously the colonies would have to pool their purses to carry out this expensive project. Article 146 of the British North America Act provided for the annexation of the lands west of Lake Superior.

With the Imperial authorities, through the Governor General, constantly jogging Ottawa on the urgency of the question, the government of the new federation wasted no time in implementing this article.[8] Early in the initial session of the first Dominion Parliament, William McDougall moved that the House of Commons consider the advisability of acquiring the Northwest. Parliament approved a resolution for this addition to the Dominion on December 5, 1867.[9] In June of the following year the British Parliament passed an act which enabled the Queen to accept the surrender of company lands and to transfer them to Canada.[10] The government at Ottawa then sent delegates to London to treat with the company about terms. After acrimonious negotiations, the company agreed to sell its title to

[7] Canadian Parliament, *Sessional Papers,* 1867, no. 19, pp. 3-4. (Canadian legislative papers hereafter identified as *Canadian.*)

[8] Lord Monck to the Duke of Buckingham, October 19, 1867, G 573 A, Secret and Confidential Despatches, 1867-1870; Sir Fredrick Bruce to Lord Edward H. S. Stanley, January 12, 1867, F. O. 5: 1104.

[9] *Canadian Commons Journals,* I, 50-51, 53, 59; *Canadian Senate Journals,* I, 142, 144-45.

[10] British Parliament, *Parliamentary Debates,* 4th ser., vol. 193, p. 1936.

the Northwest for £300,000 and the right to retain certain blocks of land and to continue its trading activities, though not its monopoly.[11] Canada accepted these terms and appointed a government for the new territory, Manitoba.

But the prospect of incorporation into Canada alarmed many in the Red River district. A primary cause of their disquiet was the land question. Some of them, particularly the métis or French halfbreeds, were squatters who had not bothered to obtain title to the land they occupied in the easygoing days of company rule. They feared that the new government would dispossess them, and the wildest rumors gained currency in the colony. The people of the Red River also resented the fact that they had not been consulted during the negotiations but sold like serfs on a medieval manor. A number of political grievances added to the tension. Some of the inhabitants had hoped that the district would become a self-governing province rather than a territory with an appointed administration. The métis also wished the same constitutional safeguards for their language and religion which their cousins in Quebec enjoyed. Moreover, the political change in the Red River would inevitably be accompanied by an economic revolution. The old order, based on the fur trade and subsistence agriculture, was almost feudal in character with its established social relationships and degree of economic security. The coming of Canada meant the coming of ruthless and aggressive nineteenth century capitalism. Canadian newcomers to the little settlement were disturbing harbingers of the impending change. Brusque, superior, and openly contemptuous of what they saw, they boasted that things would change when they were in the saddle.[12] This attitude filled with foreboding the simple métis whose property rested on custom, not on writ, and on mutual obligation, not on driving ambition.

[11] *Canadian Sessional Papers,* 1869, no. 25, pt. V.
[12] Lamb, *Thunder in the North,* 10-11; Morton, *Manitoba,* 116.

Except for the last, these grievances could have been anticipated and ameliorated. The government in Ottawa, however, ignored the audible rumblings from the west and dispatched William McDougall, newly appointed lieutenant governor of Manitoba, to his post.[13] In October, 1869, he reached the international boundary en route from St. Paul to Winnipeg. Here armed halfbreeds met him and, over his astonished protests, turned him back. Discontent had flared into rebellion, and the settlement was in the hands of the brilliant but unstable leader of the métis, Louis Riel.

American annexationists saw an opportunity to take advantage of the cloud of uncertainty which now hung over the future of western British America. It would be instructive to identify these gentlemen and their several motives as a key to understanding their subsequent activities.

The cast of this production was a variegated assortment, ranging from the urbane financier of the Atlantic seaboard to the rough-bearded fur trader of the West. The eastern headquarters of the movement was in Washington, where the annexationists were few but noisy. Their leader was Senator Alexander Ramsey of Minnesota, who desired to acquire the Red River area because it was a commercial adjunct to his state. Ramsey was seconded by Senators Zachariah Chandler and Jacob M. Brown of Michigan, who represented mercantile interests keen to acquire the British West to enhance the Great Lakes trade of Detroit. These senators expected the help of President Ulysses S. Grant, a persistent expansionist with no great sense of direction, and of Hamilton Fish, secretary of state. Fish was a nationalist, eager for expansion but handicapped by a confining conscience. He wanted to obtain British North America, not by subterranean intrigue or compulsion, but with the consent of the Imperial authorities and the desire of the

[13] *Canadian Sessional Papers,* 1870, no. 506, pt. V; J. S. Dennis to William McDougall, August 21, 1869, Howe Papers, IX, 695-98.

people concerned.[14] J. C. Bancroft Davis, the assistant secretary, was equally acquisitive and, perhaps, less scrupulous. Both men agreed on one point, and it was the flaw in their desires—they were not willing to incite, or even to risk, war with Great Britain to gain territory. They would spend dollars and diplomacy, but not blood, to gain British America.[15]

Nearby Philadelphia contributed an important expansionist, the enigmatic Jay Cooke, whose money financed the movement. What Cooke hoped to gain—and he was a firm believer in *quid pro quo*—is not entirely clear, but the evidence permits conjecture.[16] He was at this time assuming the promotion of the Northern Pacific Railroad. One possible route for it ran north of the border, but construction there might be politically unfeasible if the border continued to exist. On the other hand, if the road were built south of the line, the country north of it, in American hands, would be an important feeder area. Should Canada acquire this region, a Canadian road would be built and a tariff erected as a barrier on the lands tributary to the Northern Pacific. Cooke, then, would use political means to promote the economic welfare and future of his railroad. The empire-minded Northern Pacific greatly worried Macdonald in 1869-1870, and it would not be the last time.

Ramsey, Cooke, and the other expansionists in the East gave

[14] Richard H. Van Alstyne, "New Viewpoints in the Relations of Canada and the United States," *Canadian Historical Review*, XXV (July, 1944), 128; Charles P. Stacey, "The Military Aspects of Canada's Winning of the West, 1870-1885," *Canadian Historical Review*, XXI (March, 1940), 7; Nevins, *Hamilton Fish*, 387.

[15] An excellent description of the attitude and actions of the American government on Red River affairs is found in Alvin C. Gluek, Jr., "The Riel Rebellion and Canadian-American Relations," *Canadian Historical Review*, XXXVI (September, 1955), 199-221, especially 209-21.

[16] Henrietta M. Larson, *Jay Cooke, Private Banker* (Cambridge, Massachusetts, 1936), 335-38; Joseph Wheelock to Ramsey, April 7, 1870, Alexander Ramsey Papers (Minnesota Historical Society, St. Paul).

pecuniary and political support to the movement. For direct action, they depended upon their western allies, principally in Minnesota, which swarmed with annexationists. The reasons were not obscure. The drive for territorial expansion was a persistent force in such pioneer communities, and here it was supercharged with economic interests. Foremost was the desire to retain and expand the trade with the Red River area, already valued at close to two million dollars a year and steadily growing.[17] If Manitoba joined the Dominion, an east-west Canadian road would soon be built and would slash across this north-south commercial artery. Other railroads also shared the Northern Pacific's anticipation of benefits from annexation. The St. Paul & Pacific was building into Breckenridge, Minnesota, and hoped to bend its line northward at that point and continue up the Red River valley to Winnipeg. Its officers were fishing for a federal land grant and their lobbyists in Congress were using the expansionist agitation for bait, arguing that the road would increase the pressure on the people of the British West to join the United States. They wanted to keep the agitation alive at least until they had obtained the desired subsidy. These Minnesota expansionists had an able spokesman in the Canadian-born Joseph Wheelock, editor of the St. Paul *Daily Press*, who constantly and powerfully urged annexation and joined in the intrigues to get it.

St. Paul was not the only center of expansionism in the West. Another group was active at Pembina, Dakota Territory, where it could make its influence immediately felt in the Red River settlement just to the north. The principal here was Colonel Enos Stutsman, treasury agent at the customhouse and a wily

[17] St. Paul *Daily Press*, February 11, 1870; Alexandria (Minnesota) *Post*, August 7, 1869; J. Fletcher Williams, *A History of the City of St. Paul and of the County of Ramsey* (St. Paul, 1876), 304-306; W. G. Fonseca, "On the St. Paul Trail in the Sixties," Historical and Scientific Society of Manitoba, *Transactions*, no. 56 (January, 1900), 1-14.

politician.[18] Also prominent was Joseph Rolette, Jr., whose hirsute countenance peers frequently from the pages of Minnesota and Dakota history. The amiable Joe had reasons of his own for desiring annexation. He was a frontier type, the capitalist jack-of-all-trades, involved in land speculation, politics, and the fur trade.[19] He knew that the soil of the Red River valley was rich, that it would settle more rapidly as American than as Canadian territory, so that as a land dealer, he would reap a rich harvest if annexation came.[20]

The tentacles of the movement did not stop at Pembina but curled north into the Red River colony and even into the inner circles of Riel's group. There were several small but active groups of annexationists in Fort Garry and Winnipeg. The most vocal was the clump of American settlers and traders in the region, but they were not alone. Some of the employees of the Hudson's Bay Company were reported to be quietly urging that the settlement join the United States rather than Canada. Their motive was emotional—they did not love the Republic but they did hate Canada.[21] Another group which took a similar stand was a handful of priests. This is surprising because of the hostility of the Roman Catholic Church in general and of its local leader, Bishop Alexandre A. Taché, toward annexation.

[18] George Bryce, *The Remarkable History of the Hudson's Bay Company* (Toronto, 1910), 463; Henry V. Arnold, *The History of Old Pembina, 1780-1872* (Larimore, North Dakota, 1917), 149-50.

[19] Arnold, *Old Pembina*, 142, 159; St. Paul *Daily Press*, July 19, 1870.

[20] John P. Pritchett, "Some Red River Fur-Trade Activities," *Minnesota History Bulletin*, V (May, 1924), 413-17; Clarence W. Rife, "Norman Kittson, A Fur Trader in Pembina," *Minnesota History Bulletin*, VI (September, 1925), 234-35, 249-51.

[21] James W. Taylor to Hamilton Fish, January 25, 1870, James W. Taylor Papers (Minnesota Historical Society, St. Paul). The local officials of the company had been ignored by both Canada and British officials of the company during the negotiations for the transfer. Their future was highly uncertain and not promising. Lamb, *Thunder in the North*, 9-13.

These exceptions were French-born priests whose detestation of Britain overmatched allegiance to the polity of their superiors.[22]

Two individuals among the annexationists in the colony merit special attention. The first was General Oscar Malmros, recently arrived American consul in Winnipeg, who secretly guided the métis rebels with one hand and held the other out to Washington to beg aid for them. The other was W. E. B. O'Donoghue, a mysterious adventurer, most of whose career is lost in obscurity. He was born in Ireland and migrated to the United States, where he became a citizen. Like his kind who seem to have an instinct for impending trouble, he popped up in the Red River district shortly before the uprising—and as a theological student! He joined Riel and speedily achieved a position of prominence in the rebellion. O'Donoghue's Irish origin and his American citizenship frame the motivation of his ardent, but not always wise, efforts to promote annexation.[23]

The annexation movement was thus miscellaneous both in geography and motivation. It remains to mention the human cement which bound together this conglomerate—James Wickes Taylor. Taylor was formerly state librarian of Ohio and the greatest American authority on western British America. He peddled his knowledge to advantage. During the revolt, the Department of State employed him as a secret agent to keep Fish posted on Red River affairs; at the same time, he also served as informant and publicist for Cooke and for George Becker, general manager of the St. Paul & Pacific.[24] Taylor was more than a hack for special interests. He sincerely believed that annexation was inevitable and mutually beneficial. He knew

[22] Bryce, *Remarkable History*, 463-64; Wheelock to Ramsey, April 7, 1870, Ramsey Papers.

[23] I. Persons, "W. B. O'Donoghue," brief typescript biography in the collections of the Minnesota Historical Society.

[24] Department of State, Instructions to Special Missions, 1852-1886 (National Archives, Washington).

all of the groups of expansionists and commuted between the centers as the liaison man for the movement. Its failure was not due to any lack of ability or effort on his part.[25]

Thus the annexation movement south of the line had the ingredients for success: leadership, money, and influence. It also had opportunity north of the line, for Riel had revolted against rule from Canada, but he seemed at first to know better what he did not want than what he did want. The annexationists had a ready answer for this question. Moreover, their agitation had been going on quietly for years and the foundations of their work were laid.

Although the annexation movement began much earlier, it had slumbered for some years until Senator Ramsey abruptly reawakened it in December, 1867, by introducing a bill which would restore the Reciprocity Treaty of 1854. This was no gift. In return, Canada must abandon to the United States all territory west of ninety degrees of longitude. The American government would pay the Hudson's Bay Company six million dollars for its rights, assume the debt of British Columbia to two million dollars, and subsidize the building of the Northern Pacific Railroad to Puget Sound.[26] The fact that Canada did not own the land was beside the point. She had an option on the territory, and Ramsey proposed to buy it up.

This bill did not pass, but it spurred negotiations between Canada and the company. Their success brought no joy to Minnesota. The legislature of that state adopted a resolution of protest and forwarded it to Congress. This document denounced the fact that the Northwest had been transferred to Canada without a plebiscite of the inhabitants, "an unwarranted

[25] For a comprehensive description of his career, see Theodore C. Blegen, "James Wickes Taylor: A Biographical Sketch," *Minnesota History Bulletin*, I (November, 1915), 153-219.

[26] *Senate Miscellaneous Documents*, 40 Cong., 2 sess., no. 4. Taylor had drafted this bill and the one introduced by Banks.

interference with the principle of self-government . . . which cannot be regarded with indifference by the people of the United States." The resolution added that "the cession of Northwest British America to the United States accompanied by the construction of a Northern Pacific Railroad should be regarded by Great Britain and Canada as satisfactory provisions of a treaty which shall remove all grounds of controversy between the respective countries."[27] In brief, Minnesota proposed to trade the *Alabama* claims for western British America. Congress had this address printed but otherwise ignored it.

This indifference of the federal legislature banked the fires of annexation in the West for a time. No further protests were heard, and it seemed that the Dominion would quietly take possession of Manitoba on December 1, 1869. Manfully trying to conceal its frustration, the St. Paul *Daily Pioneer* observed that "we do not know as we want Canada very bad . . . we had better become reconstructed, secure our finances and see if we are able to take good care of what we have before assuming the charge of much more."[28]

A few rays of hope filtered into the gloomy arbor of sour grapes. One advocate of political union, noting that the government which was being established for Manitoba was a "complete proconsulship," predicted that it would be "obnoxious" to the people of the Red River.[29] As this forecast was substantiated and the soon-to-be Manitobans grew restless, the American annexationists roused up. They were neither startled nor unprepared when revolt erupted in the little settlement. In fact, it is not unlikely that American annexationists gave Riel and destiny a push forward by helping to incite the métis to rebel.[30]

Whether or not they prompted the uprising, the annexationists

[27] Minnesota, *General Laws*, 10 sess. (March, 1868).
[28] St. Paul *Daily Pioneer*, July 31, 1869.
[29] Taylor to Ramsey, June 14, 1869, Taylor Papers.
[30] Bryce, *Remarkable History*, 463.

knew an opportunity when they saw one and immeidately swung into action. Early events in the West took a favorable turn for them. Having repulsed McDougall, Riel seized Fort Garry, center of the company's power, and thereby destroyed the only government in the colony.[31] A political vacuum was thus created, and the annexationists, hoping that the United States could rush in to fill it, sought to exploit the uncertainty to gain control of the revolt. Three of them exerted their influence on Riel. The métis leader was no pliant tool, but he was willing to listen, probably hoping to play off American against Canadian influence. Colonel Stutsman was particularly active at this time, constantly commuting between Pembina and Fort Garry. Between trips he acted as Riel's unofficial "consul" at the border, issuing or denying the passes necessary to cross the line. He also joined the other inhabitants of Pembina in the agreeable sport of baiting McDougall and compounding the misery of that frustrated official, who had fled to the Dakota post after being repulsed by the métis.

Malmros, who had no pent-up sense of responsibility as the representative of a friendly power, was also active. He had anticipated the uprising—evidently having some part in its organization—and informed the Department of State that trouble threatened and that he would be glad to organize a force and seize the region for the United States when the time was ripe.[32] The meticulous and proper Fish likely approached apoplexy when he read this dispatch. If so, he recovered in time to veto Malmros' proposal sharply and to lecture him sternly on the proper behavior of American representatives in friendly nations. The consul, obviously regarding his chief as a spoilsport, took these instructions lightly. Within a short time he was reporting to a fellow worker in the annexation vineyard

[31] St. Paul *Daily Pioneer*, January 1, 1870; Alexander Begg, *The Creation of Manitoba* (Toronto, 1871), 47-50.

[32] Oscar Malmros to J. C. B. Davis, September 11, 1869, Consular Despatches, Winnipeg, I.

that he had "materially assisted in producing the present situation [of revolt] & prevented many mistakes on the part of the popular leaders."[33]

O'Donoghue, who probably carried more weight with the rebels than either Malmros or Stutsman, also worked diligently during this period to convert the uprising into an annexation movement. There is evidence that he and his associates exerted a strong influence on Riel and were largely responsible for such moves as the seizure of Fort Garry.

The annexationists thus had a dangerous grasp on the helm of the rebellion in its early months, and for a time it appeared that they might steer the colony into the United States. McDougall unwittingly helped them on their course. Thwarted and embittered, he listened to foolish advice and issued a proclamation announcing his appointment as lieutenant governor and the transfer of the region to Canada. This pronouncement played into the hands of the American party. It set the Red River colony legally adrift by canceling the company's power but providing no effective substitute for it, since McDougall could not enter the territory. To push confusion into chaos, the government in Ottawa refused to accept the transfer of the colony from the company while the rebellion persisted. By default, Riel's group was the *de facto* government, and it seemed to be seriously infiltrated by annexationists.

McDougall was not through playing the fool. He commissioned one of his lieutenants to cross the border, rally all loyal men, and attack the rebels. His call to arms was a fiasco, but it nearly provoked a disastrous bloodletting. This irresponsible action, compounded by the fear that McDougall was stirring up the Indians, drove many who mistrusted Riel into support of the métis. Thanks to its misguided representative, Canada stood repudiated in the Red River settlement for the time.

This was the loud knock of opportunity, and the annexationists

[33] Malmros to Ramsey, January 6, 1870, Ramsey Papers.

hastened to answer it. Stutsman moved from Pembina to Fort Garry and adhered to Riel, alert to press any advantage which might emerge from the uncertainty.[34] O'Donoghue, now the treasurer of the provisional government which Riel had established after McDougall's proclamation, joined Malmros and Stutsman in besieging the young métis leader with advice. But it was not enough to have Riel's ear; the annexationists broadened their base of action by striving for popular support. They bought a moribund local newspaper, the *Red River Pioneer*, for £550, an expenditure painless to all except the company, from whose strongbox the money apparently was expropriated. They rechristened the paper the *New Nation* and placed it in the hands of Major Henry Robinson, one of the coterie of American annexationists who had been buzzing about Riel.

The leading article of the first edition starkly revealed the political orientation of the paper. Entitled "Annexation our 'Manifest Destiny,'" it urged the colony to follow its purse strings into the United States rather than be tied by its heart strings to the British Empire. The article belabored the obvious fact that the Republic was market and means of communication for the Red River region and must remain so for years to come. A commercial tie with Canada was impossible across the tumbled sea of rock which intervened between Winnipeg and the nearest inhabited portions of Ontario. Union with the Republic was the order of the day, for movements to that end stretched from sea to sea, from Nova Scotia to British Columbia. It was time for Manitoba to join the rest.[35]

The annexationists thus boldly struck for the prize. But the Canadian government, now shaken out of its complacency, did not intend to let the game go by default. The Governor General issued a proclamation stating that the way was open for the

[34] Begg, *Creation of Manitoba*, 94; Taylor to Fish, January 27, 1870, Consular Despatches, Winnipeg, I.

[35] Fort Garry *New Nation*, January 14, 1870.

redress of the grievances of the Red River people. Three commissioners were appointed by Sir John A. Macdonald and sent west to probe the disaffections and allay the fears of the Manitobans. This mission offered a serious threat to the annexationists. If Canada warmly accepted Manitoban demands, chances for political union would melt away. Riel's pro-American advisers challenged the threat by persuading their leader to receive the commissioners coldly and to block them from establishing contact with the people of the settlement by keeping them as house prisoners.[36]

The future hung in the balance in January, 1870. The annexationists apparently occupied a strong position. Their leaders were close to Riel and were hawking their wares to the people through the *New Nation*. Riel had not declared for them, but his acceptance of their advice and his easy tolerance of their open agitation seemed to speak for him. On the other hand, the people of the settlement appeared eager to learn the intentions of the government in Ottawa and to cease their opposition to the Dominion if their grievances were redressed. If this were true, annexation would become a last desperate resort. The ultimate destiny of the Red River colony would be decided by the wisdom and generosity of the Canadian government, not by the machinations of agitators.

While the annexationists at Fort Garry were making their strike for success, their colleagues in the United States were also busy. In Minnesota, press, politicians, and merchants united to build up public interest in the acquisition of Manitoba. Ignatius Donnelly declared, "If the revolutionists of the Red River are encouraged and sustained by the avowed sympathy of the American people we may . . . see the Stars and Stripes wave from Fort Garry, from the waters of Puget Sound, and along the shores of Vancouver."[37] The St. Paul Chamber of Commerce

[36] Begg, *North-West,* I, 438-39.
[37] St. Paul *Daily Pioneer,* November 24, 1869.

called a public meeting and unleashed the same orator upon it. Donnelly spent an enjoyable evening in a hortatory twisting of the lion's tail, urging that the United States seize the Northwest to revenge Britain's recent sympathies for the Confederate States. Public and press reactions demonstrated the popularity of this sentiment. The leading papers of St. Paul, the *Daily Press* and the *Daily Pioneer,* clamored for Manitoba. The latter, however, soon lost interest and sourly commented that annexation was impossible because the people of the Red River district opposed it.[38] Whether this change of heart represented an objective analysis of the situation or congenital disagreement with the rival *Press* would be difficult to say. At any rate, the desertion scarcely diminished the clamor of the Minnesota expansionists.

The eastern annexationists also strove mightily. Ramsey, undeterred by the indifference to his earlier bill, sought again to stir the sluggish appetite of Congress for territory. He introduced a resolution calling on the President to submit all available information regarding the revolt. The motion passed, but the Senate was cool toward it and several members remarked that the troubles were "none of our business." Ramsey hotly retorted that the future of Manitoba was some of Minnesota's business, at least. The people of the British West, in the best democratic tradition, should be allowed to decide their own future. If they desired to join the Republic, the American government could compensate Canada by giving her commercial union.[39] President Grant presently submitted the information sought by Ramsey's resolution, but Congress ignored it.

The executive department was somewhat warmer toward the expansionist projects. As noted above, Fish wanted to acquire all of Canada, or any available part thereof, but only with the consent of the inhabitants. He had already rapped Malmros' knuckles for proposing unscrupulous actions. The consul, who

[38] St. Paul *Daily Pioneer,* January 1, 5, 29, 1870.
[39] *Congressional Globe,* 41 Cong., 2 sess., 3, 29-30, 932-34.

carefully concealed his subsequent actions from his superior, now sought to work on Fish through Ramsey. He informed the senator that the métis desired union with the United States and would fight for it if they got financial support. Success had a specific price: "$100,000 would make the annexation movement a success."[40] Ramsey was easily persuaded and suggested to Fish that the latter should tap the secret service fund for the purpose. The secretary brusquely refused to participate in subterranean practices.[41] His expansionist proclivities rose to the surface again, however, when Malmros directly informed him that many Hudson's Bay Company employees favored annexation of the settlement to the United States and had urged it upon their superiors in London. The consul maintained that the company's last governor, William Mactavish, felt that such a cession would be more to the advantage of his employers than union with Canada.[42] This "evidence" of annexation feeling in the colony met the test which Fish's squeamish conscience had assigned. The secretary at once swung into action and asked the American minister in London to probe the attitude of the company and of the British government toward cession of the territory to the United States. The quick reply dispelled Fish's illusions on these points, and the latter wistfully abandoned the idea of obtaining the Red River colony.[43]

Thus by January, 1870, success had evaded the annexationists and promised to become increasingly elusive. The American government and public, except in Minnesota, were either indifferent or had lost hope, and the foundations of the movement in the colony itself were crumbling. Several events hastened its disintegration. One of the Canadian commissioners, Donald A.

[40] Malmros to Ramsey, January 14, 1870, Ramsey Papers.

[41] Nevins, *Hamilton Fish*, 387.

[42] Malmros to Davis, December 24, 1869, Consular Despatches, Winnipeg, I.

[43] Fish to J. L. Motley, January 14, 1870, Motley to Fish, February 2, 1870, Diplomatic Instructions, Great Britain, XXII.

Smith, finally secured Riel's reluctant permission to hold a public meeting and deliver the message of the government in Ottawa. He assured the people that Canada would consider carefully their grievances and rights. All classes, except the annexationists, welcomed this intelligence. A convention was selected and drew up a list of rights to be sent to Ottawa for the consideration of the federal government. This list, as amended by Riel, asked such concessions as the admission of Manitoba as a province rather than a territory, confirmation of landholdings, protection of French rights, and a pardon for all implicated in the uprising. The selection of a committee to bear this list to Ottawa gave the American party a faint new hope; the delegates included Alfred H. Scott, who was one of them. If Scott were not an annexationist, he was shortly to seek out strange company.

In all other respects, these activities were a body blow to the American expansionists. A belligerent Canada might have driven the people of the Red River into the arms of the United States; the shrewd Macdonald was tempering their hot wrath into warm affection by his conciliatory actions, and his earlier indifference and bungling were now nearly forgotten. Moreover, Riel enjoyed the support of most elements of the population. His bold stand for Manitoban rights was winning a better deal for the entire population, white as well as métis.

As the attitude of the whites toward Riel changed, so did his attitude toward the annexationists. What the young leader actually thought of them is something of a mystery, and the conflicting reports of his contemporaries are no help in solving it. His previous acceptance of their counsel and toleration of their blatant agitation could be interpreted in several ways. Perhaps he was willing to see the colony join the United States rather than Canada if a majority of its inhabitants so desired; the reception of the commissioners from Ottawa dispelled doubt on that score. Or he may have winked at their activities and teased their hopes because he needed the support of some of the white population to give an appearance of interracial unity to his movement. A third, and plausible, explanation offered by several recent writers is that Riel was playing the United States off against Canada to force concessions from the latter while keeping the Republic as his "ace in the hole" if the Dominion proved obdurate.[44] Whatever the reason for his previous attitude toward the annexationists, he now began to tighten the tether on them. The first to be brought up short was Major Robinson, editor of the *New Nation,* who had ranged far in the columns of his paper. Riel suddenly suppressed one edition and ruthlessly censored later ones in advance, ripping out references to annexation. As a crowning token of his displeasure, he removed Robinson as editor and cast him into jail.[45]

O'Donoghue likewise fell from grace. This uninhibited spirit took it into his head to cut down the British flag which Riel had hoisted over Fort Garry and to substitute a rebel flag, featuring a concoction of shamrocks and fleurs-de-lis. Riel restored the Union Jack and pointedly warned O'Donoghue that his brains would be blown out if he again molested it. This episode abruptly ended O'Donoghue's usefulness to the cause of annexation.[46]

The attrition of American leadership continued at the expense of Malmros. The consul had enlivened his dispatches to Wash-

[44] Morton holds that Riel was fundamentally loyal but was keeping the way open to appeal for American aid if necessary. Gluek substantially agrees. Morton, *History of the Canadian West,* 896-97; Gluek, "Riel Rebellion," 199, 203.

[45] St. Paul *Daily Press,* April 22, 1870. Red River annexationists complained to an American visitor that Riel had used them to gain their support, and then discarded them when his purposes were served. The same visitor reported that both Riel and O'Donoghue told him that they favored annexation but were dutybound to take Manitoba into the Dominion if Macdonald accepted their terms. Nathaniel P. Langford to Taylor, June 12, 1870, Taylor Papers.

[46] Henry Robinson to Davis, May 10, 1870, Consular Despatches, Winnipeg, I.

ington with some delightfully indiscreet characterizations of prominent Manitobans. Perhaps feeling that it would be shameful to bury this deathless prose in the dust of a remote archive, the Department of State shared the gems with the world by publishing them. When Malmros learned this, he wrote a letter of despair to Ramsey, groaning that when the publications reached the Red River, his position would become "untenable, impracticable and, in fact, intolerable." Having made this point fairly clear, he declared his intention of leaving the colony that night, though he was ill, an Arctic wind was howling, and snow blocked the roads.[47] This he did, not even pausing to send a letter of resignation to the Department of State.

Battered by adversity, deprived of leadership, and intimidated by the lowering hostility of Riel, the annexationists in the colony abruptly ceased their agitation.[48] But their colleagues in the United States continued to work in high gear and spirits, and planned a bold stroke for success in the spring of 1870. Early in April, William Marshall, former governor of Minnesota and one of Cooke's associates, appeared in the Red River colony and closeted himself with Riel for a long interview. Although no record of this meeting appears to have survived, other evidence indicates that Marshall promised financial and military aid to Riel if he would turn his revolt into an annexation movement.[49] Meanwhile, the three delegates bearing Manitoba's "List of Rights" to Canada arrived in St. Paul. Scott soon found his way to Wheelock, and another mysterious meeting took place. Again there is no available record, but the editor, rejoicing, wrote to

[47] Malmros to Ramsey, March 15, 1870, Ramsey Papers.

[48] Langford to Taylor, July 10, 1870, Taylor Papers.

[49] Cooke had hoped to reach some tacit agreement with Riel. Larson, *Jay Cooke*, 338. Marshall's trip smacks of a secret mission, for it was not mentioned at the time in the newspapers which were printing every scrap of news and rumor they could get regarding the Red River. Over a month later, his journey received a casual mention. St. Paul *Daily Press*, May 14, 1870.

Ramsey that the list contained demands which "are preposterous and extravagant to the last degree and were obviously devised, as I am assured they were [by Scott?] for the express purpose of being rejected." Should this occur, shock and disappointment might impel Manitoba to seek the United States. Wheelock added, "Without letting Scott into the secret of the movement on foot, I assured him . . . with emphasis that if the Red River people desired to keep Canada out . . . they could depend on the co-operation of powerful interests in the United States which stood ready to lend whatever material aid was necessary." He concluded by saying that he had arranged for an interview between Scott and Cooke and by urging that Riel be supplied with "one or two batteries [of artillery] and men to work them."[50]

This letter is at once promising and provocative. It reveals that the American annexationists had a plan of action, but it leaves some questions unanswered. Precisely what was "the movement on foot"? Who were "the powerful interests in the United States," how did they intend to aid the rebels, and what would be the reaction of the American government to such adventures? Scraps of evidence indicate that the annexationists mooted an armed expedition to aid Riel if he diverted his movement into the desired channels. Certainly the nation which had produced William Walker could spawn another "grey-eyed man of destiny" to lead filibusters to the north. Whatever the coup that was planned, it was never delivered. Perhaps Riel rejected the suggestion of an armed expedition, if, indeed, Marshall proposed it to him. Or the results of the Manitoban mission to Ottawa, to be recounted below, may have convinced the Americans that the game was hopelessly lost. In any event, they made no further moves.

The game was also approaching a losing conclusion in Washington, despite the efforts of Ramsey and Chandler. The latter introduced a resolution into the Senate in April, 1870, requesting

[50] Wheelock to Ramsey, April 7, 1870, Ramsey Papers.

the President to appoint two commissioners to negotiate with the people of Winnipeg for annexation. The Senate debated the motion on April 22, and Chandler enlivened the occasion by hurling some verbal thunderbolts. He charged that the British and American systems of government and landholding were incompatible and could not long continue to exist side by side. Canada was a nuisance which the United States must abate. He concluded, in typical spread-eagle oratory, that the American army and militia, the finest in the world, would overwhelm a pathetically undermanned Canadian defense in a march which would carry the American flag to the desolate shores of the Arctic Ocean. "This continent is ours and we may as well notify the world . . . that we will fight for our own if we must."[51]

This effort evoked no response from Chandler's colleagues other than an "amused smile of recognition" of the fact that the senator was riding a favorite hobbyhorse. Even the British minister at Washington, who trembled at every will-o'-the-wisp threat to British possessions, realized that Chandler stood virtually alone in his desire to acquire any part of British America by force.[52]

This indifference in Congress reflected the obvious fact that the annexation movement, so far as the Red River was concerned, was dead. It received its coup de grace when the Canadian government incorporated most of the Red River's "List of Rights" in the Manitoba Act which was pushed through Parliament. This bill admitted Manitoba as a province, confirmed existing land titles and occupations, reserved 1,400,000 acres of land for the halfbreeds and their children, and established a separate school system.[53] To pacify Ontario, furious

[51] *Congressional Globe*, 41 Cong., 2 sess., 2887-89.

[52] Edward Thornton to the Earl of Clarendon, 167, April 5, 1870, F. O. 5: 1192; Thornton to Sir John Young, April 23, 1870, G 147, 1417 (Public Archives, Ottawa).

[53] Creighton, *Macdonald*, 65-69; Morton, *Manitoba*, 141-42.

at this coddling of French halfbreed rebels, an armed expedition was to be sent to confirm Canadian possession.[54] As this act conceded more than the people of the Red River had expected, the proposed military expedition was now the only straw at which the annexationists could clutch. From the safe vantage of his editorial chair, Wheelock bravely urged the Red River people to resist this "armed invasion," slyly hinting that there were numerous places where it might be ambushed and reporting that Fenians were gathering near the border to go to the aid of Riel.[55] The Manitobans ignored these suggestions, and the paper bullets from St. Paul were the only ones fired at the expedition. It reached the Red River country late in August and found that Riel had discreetly left Fort Garry to go into exile. The métis army dispersed and Manitoba entered the Dominion as its fifth province.

But the dying storm still sent forth mutterings of thunder. A number of the métis felt that they had been the victims of unscrupulous practice. The Dominion's emissaries had led them to believe that a pardon would be granted to all rebels. Performance did not match promise; the amnesty was not all-inclusive, and Riel and others consider it politic to fly to the United States. This angered many of his followers, who were heard to exclaim, "Oh, for the States! the States!"[56] These malcontents sought aid in Washington, dispatching a memorial to President Grant. This document recited the history of the rebellion, promises presumably made and broken by Macdonald, and outrages committed by the military expedition from Canada.

[54] English-speaking Canadians were especially outraged because Riel had executed an Ontario Orangeman, Thomas Scott. This unfortunate episode revived French-English bitterness in Canada and was partly responsible for the sending of the expedition and for Riel's flight to the United States. Ontario did not forget Scott.

[55] St. Paul *Daily Press*, May 18, 1870.

[56] Taylor to J. C. B. Davis, November 22, 1870, Consular Despatches, Winnipeg, I. Taylor had succeeded Malmros as consul.

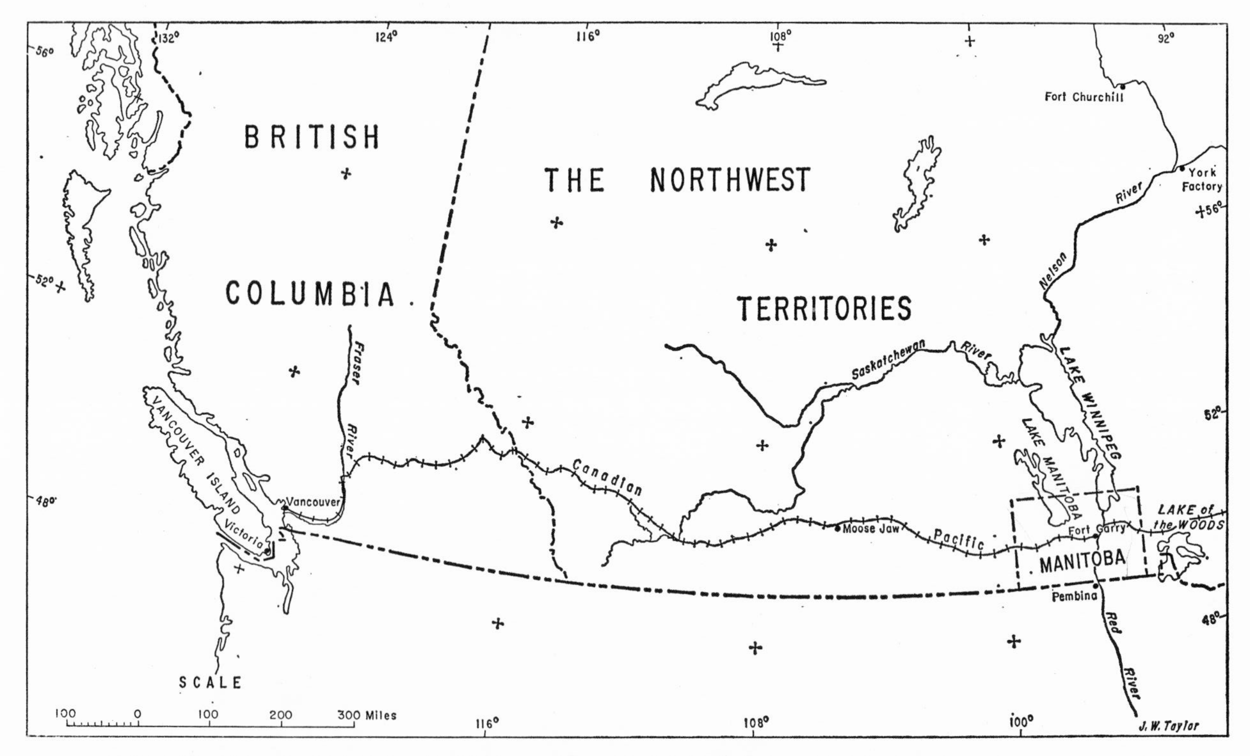

WESTERN CANADA AFTER THE ADMISSION OF BRITISH COLUMBIA

In conclusion, the petitioners requested Grant "to intercede in our behalf . . . to enable us to enjoy the blessings of life, liberty, property, and the pursuit of happiness, under a Government of our own choice or in Union with a people with whom we may think we can enjoy these blessings."[57] Though Grant ignored the memorial, annexationism was not quite dead. In 1871 the persistent O'Donoghue who had also fled into exile in the United States, organized a raid upon Manitoba. Ostensibly under Fenian auspices, this incursion had annexation as its goal; it was a miserable fiasco.[58]

For over a decade thereafter, the movement to add the British Northwest to the United States was to slumber. The reasons for its failure were several. Most obviously, it did not succeed because the people of the Red River settlement preferred Canada to the United States. The métis in general were hostile to annexation because it would abort the plans of the Roman Catholic hierarchy who hoped to make Manitoba into a new Quebec, peopled with the surplus population of that province.[59] Moreover, the American Constitution did not offer the special position and privileges which the church and other French institutions enjoyed under British rule. Hence the métis, the bulk of the population, were as impervious to the annexation infiltration as their cousins in Quebec, and for the same reasons. The white population, aside from the exceptions noted, also opposed union with the Republic. Some of them had recently come from Canada and were eager for political reunion with it. Most of the rest were from the British Isles and had brought

[57] Petition written "by authority of the people," dated at the Red River, October 3, 1870, and printed in full in New York *Times,* January 31, 1871. It was presented to Grant January 28.

[58] John P. Pritchett, "The Origins of the So-Called Fenian Raid on Manitoba in 1871," *Canadian Historical Review,* X (March, 1929), 23-42.

[59] Chester Martin, "Confederation and the West," Canadian Historical Association, *Annual Report, 1927,* p. 22; St. Paul *Daily Pioneer,* May 18, 1870.

with them both a love of their native land and an aversion to the United States.

Deep-seated and unremedied grievances against Canada and the Imperial government might have upset the loyalties of both the métis and the whites and driven them into the arms of the United States. The dissatisfaction, however, was susceptible of redress. When Macdonald awoke to the danger of the situation and promised the desired concessions, resistance to Canada melted and washed away the hopes of the expansionists. It was evident that there was relatively little demand in the British Northwest for annexation to the United States. This meant that American expansionists must either use force or abandon hope. Some of them might have fought if there had been a chance of success, but there was none. They were too few, their government offered no help, and their countrymen were indifferent.

Thus the movement failed for lack of support, but it was important. It indicated that expansionism had not died with the Civil War. Also, it is an example of the power and activities of the railroad builders, one of the most important and aggressive groups in the United States at that time. Their money and influence made this one of the few annexation movements directed at British North America which had organization and substantial financing. Finally, the movement had significant effects on Canada's history. It gave Riel the perfect foil for his duel with Macdonald to gain rights for Manitoba, and was partly responsible for the excellent terms which the people of the Red River received for entering the Dominion. With the United States in the contest, even though unofficially, Macdonald bid high for the prize. Ironically, the annexation movement again promoted what it was designed to prevent. In the east it had hastened the coming of confederation, and in the west it had helped to bring the union of the British Northwest with the Dominion.

The outcome of the Red River crisis was decisive for the future of the entire British West. In the hands of Canada,

Manitoba was an opened door to further westward expansion, even to the Pacific; in the hands of the United States, it would have been a wall, forever containing the new Dominion to the eastern half of the continent. The British settlements on the Pacific would become an insignificant region environed by American territory, culture, and economy, and a prey to absorption.

Though the path of the Dominion to the Pacific was clear in 1870, it appeared that as in the case of Manitoba, Canada must hasten if it would forestall the United States, for the British Pacific settlements were becoming Americanized.[60] Geography was partly responsible. With the Dominion thousands of miles away and Britain at the other end of the earth, San Francisco had become the entrepôt of British Columbia and its link with the outside world. The completion of the Union Pacific and Central Pacific railroads increased this commercial dependence. A sentimental attachment also enhanced the economic connections with the Republic. The gold rush of 1858-1859 into the Fraser Valley brought perhaps thirty thousand from California and other parts of the United States. These argonauts awoke the tiny colony drowsing by the sea, injected vitality and American institutions, and hoped to add it to their native land.[61] Thus the weak and detached settlement was besieged within and without by American influence.

It was also beset with political grievance and economic distress, those fertile seeds of annexationism. The mainland, or British Columbia, and Vancouver Island were administered by one governor, James Douglas, who ruled with an iron hand and

[60] The general accounts used for the political narrative in British Columbia include Frederic W. Howay, Walter N. Sage, and Henry F. Angus, *British Columbia and the United States* (Toronto, 1942); Walter N. Sage, "The Annexation Movement in British Columbia," Royal Society of Canada, *Transactions*, 3d ser., XXI (1927), 97-110; Hugh Keenleyside, "British Columbia, Annexation or Confederation," Canadian Historical Association, *Annual Report*, 1928, pp. 34-40.

[61] Howay, *British Columbia*, 184-88.

a nominated council. Petitions of protest from the inhabitants finally persuaded the reluctant Imperial authorities to concede a partly elected legislature. This compromise between the old autocracy and the desired self-government was an inadequate improvement. The government gave other grounds for dissatisfaction. Tailored to fit the earlier and prosperous days, it saddled a now shrunken population with supernumerary officials, annual deficits, and mounting debt. The inhabitants did not seem to recognize that this was partly the product of the situation. Mining enterprise necessitated a network of roads to carry in supplies and to transport out bulky loads of ore. Since the camps were tucked into the narrow and twisting gorges of mountain streams, the problems of roadbuilding were the despair alike of the engineer and of the colony's treasury. But without roads, there would be little mining or settlement.

Prosperity might have carried the burdens of an expensive road system and a bloated government, but prosperity had fled after 1862. The placer deposits on riverbars had never supported the crowds which came to work them. As they panned out, thousands who had rushed in drifted away, leaving a residue of less than ten thousand by the mid-1860's. As the production of gold, largest income of the colony, declined annually, the formerly dynamic economy of earlier days sank into lethargy. Bankruptcy practiced its attrition among businessmen, and the survivors lived hopelessly day by day, their pain sharpened by the awareness that neighboring American states rejoiced in prosperity and low taxes.[62]

Experience had taught the Imperial government that this was the classic pattern of conditions from which annexationism could emerge. They first sought to deal with the situation by uniting British Columbia and Vancouver Island in 1866 into

[62] Sage, "Annexation Movement," 97-100; Victoria *Daily British Colonist and Chronicle*, July 12, 1867; San Francisco *Daily Alta California*, February 1, 1868, enclosed in Miscellaneous Letters to the Department of State, 1868, February, I; Sarnia *Observor*, February 15, 1867.

a single colony and administration to reduce the costs of government to bearable proportions.[63] Furious opposition at once arose on the island, whose inhabitants were rankled by the fusion of the mainland's debt of more than $1,000,000 with their debt of $300,000 as a common burden for all to bear. The merchants of Victoria had another grievance. Their town was attracting a thriving trade as a "free port," an eastern Pacific counterpart of Hong Kong's Victoria. Union would cloud its future by stretching British Columbia's tariff, ranging from 10 to 40 percent, around the island as well.[64] This was a hard knock, and it represented a trend. The islanders would be a minority in the population and legislature of the colony, their interests and rights at the mercy of the decisions of the mainland majority. Their attitude toward the union paralleled that of Nova Scotia toward confederation; a minority with peculiar interests, they saw little to gain and much to lose by the change of status. And to cap their discontent, the union did not achieve even the modest goal assigned to it. The governor, "a well-meaning and easy-going mediocrity," lacked the fortitude to cull out surplus officials after the amalgamation, and taxes and deficits continued to mount.[65]

It would have been strange if such afflictions had not produced an annexation movement in such a location. The agitation began in 1866 and became a perennial force, with varying intensity, until 1871, when British Columbia joined Canada. Its center was Vancouver Island, and particularly the commercial city of Victoria, though it also had some support on the mainland.

The movement came into the open in a public meeting held at Victoria on September 29, 1866, called by Leonard McClure,

[63] Howay, *British Columbia,* 180-81.

[64] Victoria *British Colonist,* September 15, 24, 25, 26, 1866, summarizes the grievances of the island.

[65] Howay, *British Columbia,* 180-81; Sage, "Annexation Movement," 100.

editor of the *Evening Telegraph*, a paper which had reflected strong annexationist proclivities. Confusion and turbulence characterized the gathering. A bewildering series of conflicting resolutions were introduced and defeated, with the single exception of one which endorsed reciprocity with the United States. Tiring of this bootless turmoil, someone moved adjournment, and after giving three cheers for the Queen, the crowd began to stream out.

But this did not end the affair. Of the six hundred originally in attendance, some hundred and fifty remained and began a rump session which developed subversive overtones. A resolution was introduced denouncing union with the mainland and urging the British government to grant self-government and to negotiate reciprocity with the United States for the colony. If this proved impossible, arrangements should be made for annexation, for the colony could not long remain in its existing wretched condition. After acrimonious debate, this resolution passed by a small majority.[66]

Though tumult discredited this meeting, its proceedings indicated that change must soon come, for discontent was seeking dangerous channels of expression. The annexationists by their bold agitation and plausible arguments were shaking the loyalty of some of the islanders. To counter them with a loyal alternative, another party arose advocating the union of British Columbia with the impending confederation of British colonies to the east.[67]

This group operated under serious handicaps. The Dominion was not yet a reality and might be stillborn unless eastern opposition to it were overcome. Even if it came into existence, there was no practical means of transportation and communication over the thousands of miles which intervened between it and

[66] Victoria *British Colonist,* October 1, 1866.

[67] Victoria *British Colonist,* December 17, 1866, March 25, 1867; Sage, "Annexation Movement," 100.

British Columbia. Annexationists insisted that a union with the Dominion would be artificial, tenuous, and short-lived. On the other hand, settled areas of the United States were nearby and easily reached by established trade lines.

Events as well as conditions favored the United States rather than Canada. In 1866 the threat of Fenian invasion alarmed the people of British Columbia, who felt defenseless against serious attack.[68] This fright passed only to be replaced by another disturbance. Canadians and British Columbians could imagine only one purpose for the purchase of Alaska by the United States in 1867. The new American possession had no apparent economic value and must have been acquired to put unbearable pressure on the British Pacific coast. British Columbia, sandwiched between blocks of American territory, would soon be gobbled up. Even the most loyal were in despair at this situation and in wrath at British "imbecility, ignorance or neglect" which had permitted Seward to strike this shrewd blow.[69] Another alarm soon waited upon the longsuffering colonists—the rumor that the Imperial government intended to cede British Columbia to the United States in satisfaction for the *Alabama* claims. This tale sounded plausible. The home government had allowed Seward to put British Columbia into an impossible position, and it was logical that they would get what they could for the colony while they still had it.[70]

This was indeed the winter of British Columbia's discontent. Beset by depression, burdened by costly and inept government, ringed about by acquisitive neighbors, apparently neglected, even

[68] Sage, "Annexation Movement," 102.

[69] Statements illustrating this point of view may be found in Quebec *Morning Chronicle*, April 3, 1867; Sarnia *Observor*, April 26, 1867; Victoria *British Colonist*, April 17, May 16, 1867. Some American congressmen voted for the purchase in hopes of increasing the possibility of acquiring the British Pacific coast. Harrington, *Banks*, 182-83.

[70] Sage, "Annexation Movement," 102; Victoria *British Colonist*, April 25, 1867.

scorned, by the motherland, it is not strange that devoted and loyal citizens were shaken with doubts. The annexationists saw fruitful possibilities in the gloomy foreboding of their fellow citizens. Their argument that union with the United States was the inevitable and best future for the colony, and that it was useless to struggle against it, gained headway among the disheartened. Victoria's stanchest advocate of joining Canada admitted that "since no change could be for the worse, they [the local inhabitants] would welcome annexation to the United States to continuing in a state of poverty and wretchedness. In writing this, we know we speak the mind of nine out of every ten men in the colony. . . . The sentiment is heard at every street corner—at social gatherings—in business circles—at the theatre—in the saloons—in all places." And it was the indifference of Imperial authorities toward the colony which had produced this situation.[71]

This outburst came at the nadir of despair in the early spring of 1867. Time soon eroded the anger of the loyal, and sober second thought revealed flaws in the plausible arguments of the annexationists. The persistence with which the British pushed for confederation in the east indicated that the Imperial government did care what happened to its colonies and would not let them slip into the United States. Nor was it certain that annexation would cure the local economic disease. If British Columbia joined the Dominion, a railroad would ultimately be constructed across the continent, and its only logical western terminus, Victoria, would become a Pacific metropolis. The United States also intended to build a northern transcontinental line, but it would seek the sea through the gentler passes leading to Seattle. Thus, argued the confederationists, if Victoria wished to remain a city, it must remain a British city.[72]

So the loyalists in the colony climbed from the pit of their

[71] Victoria *British Colonist*, April 29, 1867.
[72] Victoria *British Colonist*, May 18, 23, 1867.

despair and again began vigorously to agitate for a union with Canada. This revival did not damp the annexationists, who proceeded to draw up and circulate a petition to the Queen, requesting that British Columbia be allowed to secede from the Empire.[73] No reply was received.

When 1867 drew to a close, the future of the colony still dangled in uncertainty. While the crisis of the Alaska purchase and the rumors of the *Alabama* settlement had been surmounted without mortally wounding the Imperial connection, annexationism was still boldly and ingeniously pressed by an influential segment of the population.

The struggle for control of the future continued in 1868 without letup. Though the confederationists now had the support of most of the population, their path was still cluttered with obstacles. On Vancouver Island, petitions against the proposed union with Canada were being circulated by "men who still cling to the wild delusive hope that England will eventually relinquish her hold on this colony and pass it over to the tender care of Uncle Sam."[74] Weightier opposition came from higher sources. Governor Frederick Seymour and his official coterie did all in their power to block union with the Dominion, probably from selfish motives.[75] To discredit the plan, they threw their influence behind anticonfederationist candidates in the legislative election of 1868. The pro-Canadian party fought back as best it could, holding numerous public meetings and forming a Confederation League.[76] But these efforts were not enough. A majority opposed to union with Canada was returned, including

[73] Sage, "Annexation Movement," 103-104; Victoria *British Colonist,* May 18, August 1, October 8, November 23, 1867.

[74] Victoria *British Colonist,* February 5, 1868.

[75] Sage, "Annexation Movement," 104; Howay, *British Columbia,* 194. The British government at this time was not pressing for union with Canada.

[76] Victoria *British Colonist,* January 25, 29, 30, April 5, 24, May 8, July 18, August 7, 1868, contains accounts of public meetings in support of union with Canada. See also Howay, *British Columbia,* 212-13.

all four representatives from Vancouver Island.[77] The movement to join the Dominion would obviously be futile while Seymour remained in office. It was also clear that the governor had, unwittingly, helped the annexationists. The existing situation was intolerable and change was imperative. If the gate into Canada were barred, the way to the United States might still swing open. Thus the results of the election breathed new hope into the advocates of American union.

Some interested spectators in the United States had been watching with anticipation the varying fortunes of this struggle. They wished to acquire British Columbia both for itself and to frustrate Britain's North American strategy. Unable to prevent the birth of the infant Dominion, the United States might still stunt its growth by blocking its expansion to the Pacific. Seward admitted what British Columbians had suspected—that the purchase of Alaska was designed to hem them in and press them from the north as well and from the south, a consideration which eased the path of the treaty with Russia through the Senate.[78] The British minister at Washington warned his government that the purchase of Alaska had increased the American desire and opportunity to gain British Columbia.[79]

Despite this activity and seeming interest, few members of Congress indicated an acquisitive attitude toward the British Pacific regions. In November, 1867, Representative George F. Miller of Pennsylvania introduced a resolution for the annexation of British Columbia on terms mutually satisfactory to Great Britain and the United States.[80] Congress was not interested, the resolution did not come to a vote, and no public response awoke except in the West. In the following month,

[77] Victoria *British Colonist,* November 4, 13, 1868.

[78] John W. Foster, *A Century of American Diplomacy* (Boston, 1900), 409.

[79] Sir Fredrick Bruce to Lord Stanley, April 2, 1867, F. O. 5: 1106.

[80] *Congressional Globe,* 40 Cong., 1 sess., 813.

Ramsey presented his bill, previously mentioned, for the admission of British Columbia and Manitoba; this also failed to come to a vote. After a lapse of several years, Senator Henry Corbett renewed the attempts to conjure up a demand for British Columbia. He read his colleagues an annexation petition from that colony and moved that the secretary of state arrange for its transfer to the United States. Only a handful of western senators supported the motion, which never emerged from that graveyard of annexation proposals, the Committee on Foreign Relations.[81]

The only demand for the acquisition of British Columbia came from the Pacific states, and particularly San Francisco.[82] The motive here was economic. Californians wanted to acquire the coalfields of the colony to fill a lacking requisite for industrialization. They also hoped to prevent the construction of a transcontinental railroad to the colony which would enable Victoria, appreciably closer to the Orient than San Francisco, to outstrip the latter in the race for Asiatic trade.[83] This concern took form in a resolution, introduced into the California legislature early in 1868, which pointed out that it was important to the entire United States that the British intended to merge British Columbia into Canada, thus creating "a Kingly Empire along our entire northern border and between us and our new possession of Alaska." This would "result in establishing monarchical institutions upon one half of the continent of North

[81] The popular support of these annexation proposals came entirely from the West. One publisher urged Seward to buy British Columbia and promised the support of his paper, the St. Louis *Times*, for the project. D. A. Mahony to Seward, April 10, 1867, Miscellaneous Letters to the Department of State, 1867, April, I.

[82] San Francisco *Daily Alta California*, February 1, 2, 3, 1868, and San Francisco *Evening Bulletin*, February 10, 1869, enclosed in Miscellaneous Letters to the Department of State, 1869, February, I.

[83] Hamilton *Spectator*, undated, quoted in Victoria *British Colonist*, May 13, 1868.

America in violation of our traditional policy." For this reason, it was essential that British Columbia be annexed to the United States, and California's representatives in Washington were admonished to urge the federal government to employ "all fair and honorable means" to acquire the colony. The resolution was debated at length and engrossed.[84]

Annexationism also had its advocates in Oregon. The Portland *Herald*, indignant that the British had fortified "an American island," San Juan, and that no ships could reach Puget Sound without going under British guns, proposed a sanguine solution: "the Fenians of the Pacific and a few thousand willing Americans and Germans will take away all that country from the British. We will lower their flag in six months." Financing a filibuster presented no problems; "We will give our notes at ninety days for an outfit, and be back with the spoils of Victoria to pay them before they are due."[85] Fortunately, the *Herald's* followers were unable to blood their weapons on the no doubt terror-stricken citizens of Victoria. Whether the *Herald* could not find the proper number of "willing Americans and Germans" or get takers for its ninety-day notes is not clear. At any rate, the expedition did not leave the columns of the paper.

Not dismayed by the lack of interest in most of the United States, the annexationists of British Columbia continued their activities in 1869.[86] A number of meetings were held and a second petition for union with the United States was drafted and signed by 104 persons, mostly Germans, Jews, and Irish. This document stated that separation from the Crown was imminent and British Columbia needed a new connection to insure its well-being. Canada could not be that connection, for

[84] Victoria *British Colonist*, February 25, 28, 1868.

[85] Portland *Oregon Herald*, undated, quoted in Victoria *British Colonist*, September 9, 1869.

[86] Victoria *British Colonist*, May 10, 21, June 4, July 6, 1869.

it would not furnish the immigration, markets, or protection needed by the colony. Annexation to the United States, on the other hand, would yield an impressive array of assets: an outlet for its products, an influx of population, an injection of capital, regular postal service, self-government, and adequate protection.[87] The petition, addressed to President Grant, was entrusted to Vincent Collyer, an American traveler, who delivered it late in December, 1869. The President responded with a customarily sparkling remark that the document was "interesting," and turned it over to the Department of State, which tucked it away in the appropriate file.[88]

Though the petition failed to excite its recipient, it stirred a gratifying interest in the place of its origin. Again the future of the colony became the major topic of public discussion. The London *Times* chose this moment for an unfortunate intrusion of views delivered in the toplofty manner which had been the despair of loyalists in other colonies. The Thunderer pointed out that the distance and arduous obstacles which intervened between Canada and British Columbia was nature's veto upon a union between that colony and the Dominion. Moreover, the *Times* continued, British Columbia had numerous American-born inhabitants; trade, contiguity, and ease of communication bound it to the United States. These facts plodded toward an obvious verdict—if British Columbia showed any inclination toward union with the United States, Great Britain should place no obstacle in its way.[89]

[87] People of British Columbia to U. S. Grant, November 30, 1869, Miscellaneous Letters to the Department of State, 1869, November, II. Analysis of signers in Howay, *British Columbia*, 206-207.

[88] Montreal *Pays*, January 4, 1870. A copy was sent to the American minister in London, who discussed it with the British foreign secretary. The latter offered no objection to the idea of annexation unless force were used to carry it out. Howay, *British Columbia*, 200.

[89] London Times, undated, quoted in Victoria *British Colonist*, January 26, 1870.

Thus the loyalists of the colony had the rug upon which they had taken a firm stance yanked out from under them. Even the stanch *British Colonist* wavered before this test: "It would be idle to disguise the fact that the *Times* article has had the effect of giving new life and vitality, if, indeed, it has not given new recruits to the Annexation Party of Victoria. Annexation may now be said to be rampant in this community. It no longer lurks in secret places . . . but with firm step and almost defiant air it stalks our streets at noonday." It was found in the countinghouses and hotels and on the street corners, and it might soon boldly mount to the public platform. The hour of decision approached. British Columbia would not remain a colony but must become a province or a state. If Britain abandoned her Empire, Canada could not build a transcontinental railroad and British Columbia must consider the possibilities of annexation "in a business spirit."[90]

Encouraged by these sentiments, various advocates of union with the United States wrote in to air their views. A typical letter reveals the brotherhood of the western and eastern annexationists: "not that Annexation is desired from any special love or admiration of the United States [but because] it is the only prompt and permanent remedy for most of the evils from which the colony is suffering." Loyalty was not the issue, for "in our present condition, the great question is that of dollars and cents." Annexation would bring a migration of American settlers and American capital which was currently inhibited by legal restrictions on the acquisition of land by foreigners.[91]

The open advocates of annexation included a number of prominent and influential men such as J. D. Pemberton, formerly a member of the colony's executive as colonial surveyor, and perhaps Dr. John S. Helmcken, a leader in the legislative

[90] Victoria *British Colonist,* January 28, 1870.
[91] Letter from Robert Jenkinson in Victoria *British Colonist,* February 10, 1870.

assembly.[92] To outward appearances, the ties of the little colony with the British Empire were badly frayed.

Actually, the movement was more froth than substance. It was largely confined to Vancouver Island and was undoubtedly a minority even there.[93] The mainland population was either hostile or indifferent to the movement. At the same time, other and effective forces were quietly working for union with Canada. Throughout 1869, numerous public meetings were held to promote this amalgamation. In June, even death lent a helping hand by removing Governor Seymour. Macdonald, anxious to consummate Canada's expansion to the Pacific, quietly used his influence to secure the transfer of an advocate of confederation, Anthony Musgrave, from the governorship of Newfoundland to the vacant post in British Columbia.

To the east, the sun of confederation for British Columbia was also rising. One cogent annexationist argument was removed when Canada acquired the territories of the Hudson's Bay Company. Despite the Riel rebellion, union with Canada became practical. These changes had their effect. By 1870, support for confederation had become overwhelming and the annexation movement was rapidly dwindling.[94] Unvexed by executive interference, the assembly dispatched delegates to Ottawa to negotiate with the Canadian government. Though one of this group, the dubious Dr. Helmcken, dragged his feet, agreement was soon reached on the terms of admission for the colony.[95] Canada promised to assume the burden of British

[92] Sage, "Annexation Movement," 106-107; Victoria *British Colonist,* January 26, 29, February 1, March 9, 1870. The evidence is not conclusive, but Helmcken denied that he was an annexationist. Howay, *British Columbia,* 208.

[93] Victoria *British Colonist,* January 29, 1870; Sage, "Annexation Movement," 106-107.

[94] Victoria *British Colonist,* November 4, 1869.

[95] Trotter, *Federation,* 293-95; Victoria *British Colonist,* March 10, 1870.

Columbia's debt and, within ten years, to complete a railroad to the Pacific to break the economic grip of the United States on the British Pacific region. The government of the colony could not refuse such terms. The political union movement, now defunct, finally served a useful purpose. When the Liberals in the Dominion Parliament protested the extravagant commitments made to British Columbia, the Conservatives used the threat of the annexation movement to propel through the Commons the measure to admit British Columbia as the sixth province of the Dominion in 1871.[96]

The failure and collapse of the annexation movement in British Columbia ensued from causes already discernible. Almost its entire strength was localized in Vancouver Island and was never a controlling element even there; the mainland evinced little interest in the movement.[97] The willingness of the Dominion government to remove the serious grievances of the colony by assuming its debt and sharing the expenses of its government was fatal to the cause of annexationism. The promised transcontinental railroad opened a new future. It would break the American grip on the trade of British Columbia and bring settlers and capital to it because the new province would become the middle link of a faster new trade route between Europe and the Orient.[98] British Columbia would be the point of transshipment, and the stream of new trade would stir up the commercial stagnation of the colony.

Sentiment also helped to save British Columbia from the United States. This was the most British of the North American colonies, with the highest percentage of people born in the mother country. Neither time nor adversity dulled the love of most of these people for their native "fast-anchored isle." On the other hand, many of the Americans attracted by the gold rush had drifted away during the days of economic blight.

[96] *Canadian Commons Debates, 1871*, pp. 671, 909.
[97] Howay, *British Columbia*, 208.
[98] Trotter, *Federation*, 240.

The annexation movement in British Columbia resembled that in Manitoba in some respects. Threat of Americanization hung over each of them, for both were economically linked to, and partially peopled from, the United States. Both had serious political grievances. Identity ended here and contrast began. Economic distress, the strongest impetus to annexationism in British Columbia, was lacking in Manitoba. The loyalties of the two were also diverse. British Columbians were attached to Great Britain; the loyalty of the métis of Manitoba was incidentally British, but primarily to nationalité, culture, and religion, for which Canada offered fast constitutional guarantees.

The failure to add the British West to the United States did not disappoint many Americans, for the sectional character of the annexation movement in the Republic became apparent at this time. Eastern expansionists—Banks, Sumner, Pomeroy, and Henry Wilson, for example—tried to pry the Dominion from the Empire, but uttered no word or act to help Ramsey, Chandler, and Corbett to gain the Northwest and the Pacific littoral. The possession of these distant marches was a matter of indifference to the East, which had little to gain from them. Even in the West, only Ramsey showed an interest in gaining both the Red River and British Columbia. The annexation movement in the United States, already weak, was all the weaker for being sectional.

American expansionists could console themselves that Canada might have overmatched her strength with her commitments. The Liberals had charged that Macdonald's drive to get the West brought onerous pledges whose redemption might smash the Dominion financially. Moreover, the gain had been in length, not in depth, attenuating an already slender pattern of population. A country over three thousand miles long but less than a hundred miles deep might be buckled and broken at almost any point. Thus the Dominion dare not relax its anxious vigil over its farflung territories and over the activities of its neighbor.

CHAPTER FIVE

Changing Conditions in the Dominion 1873-1885

The postconfederation annexation movement, surprisingly, was killed rather than strengthened by the Panic of 1873. The condition of the Republic explains this. The two previous movements had occurred when Canada was distressed and the United States prospered, a contrast which suggested that Canadians could improve their lot by becoming Americans. But from 1873 to 1878, Americans might well have preferred to become Canadians.

This disparity was a result of the Civil War and its aftermath. The conflict swelled both the demand for produce and the volume of the currency. Money and credit were easy, prices were rising, and profits were enormous. These factors had bred a frenzy of speculation. The boom did have a solid foundation in the growth of industry, the rapid peopling of public lands, and the westward thrust of the steel of transcontinental railroads. But as virtue exaggerated becomes vice, healthy economic progress was distended into an unhealthy boom. Railroads were overbuilt, production outstripped consumption, and there was rampant speculation. In the wild scramble for easy wealth, scruples were cast aside as stock was watered, markets manipulated, and a gullible public snapped up shares in almost everything except the moon.

In 1873 the United States paid for its orgy. A disastrous crash followed the collapse of Jay Cooke & Company, considered the Gibraltar of American finance. No section or class in the Republic escaped the punishment of the ensuing depression. Hard times also visited the Canadians, but their condition was obviously better than that of their neighbors. Since they had not flown so high, they did not fall so far, and they showed no desire to join a country whose economic structure seemed to be lying in shattered ruins.

This was not the whole explanation of the absence of annexationism in the 1870's. Bitterness toward the United States growing from the negotiations of the Treaty of Washington still lingered. It will be remembered that the Republic used the *Alabama* claims to force Canada to open its inshore fisheries, and then had flatly refused to discuss the claims arising from the Fenian raids, Canada's equivalent to the *Alabama*. This fresh experience made the mere suggestion of annexation repulsive to Canadians in the 1870's. Moreover, the complete collapse of the previous agitation in 1871 discouraged any early attempts to revive it.

These impediments to annexation slowly wore away. Canadian resentment against the United States cooled, and economic conditions in the Republic began to improve. The bitter medicine of 1873 purged American business. Sound enterprises survived, natural growth continued, and the United States began to pull out of the depression. At the same time, Canada was sinking deeper, and by the end of the decade it was apparent that conditions had reversed and the Republic enjoyed better economic health than its northern neighbor.

This contrast had the usual effect of suggesting annexation to some Canadians, particularly in the business and commercial classes. The American consul at Port Stanley and St. Thomas toured Ontario in 1880 and informed his superiors in Washington that one-third of those whom he met were "outspoken" in their desire for political union.[1] Allowing for exaggeration, there was a basis of truth in the statement. Other evidence

[1] P. Carroll to the Department of State, May 6, 1880, Consular Despatches, Port Stanley and St. Thomas, I.

indicates the existence of a considerable agitation in such centers as Toronto, London, and Hamilton.[2] Local politicians and businessmen were hatching another movement in Montreal, incubator of annexationism.[3] In New Brunswick also the movement gained substantial footing.[4] Everywhere the agitation in 1880 was primarily urban, drawing its support from the merchants and producers who hoped to rebuild the export trade which had dwindled after 1873.[5]

The movement in Canada evoked no warm response in the United States. The New York *Sun*, once belligerently expansionist, coldly commented that "we have really nothing to gain from it [annexation] in a social and intellectual point of view and next to nothing in a commercial way." Even if Canada begged for admission to the Union, the *Sun* doubted that Congress, or the country, would honor the petition.[6] The other American papers which deigned to notice the movement generally frowned on it, and individuals who tried to call an international political union convention at Niagara Falls in 1881 got no response.[7] The American government was similarly indif-

[2] Howells to Department of State, undated but filed under January, 1880, Consular Despatches, Toronto, VI, 26; Toronto *Evening Telegram*, January 2, 1880, quoted in Chicago *Tribune*, January 5, 1880; New York *Herald*, January 6, 1880.

[3] The Political Economy Club of that city was the spearhead of the movement, and its leader, J. Perrault, was a notorious annexationist. Toronto *Globe*, January 3, December 14, 1880; J. Burnley to John Campbell, Marquis of Lorne, June 1, 1880, Macdonald Papers, Governor Generals' Correspondence, VIII, Lord Lorne, 1880-1881; Howells to the Department of State, January 7, 1880, Consular Despatches, Toronto, VI; P. Carroll to the Department of State, January 25, 1881, Consular Despatches, Port Stanley and St. Thomas, I, 14.

[4] Toronto *Bystander*, August, 1880.

[5] Annexation letter in Toronto *Globe*, December 18, 1880.

[6] New York *Sun*, January 9, 1881.

[7] New York *Herald*, March 10, 1880; New York *Times*, November 30, 1881; and New York *Sun*, August 18, 1881, express typical opinions. Only two prominent papers, the Chicago *Tribune* and the Buffalo *Courier*, seem to have favored annexation.

ferent. Congress heard no mention of the topic; William M. Evarts, the secretary of state, ignored a letter from a Canadian politician who generously offered to arrange for annexation;[8] and the business and commercial men of the border states, eager participants in former agitations, were strangely still.

Americans lost no golden opportunity when they neglected to exploit this movement in Canada. Annexationists there may have been fairly numerous, but they lacked the courage to voice their desires and to organize their agitation, which fell an easy victim to the temporary return of prosperity in the early 1880's.

For a few years, the agitation for continental union lay dormant. Then it was revived, stronger than ever, but so was the resistance which it aroused. Conditions in Canada had been changing for over a decade, and it is necessary to examine them to understand why annexationism was launched again and what was the nature of the formidable opposition on which it broke.

It is appropriate to consider first the developments which piled up impediments to annexationism. Perhaps the most significant of these was the growth of nationalism. Legally, the Dominion was a political unit in 1873, but so long as it lacked real cohesion, the specter of annexation would continue to hover over it. Therefore, Canadians made every effort to knit their sprawling provinces together into a nation, economically, physically, and spiritually as well as legally, to counteract the pull to the south.

The first step, the physical union of the Dominion, had been achieved in 1885 by railroads which extended from Halifax to Vancouver. This system of communication was a necessity, not a luxury, a great steel spike driven through Canada from end to end to stiffen its resistance against the attraction of the United States. The "Fathers of Confederation," foreseeing this need, had provided in the British North America Act (Article 145)

[8] R. W. Phipps to Evarts, September 19, 1879, Miscellaneous Letters to the Department of State, 1879, September, II.

that the federal government must shortly begin the construction of the Intercolonial Railroad to connect Quebec with Halifax. To finance it, the Canadian government borrowed money, and the Imperial Parliament guaranteed the interest on further loans to the Dominion. The road was completed in 1876. For military reasons, it did not pursue the shortest route, which hugged the American boundary, but ran on the fringe of river and sea, where the ubiquitous British navy could protect it. This uneconomic elongation of the road increased the cost of an enterprise which was intended to produce not an economic profit but political unity by tying the Maritime Provinces to the St. Lawrence Valley. Most Canadians saw the Intercolonial Railroad as part of the necessary price of confederation and of nationality.

Before the Intercolonial was completed, the Dominion had shouldered an even more staggering burden. As noted in the previous chapter, the government at Ottawa had won British Columbia with the promise of a magnificent dowry, the construction of a railroad to the Pacific within ten years. Assurance of communication with Canada was a *sine qua non* to the acquisition of the West, as it had been to the union with the Maritimes. Yet the Pacific railroad might be a burden which would overtax the strength of a new country of slender resources. Macdonald and his government had hoped to build it as a public work, but the magnitude of the task appalled them. They also hoped for aid from the Imperial government, but this was denied. Private enterprise was willing to tackle the project if endowed with a substantial subsidy, for the Pacific railroad, unlike the Intercolonial, could be made to pay. Two groups of capitalists submitted bids for the construction contract. One consisted of Torontonians, headed by David Macpherson; the other, largely of Montreal men with Sir Hugh Allen as its chief. The latter syndicate had richer resources, but the taint of American money and personnel. Macdonald refused the risk of having any American hands on the controls of an instrument vital to his policy and perhaps to Canada's existence.[9] He would not give the contract to either group but suggested that they amalgamate and purge themselves of American interests.

The general election of 1872 occurred while these negotiations were in course. Allen and his associates, solicited by the Conservatives, poured over $150,000 into their war chest, an important factor in their victory. Parliament then granted the railroad charter to a new company which Allen had formed, leaving his former American colleagues out in the cold. But their indigation kept them warm. They had joined in the lavish contributions to the Conservatives, only to be dropped when they were no longer useful. Now they sought and gained revenge by pouring their story into the willing ears of the Liberals. The latter accused the Prime Minister of corruptly bartering the railroad contract for campaign contributions. Subsequent investigations led to the resignation of the Macdonald government and its defeat in the ensuing election of 1873. Sir John was the victim of his fears of American influence.[10]

The chief of the Liberals and new premier was Alexander Mackenzie, a saint in politics and a John Knox on the hustings. He was no "hot termagent Scot," but a cool and calculating one whose watchword was economy. Lacking Macdonald's imperial vision, Mackenzie failed to see the significant place of the Pacific railroad in the architecture of nationhood. He considered it an illusory enterprise which would never repay its cost and would remain a clumsy burden on a nation unready to carry it. The Allen company had abandoned its charter after the fall of Macdonald, leaving the railroad project a foundling on the doorstep of the new administration. Mackenzie tried to avoid this commitment, even offering British Columbia a payment in lieu

[9] Creighton, *Macdonald*, 112-13.

[10] Joseph Pope, *Memoirs of the Right Honorable Sir John Alexander Macdonald* (London, 1930), II, 161-96.

of the promised road. This attitude angered the people of the province, who bitterly accused Ottawa of violating a sacred pledge and began to speak of secession from the Dominion and annexation to the United States. The threat had its usual effect. Henry Herbert, Earl of Carnarvon, the colonial secretary, hastened to mediate between the Dominion and its fractious province. He proposed the so-called "Carnarvon terms"; the Dominion should begin building at once in British Columbia and complete the road to the East before 1890. Both parties accepted this compromise, but the federal government was dilatory in construction and the British Columbians again became dangerously sullen.[11]

Macdonald returned to power in 1878 and, with less than one-fourth of the road completed, again sought private interests to relieve the Dominion of its task. A corporation of five men undertook to build the road in return for a subsidy of twenty-five million acres of land, twenty-five million dollars in cash, and other considerations. Vigor replaced dawdling, and within a short time the rails were pushed across the prairie, up the Kicking Horse Pass, and threaded through the Fraser Canyon to the western threshold, present Vancouver. To the east, the company blasted rocks, felled trees, and filled in the almost bottomless swamps and mires of quicksand in the jungle of boulders and forest north of Lake Superior. It had underestimated the costs of construction and its finances were touch and go many times, but it squirmed through each crisis, thanks to additional government aid, and saw the last spike driven on November 7, 1885. The railroad builders had pulled down the mountains and bridged the wilderness to seam the four inhabited sections of Canada with their tough threads of steel.

Uniting the provinces was not the only significant function of the Intercolonial and the Canadian Pacific. The new east-

[11] *Canadian Commons Debates, 1876,* pp. 901, 1133; Creighton, *Macdonald,* 196-98.

west communication which they established cut across the old north-south channels, loosened the taut lines of trade between the United States and Canada, and eased the unceasing pull to the south. Canadians no longer needed to traverse the United States to go from one part of their own country to another. In the winter they did not have to import necessaries and to export surpluses through the ice-free ports of the Republic. Canada was becoming commercially emancipated from the United States.

But the Dominion needed more than a system of communication to become a nation. Particularism and popular indifference to the new federation still dangerously inhibited the growth of nationalism. Farsighted loyalists in Canada saw the need for nurturing patriotism and unity. Unfortunately, nationalism could not be built, as railroads were, by parliamentary grants but by time and association.

Various attempts were made to evoke a spirit of patriotism. Probably the most successful of these was the Canada First movement which grew out of the conversations of five young men, George Denison, Charles Mair, Henry Morgan, W. A. Foster, and Robert Haliburton, who chanced to meet in Ottawa in the spring of 1868. Enthusiastic about the future of the Dominion but sensitive to its weaknesses, they pledged themselves to work for the growth of a national consciousness. To this end they formed an organization pointedly entitled "Canada First." Riel's rebellion brought an opportunity to launch the movement with eclat. They organized numerous meetings to protest the action of the métis as an insult to the national honor of the Dominion. The striking success of these ventures and the gratifying publicity which they received encouraged some of the members to attempt the formation of a political party to advance their cause. George Denison, their leader, disapproved, pointing out that the Conservatives and Liberals would be driven in self-preservation to attack the new party, to the injury of its cause of nationalism. Despite this sound advice, a Canada First Party was established in 1874 and speedily proved the validity of Denison's fears by crumbling under the assaults of the major parties and their press.[12]

But the movement had not lived in vain. The lectures, pamphlets, and press notices which it evoked penetrated all parts of the Dominion. Its votaries were possibly misunderstood by many, their message was probably ahead of the times, but they certainly spoke with prophetic voice. The five young men had preached the gospel of pride in Canada and the virtue of casting down the false gods of provincialism and particularism, and echoes of their evangelism did not recede into silence. As the poet of the group, Charles Mair, declared: "The seed they sowed has sprung up at last, And grows and blossoms through the land."[13]

With all this, time quietly and without exploit or feat accomplished more for nationalism than speeches or frenetic activity. Canadians first became accustomed to the Dominion and then began to grow proud of it. Canada had done much in a short time and with limited resources. It had thrust out its boundaries as far in six years as the United States had in half a century; it had built two great railroads; it had repressed a dangerous revolt almost without the letting of blood. The railroads brought closer contact between the provinces and, with it, better understanding. The Nova Scotian "Bluenose" learned that the Manitoban and Ontarian was very like himself and, amazing discovery, all were citizens of a common country. The continental expansion of political parties increased this contact and helped men to lift up their eyes to the plane of the national scene. Here was much of Macdonald's genius. He stressed common interests and repressed divisive quarrels. With the sure

[12] George T. Denison, *The Struggle for Imperial Unity* (London, 1909), 56-61.
[13] Denison, 10, 50-55.

touch of the master political craftsman, he cemented a political conglomerate into the Conservative Party, combining the capitalist and laborer, the Roman Catholic and the Orangeman, the British Columbian and the Nova Scotian.

Passing time dulled the edge of provincialism and drugged the memories of the day when each province was a separate colony. Now a new generation was approaching adulthood which had been either unborn or in the cradle on that first Dominion Day of July 1, 1867. As long as they could remember, the provinces had been subordinate to the central government, and it was not easy for them to reverse the two in their mental hierarchy of power relationships.

This is not to say that particularism was either dead or moribund, but rather that, to many Canadians, it occupied second place to the nation by the middle of the 1880's. Spiritually, as well as physically, the Dominion was far more united in 1887 than it had been in 1867. The ever-present danger of absorption had compelled Canadians to recognize their common identity vis-a-vis the United States, and the passing of time, and of men, was tightening their union.

A great danger remained: the lack of economic integration in the Dominion. The ancient desire for reciprocity with the United States persisted, and the government of Canada must try to get a new treaty. But all was in vain. The vested interests in the United States, securely gripping Congress, would allow no tampering with their sacred system of protection. Canadian resentment mounted, then flared into retaliation. In 1870 the Dominion excluded American fishermen from its inshore waters where, since 1866, they had been permitted to fish upon payment of annual license fees. British cruisers patrolled the area, boarding many vessels and confiscating fifteen. This hurt American fishermen, whose annual catch in Canadian territorial waters had been six million dollars.[14] Canada had now created a *quid*

[14] Nevins, *Hamilton Fish*, 414.

pro quo to offer for reciprocity, and soon found an opportunity to try it. A Joint High Commission met in Washington in 1871 to settle questions outstanding between the United States and Canada and Great Britain. Sir John A. Macdonald, who was one of the British commissioners, hopefully suggested a renewal of the treaty of 1854 in exchange for fishing privileges in Canadian territorial waters. Hamilton Fish, the secretary of state, was inclined to make the trade, but he feared the growls of touchy protectionists in the Senate. After much haggling and the dispatch and receipt of reams of cables and telegrams, a bargain was struck. In exchange for fishing rights, the United States would admit Canadian fish duty-free and pay to Canada a sum of money to be determined later by a tribunal. The agreement would last for ten years, after which time either party could terminate it upon two years' notice.[15] Macdonald signed this agreement under protest and only after the other British commissioners warned him that his failure to do so would scuttle the whole agreement, including the settlement of the dangerous *Alabama* question. His irritation was increased when the United States refused to discuss the Fenian claims, which had been left off the official agenda. Canadians at home were as angry as Macdonald as the results of this conference. They felt that in its anxiety to settle the *Alabama* matter, the British government had bartered their interests to retrieve its own. Though the treaty satisfied the Nova Scotians, who now had a market for their fish, it left the rest of the Dominion as far from reciprocity as ever. However, the cavalier attitude of the United States in the negotiations had reduced the desire of Canadians for such an agreement and had stimulated their nationalism.

Then the world depression of 1873 began to contract foreign markets and revived the desire for freer trade with the United

[15] Shippee, *Canadian-American Relations,* 262-87, 348-76, 426-71; Nevins, *Hamilton Fish,* 474-81.

States. Canadian exports shrank from $90,000,000 in 1873 to $75,323,000 in 1877 and continued to slip down to $71,491,000 in 1878.[16] The government of the Dominion again sought the old cure for their distress. George Brown, editor of the Toronto *Globe,* was sent to Washington to aid Sir Edward Thornton, the British minister, in negotiating a treaty of reciprocity. On June 18, 1874, President Grant unenthusiastically submitted an unsigned draft to the Senate, which refused to consider it.[17]

Canadians were offended by this rude rebuff, but it proved to be the ill wind which blew good to the Conservatives, who were then out of power. They contended that reciprocity would probably lead to annexation; besides, they had a better solution for the depression. This turned out to be the National Policy, a system of protective tariffs. It met the demands of Canadian manufacturers who had been clamoring for protection of their markets against the dumping of American goods. Others wanted a higher tariff to increase the revenues of the government. Most Canadians, however, favored the change because of its political implications. It would promote interprovincial trade by discouraging importation and by stimulating local industry. In proportion as internal commerce and production increased, economic dependence on the United States would decrease. In short, the tariff would serve economic nationalism as Canada First had served political nationalism.

The new policy was not a peculiarly Canadian development, but simply the local manifestation of a general world movement; actually, it was somewhat late in arriving in the Dominion. The nations of the western world were looking inward rather than

[16] Canada, *Statistical Abstract and Record* (1886), 125-26; William Howells to W. M. Evarts, October 3, 1877, Consular Despatches, Toronto, VI, 60. Prices decreased greatly. Wheat dropped from $1.30 a bushel in 1873 to $0.76 in 1886, barley from $1.06 to $0.63, and cattle from $6.00 per hundredweight to $4.00. *Canadian Commons Debates, 1886,* p. 444.

[17] Shippee, *Canadian-American Relations,* 464-68.

outward economically, and a maze of tariff walls was being constructed. The United States presented an extreme and provocative example of the trend. Canada could hardly escape being caught up and carried away in this universal current.

Moreover, nationalism paid dividends in partisan politics. Its popular appeal helped to carry the Conservatives into power in 1878. The following year they put the new program into effect and were delighted, and perhaps surprised, when economic conditions began to improve. Agricultural production rose above normal and commodity prices accompanied it. Exports climbed from $71,491,000 in 1878 to $102,137,000 in 1882.[18] The annual value of the fisheries, which had rarely fluctuated, increased rapidly and soothed the Nova Scotians who had grumbled about the new tariff.[19] The number of business failures decreased, and optimism gradually returned to the Dominion as the fog of depression lifted.

The Conservatives easily accepted this blessing as a token of the pleasure of providence that Canada had returned to righteousness after the deplorable fall from grace between 1873 and 1878. In the name of the National Policy, they modestly accepted the responsibility for prosperity and did not neglect the obvious lesson that nationalism was economically as well as politically profitable. Canada would never again need to beg the United States for commercial favors.

This *post hoc ergo propter hoc* reasoning was seductive. To be sure, a few scoffers pointed out that prosperity might be due less to the new policy than to the improvement in business and the extensive railroad building in the United States and the crop failure in England, all of which stimulated the demand for Canadian products. The people of the Dominion ignored such

[18] Canada, *Statistical Abstract* (1886), 125-26.

[19] United States, *Consular Reports, 1887*, XXI, 351. The increase in exports of fish amounted to $2,300,000 in a single year.

hardened cynics and rewarded the sagacity of the Conservatives by returning them in the landslide election of 1882. A vista of prosperity seemed to stretch, limitless and enticing, before Canada.[20]

Then came a rude jolt. For all its talk of industrial development, Canada's economy still rested on the export of staples, and world prices for raw products began to sag in 1882. By September the Canadian farmer was receiving from 10 to 30 percent less for his produce than he had the preceding June. The western world was slipping back into depression. Exports from the Dominion dropped by $10,700,000 by 1884, and many industries hung on the brink of bankruptcy.[21] The government also had its problems as deficits ate up the surpluses of earlier years and the national debt climbed to $270,000,000. The depression lasted from 1883 to 1896 and seemed to be chronic. As prices for primary products slowly sank in world markets, they dragged Canadian income down with them.

Depression had been the milieu for the propagation of annexationism, and that of the 1880's was much the worst that British North America had experienced, both in its protracted endurance and the universality of its impact. Former economic declines had fallen primarily upon the commercial classes, affecting others slightly and indirectly. In the 1880's, no class escaped. The farmer, the lumberman, the fisherman, and the merchant suffered alike.

The economic condition of the Dominion taxed the loyalty of its people, and the Conservatives had done their bit to increase this strain. They had modestly and complacently accepted credit in the name of the National Policy for the prosperity from

[20] P. Carroll to the Department of State, June 22, 1882, Consular Despatches, Port Stanley and St. Thomas, I, 69.

[21] A. Roberts to the Department of State, October 29, 1883, Consular Despatches, Hamilton, V, 16; J. Smith to the Department of State, December 24, 1882, Consular Despatches, Montreal, XVIII.

1880 to 1882, and for having found the antidote for future depressions. The subsequent slump brought a reaction, and it was rather violent. Many who had praised the tariff for the good times now bitterly accused it of causing their distress. The plan of economic nationalism sank in popular esteem and the desire for closer economic relations with the United States rose again. The first had failed; now the second should be tried.

The opposition party naturally fostered this belief. They delivered innumerable jeremiads upon the state of Canada, bolstering their lugubrious oratory with a baffling array of statistics until it seemed that these ornaments of public life and journalism were mathematicians, not speakers and writers.

The Liberals kept two interlocking ideas constantly before the country: Canada was in a slough of depression, and closer trade ties with the United States were needed to pull her out. Her Majesty's Loyal Opposition were unwittingly disloyal to an extent, for they thus undermined the nascent economic nationalism which could be one of the sturdiest barriers against annexation. And they were giving new life to the old idea that Canada was economically dependent upon the United States. If negotiation could not gain reciprocity, annexation would. The longer the depression and the Liberal campaign for reciprocity continued, the greater this danger became. Moreover, the persistence of the depression bred pessimism with regard to the future of the Dominion. It seemed to many that Canada lacked the requisite population and capital to achieve economic nationalism or political nationhood. Despair and the fear of continuing distress gnawed at their loyalty.

At the same time, the contrast between conditions in the United States and in Canada enhanced the attractions of reciprocity. American business was reviving, railroads and industrial interests were expanding, and the West was filling up. Many Canadians, unwilling to await the uncertain prospects of reciprocity or political union with this thriving economy, annexed themselves to it by migration to the United States. It was estimated that one-quarter of those born in the Dominion eventually settled permanently in the Republic, an intolerable drain upon a slender population.[22] Those who departed were often aggressive and intelligent young men whose loss deprived Canada of potential leaders.[23] This drain of population continued until the American West filled up and the trend of internal North American migration reversed and flowed north into the Canadian West. Before this change occurred, Canadians were deeply disturbed at their losses, and some urged annexation to bring opportunity to Canada so that its younger generation would not have to leave home to seek it.

The National Policy not only failed to bring such opportunities or to prevent the depression, but it also caught the people of the Dominion in the pinch of increasing costs of living.[24] Canadians had had to import many necessaries, principally manufactured goods. When the National Policy began to stimulate the production of such articles in Canada, the result too commonly was an increase in price and a decline in quality. Often the disparity was so great that Canadians found it cheaper to import the goods and pay the duties. Some Canadian industries which needed no protection received it anyway, promptly raised their prices proportionally, and pocketed wind-

[22] The American census of 1890 showed that 980,938 persons born in Canada were residing in the United States. *Compendium of the Eleventh Census of the United States,* III, 47-48.

[23] The Maritimes were particularly hard hit. From 1881 to 1891 they lost 103,785 persons by migration to the United States, including about 50,000 between the ages of fifteen and nineteen. The population of these provinces grew by only 10,041 during this decade, whereas it had increased over 100,000 in the previous decade. Canadian Bureau of Statistics, *The Maritime Provinces since Confederation* (Ottawa, 1927), 4-5, 7, 76.

[24] One set of figures indicated that the new tariff increased the cost of living for the average family by $30.44 annually. Toronto *Globe,* August 14, 1880.

fall profits.[25] As the cost of living rose, those who paid the difference saw no apparent compensatory gains to themselves. Labor was underpaid, and producers of raw materials found that their prices received showed little or no advance. The profits from new industries went to the shareholders or entrepreneurs, or were ploughed back into new capital goods. The concentration of wealth and profits in the hands of relatively few was becoming an old story in the United States and other more mature economies, but it was a new and unwelcome experience for Canada.

Even for the industrialists the National Policy was not a universal blessing. It led to overbuilding in some industries, such as refining and textiles. The home market could not absorb the swelling production, and export was often impossible because the costs of small Canadian manufacturers were higher than those of mass producers abroad.

It was unfortunate mischance that these dislocations incident to the revolution in fiscal policy—higher costs of living, overproduction, low wages, and failures—should have coincided with the resumption of the depression. Squeezed in the pressures of distress, many Canadians failed to realize that such conditions were temporary or to weigh the political value of economic nationalism in the scales of judgment. Thus the protective tariff often aggravated the effects of the depression to endanger loyalty.

Special circumstances maximized the impact of hard times on the Maritime Provinces. Their people had to pay for the support of industries which pushed some smaller Maritime factories to the wall.[26] Several developments, coincident but

[25] One Canadian mill, prosperous before the National Policy, the year after the tariff went up paid 38 percent dividends on $1,250,000 worth of stock, of which all but $285,000 was water. Interview with the owner in Toronto *Globe*, May 24, 1882.

[26] New Glasgow *Plaindealer*, undated, quoted in Toronto *Globe*, August 7, 1880.

not connected with the depression, deepened their gloomy prospects. Iron was superseding wood in shipbuilding. The shipyards of Nova Scotia and New Brunswick, founded on the abundant local supply of timber, were not adapted to the new techniques, and their business decayed. This decline of a basic industry was a body blow, and it affected subsidiary enterprises such as lumbering, which was also afflicted with a decline in its American market.[27]

Then the American government compounded the difficulties of the Maritimes by slamming the door shut on imports of fish from the Dominion. As a result of the Treaty of Washington, the United States had agreed to make a cash payment to Canada as well as opening the American market to Canadian fish in return for the right to use Canada's inshore fisheries. The Halifax Commission set the sum at $5,500,000, an amount in excess of American expectations or Canadian hopes. Washington sent Ottawa the cash and enclosed a vigorous protest. Then nature played a prank which increased American resentment. New England fishermen discovered to their consternation that their favorite prey, the mackerel, had deserted the inshore waters of Canada and appeared off the American coast. This made the Treaty of Washington more a liability than an asset, and the United States abrogated it July 1, 1885, and deprived Nova Scotians of free access to their best market.[28] Exports of fish to the United States declined from $3,147,000 in 1884 to $1,502,000 in 1886.[29]

Political troubles came on the heels of economic distress. Some American fishermen continued to frequent the fisheries of the Dominion and boldly used the expired privileges. The

[27] Consular Despatches, Halifax, XV, 265; *Consular Reports, 1886*, XIX, 601-602, contains special information on lumbering. Exports to the United States fell off over five million dollars in one year. See also New York *Times*, August 15, 1887.
[28] Callahan, *Canadian Relations*, 362-63.
[29] *Consular Reports*, 1887, XXIII, 218.

Canadian government responded with a proclamation in March, 1886, forbidding Americans to fish or to buy bait or provisions within Canadian territorial waters.[30] Fisheries cruisers sent to enforce these regulations confiscated a number of American ships found violating them.[31] In retaliation, the United States sent an armed vessel to protect its nationals. The situation grew more serious as the fisheries question resumed its accustomed place as the plague spot of Canadian-American relations.

The people of the Maritimes were in a dilemma. The fisheries, as a principal source of income, must be protected. This necessitated stern measures which would provoke the United States —possibly to war—and decrease the chance of regaining any privileges in the American market. In their frustration, some Maritimers irrationally blamed the Canadian government for their predicament and again raised the cry for secession.

The Maritimes were not the only provinces with special grievances in the 1880's. Manitoba was again unhappy. Its plaints echoed those so loudly voiced at the same time in the western American states against the railroads. As a wheat country, Manitoba must have cheap transportation to world markets. She was not getting it. The federal government had given a charter monopoly to the Canadian Pacific for twenty years as the price of inducing it to build its line north of Lake Superior through the rocky and unsettled Laurentian Shield instead of using existing American lines south of the Great Lakes. The government promised to prevent the charter of any railroad running within fifteen miles of the American border in the Northwest. This monopoly was the price which the Dominion must pay for an all-Canadian railroad, a foundation

[30] A copy of the proclamation in W. Phelan to J. Porter, March 30, 1886, Consular Despatches, Halifax, XIV.

[31] W. Phelan to J. Porter, May 3, 8, 17, 1886, *et passim,* Consular Despatches, Halifax, XIV. These dispatches reported a number of cases in which Phelan considered the Canadians too severe and meticulous in their enforcement proceedings.

stone of economic nationalism. A road partly in Canada and partly in the United States would stress continentalism and contradict nationalism.

Again the Canadian government had to balance economic loss and political gain. Since nationalism had become the basic political commitment of his career, Macdonald insisted that the Canadian Pacific monopoly remain inviolate and warned Manitoba that he would disallow any provincial legislation for the construction of a competitor.[32] This brought the issue to a dangerous impasse, for Manitobans were less impressed with the possibilities of vague future political gains than with their present economic distress. They must have lower freight rates or be driven from the markets which paid their living. Competition seemed the only certain way to obtain those lower rates, and in their eyes, the Macdonald government was corruptly coddling its favorite vested interest at their expense. This conviction strained their loyalty.

The depression and coincident economic evils in themselves had made Canada a sick nation in the 1880's. But this was not all. Perverse fate had apparently willed that depressions must be accompanied by renewed antipathy between the French and the English. Passions had been smoldering since the execution of Thomas Scott in the first Riel rebellion and flared up again during the second rebellion in 1885. Other episodes followed in sorry procession, to be more fully described below, liberally salting the reopened wounds until many of each nationality insisted that they preferred annexation to the danger of domination by the other.

This friction fanned the flames of discontent kindled by economic distress. Conditions in Canada in the 1880's were the worst that that country had known. Distress was psycho-

[32] Macdonald to Martin J. Griffin, October 31, 1881, Macdonald to John Norquay, November 5, 1881, Macdonald Papers, Macdonald Letter Books, XII.

logical as well as physical. The inability of their government to alleviate the situation, the failure of the National Policy as a panacea, drove many to desperation. It seemed to some that anything different would be an improvement, and they looked southward toward the obvious change.

A similar situation and complex of problems occurring in 1849 or 1867 might have been fatal to Canada. It was well for those who wished to remain British that the new, if yet shaky, buttress of Canadian nationalism reinforced Imperial allegiance in this dark era. The efforts of Macdonald and others to arouse a spirit of patriotism had been successful within the limits imposed by time and circumstance. In the hearts of most of its citizens there was a growing love of Canada. During the 1880's, annexationism had to dispute with two foes for the possession of the Dominion: loyalty to the Empire and loyalty to the Dominion. Consequently, though the forces which pushed Canada toward union with the United States were stronger than ever before, so was the resistance to that pressure stronger. The ensuing movement for the annexation of Canada to the United States was the greatest—and the last.

CHAPTER SIX

The Rebirth of Continental Union 1883-1887

In Manitoba the curtain rose on the final act of the continental union drama. Many grievances sorely beset this province in the 1880's, and the Canadian Pacific Railroad was the greatest of these. This road, as noted above, had a legal transportation monopoly in the West which it mercilessly exploited. As the depression of 1883 set in, it raised its rates until they exceeded American rail charges, already so high that they were causing farmers in the United States to complain bitterly.[1] This was a heavy and untimely tribute to exact from a poor community. Moreover, it cast a shadow over the future of Manitoba. That province could not compete for immigrants with Minnesota and Dakota while the cost of its transportation compared unfavorably with theirs. Nor was the Canadian Pacific responsive to pleas for relief or sensitive to criticism of its policies. Too often it answered both with threats of punitive action.[2] It is little wonder that many Manitobans were bitter against the road and resolved to go to great lengths to escape its iron grip.

Hostility to the railroad increased the bitterness resulting from another grievance, the land question. The Dominion government held title to the public lands in the Northwest, and its policy of disposal provoked much protest. The authorities in Ottawa had heavily subsidized the Canadian Pacific with land; other choice sections were granted to political favorites and to speculators. This left the impression that little good land remained for settlers. Moreover, the inhabited areas were badly broken up, interlaced with blocks of land held off the market awaiting an increment in value.[3]

The land grievances were probably less important than those against the elevators and grain buyers. These interests, like the Canadian Pacific, had established a monopoly situation, and there were no standard grades or regulation to protect the producer. The result was undergrading, mixing, and exorbitant charges and commissions.[4]

The tariff of the National Policy offered a further cause for discontent. Living in a pioneer community, Manitobans had to import many necessaries. If they purchased American goods, the tariff raised the cost. For example, the agricultural implements then manufactured in Canada were unsuited to the heavy soil and thick straw characteristic of prairie agriculture, and so Manitoban farmers bought machinery from the United States.[5] If they purchased Canadian implements to escape the tariff, they received an inferior product and had to pay the heavy transportation charges imposed by the Canadian Pacific. Thus the tariff and the Canadian Pacific gave the people of the Northwest a choice which cost them dearly whatever their decision.

The financial plight of Manitoba also concerned its inhabitants. They complained that their contributions to the support of the federal government were much in excess of charges on

[1] Harold A. Innis, A *History of the Canadian Pacific Railway* (Toronto, 1923), 175-76, discusses railroad rates. See also Morton, *Manitoba*, 208.

[2] Toronto *Globe*, February 18, 1884; St. Paul *Pioneer Press*, May 13, 1887.

[3] Toronto *Globe*, July 31, 1882; St. Paul *Pioneer Press*, November 15, 1883. The cumbersome system set up by the Canadian government made it difficult to get title to the land which the settler had "proved up" under the homestead provisions. Macdonald Papers, Manitoba and North West Territories, Land Matters, I.

[4] Macdonald Papers, North West Territories, 1883-1886; Toronto *Globe*, January 8, 1884; St. Paul *Pioneer Press*, March 7, December 21, 22, 1884.

[5] Begg, *North-West*, III, 62-63.

citizens of the other provinces.[6] Their hard-pressed provincial government desperately needed this tribute exacted by Ottawa, for the British North America Act had deprived the provinces of certain sources of revenue, giving them in return annual federal subsidies which covered only half of the local expenses in Manitoba.[7] This complaint was not peculiar to Manitoba; all provinces grieved over the penuriousness of the federal subsidy and, with tears, launched movements for "Better Terms"—for which read, "More Money."

These grievances filled the minds of the Manitobans and impelled them to action, for the western Canadian, like his American counterpart, adopted no philosophy of kismet toward his sufferings. When he was kicked, he kicked back.

The railroad situation, which interlocked with several other grievances, seemed to be the key log in this jam, and the Manitobans turned to pry it out, hoping to break the local exploitive monopolies by gaining access to both American transportation and markets. Accordingly, the provincial government, early in the 1880's, chartered a railroad to run to the border and connect there with lines in the United States. The federal government promptly disallowed this act because it violated the spirit of the Canadian Pacific charter and might release that road from its obligation to build the costly line north of Lake Superior.[8] It also violated the assumptions of a national economy by opening the way for an American invasion of the sensitive

[6] Begg, *North-West*, III, 73. Ontarians paid $3.82 per capita annually to the Dominion, Nova Scotians, $3.99, and the inhabitants of Quebec, $6.75, but it cost the Manitoban $16.00 a year.

[7] St. Paul *Pioneer Press*, December 22, 1884; New York *Sun*, February 28, 1884.

[8] Macdonald to John Norquay, November 5, 1881, Macdonald to Andrew Simpson, November 9, 1882, Macdonald Papers, Macdonald Letter Books, XXII. Macdonald had warned Norquay, the provincial premier, that he would disallow any charter passed. Manitoba's government argued that the monopoly pledge applied only to the federal government, and insisted on its right to charter intraprovincial railroads.

area where east-west lines of communication must be developed to replace the politically dangerous north-south lines which had dominated in prerailroad days. The fact that the connecting line at the border would be his old bête noire, the Northern Pacific, did nothing to reconcile Macdonald to the provincial charter.

This frustration infuriated Manitobans, who considered it both an injustice and an invasion of provincial rights. They might lack cash and economic power, but they had numbers and votes and knew how to use them. Accordingly, they formed various organizations such as the Manitoba Rights League and the Manitoba and North West Farmers' Union, similar to the Grangers in the United States.[9] They planned to petition the federal government for the redress of their grievances. If this failed, they would form a political party to elect representatives to the federal Parliament. They defined their goals in a declaration of rights issued in the fall of 1883, calling for local control of public lands, removal or lowering of the tariff on necessaries, and acknowledgment of the provincial right to charter railroads and the municipal right to construct mills and elevators.[10] This plan of action was loyal and constitutional in form, but it harbored a latent menace to the Dominion. Like the Nova Scotians on the morrow of confederation, Manitobans who could not get relief in one way might try another.

Several elements in the population were inclined to channel the discontent into an annexationist course. One of these was the group of American-born settlers, who, as in the days of Riel,

[9] These organizations claimed a membership of 100,000, probably an exaggeration. Toronto *Globe*, February 18, 1884. Part of the ensuing material relating to annexationism in the farmer organizations has already appeared in the author's article, "The Farmers' Alliance and the Farmers' Union: An American-Canadian Parallelism," *Agricultural History*, XXIII (January, 1949), 9-19, and is used again herein with the permission of the editor, C. Clyde Jones.

[10] New York *Times*, November 27, 1883.

were fairly numerous and unquenchably vocal. From their lofty insight, they were able to inform their neighbors of the superiority of the American government and land system (which they themselves had voluntarily left) and, more effectively, to add that the state of Manitoba, unlike the province of Manitoba, could build all the railroads it wished.

Another element was more dangerous. It consisted of footloose adventurers, economic soldiers of fortune, whose basic loyalty was to their wallets. This type was common to all frontiers but especially numerous in Manitoba because of circumstances. The building of the Canadian Pacific had induced a burning fever of speculation in the lands along its tracks from Winnipeg to Moose Jaw. One railroad man disgustedly wrote, "Wherever there's a siding, that's a town; and where there's a siding and a tank, that's a city."[11] The "boom" news brought crowds of fortune hunters to Winnipeg, and the pace of real estate transactions became frantic. Everyone was buying land on margin, financing each transaction by the proceeds of its predecessor; the value of choice lots often appreciated 1,000 percent in a week![12] These adventurers so distended the bubble that it soon burst, leaving many penniless and possessed of land worth but a fraction of what they had paid for it. They thenceforth lived only to retrieve what they had lost, by whatever means offered.[13] Annexation seemed the best solvent for their troubles, because American land generally commanded a higher price than Canadian land, for which the demand was not so great.

These disloyal elements in the province joined the Manitoba and North West Farmers' Union and sought to infect its mem-

[11] Begg, *North-West*, III, 70.

[12] St. Paul *Pioneer Press*, March 25, 1882; Begg, *North-West*, III, 69.

[13] A frosted crop in 1883 was the immediate cause of the crash. Creighton, *Macdonald*, 369-70; Morton, *Manitoba*, 200-201; William McDougall to Macdonald, August 14, 1884, Macdonald Papers, General Letters, 1884.

bers. Their persuasions began to have effect, and Dominion authorities in the province warned Macdonald that the situation could become serious. The validity of these predictions was soon confirmed. In the fall of 1883, political union with the United States became a subject of public discussion in Manitoba for the first time in a decade. The Farmers' Union called a convention of its members to meet in Winnipeg on December 18. When the local branches of the organization met to elect delegates to this conference, lively and startling results ensued. The members, who lived on isolated farms without opportunity to discuss their grievances with others, had been brooding over their troubles and storing their wrath. They were well charged when the meetings of the local unions were held, and many exploded in violent annexation speeches.[14]

This venting of emotion had a salutory effect, for the convention at Winnipeg was comparatively mild and innocuous. The few annexationists who dared to raise their heads submitted a motion for the secession of Manitoba, but they were severely punished in the voting. Extreme measures seemed unnecessary to the other members; since the union commanded the support of practically the entire population of the province, the federal government surely could not resist their demands.[15] The convention then proceeded to draw up a "Declaration of Rights," demanding such concessions as a lower tariff, local control of local public lands, and the charter of provincial railroads without federal interference. The provincial premier, John Norquay, although a Conservative, moved with alacrity to keep his fences in order by allying his government to the union. Shortly thereafter, both Norquay and the union sent missions to Ottawa to press their demands on Macdonald. The Prime Minister was

[14] J. C. Aitkins (lieutenant governor of Manitoba) to Macdonald, November 30, 1883, Macdonald Papers, Honorable J. C. Aitkins, 1871-1891; Begg, *North-West*, III, 85; New York *Times*, December 8, 1883.
[15] Winnipeg *Manitoba Weekly Free Press*, January 10, 1884.

noncommittal. He refused a decision, pleading the need to study the situation and to await the convening of Parliament, which would have to approve any commitments he made. He implied, however, that he would be adamant in retaining the railroad monopoly and the protective tariff; he could not do less without mortal hurt to his basic policy. The Canadian Pacific, now alarmed enough to be amenable to pressures, lowered its rates by one-quarter.[16] So the Manitobans returned, otherwise empty-handed, from the first of a series of hegiras to Ottawa.

The Farmers' Union did not accept this rebuff gracefully. Its officers called another convention to meet in Winnipeg on March 5, 1884, to plot the course of future action. The strength of the annexationists had increased sharply after the federal refusal of redress, and they now made their presence felt.[17] Several speakers boldly discussed the advantages of union with the United States, and no one rose to rebuke them. Rumors of a rebellion in the province and of a Fenian invasion from the United States to aid it were thick in the air.[18] The convention adopted a resolution of loyalty but promptly nullified any good effects of this action by entertaining a motion for the secession of Manitoba from the Dominion if Ottawa did not do them justice.[19] Though the resolution was later withdrawn, the damage had been done. Canadians outside the province began to suspect the loyalty of the Farmers' Union.

Having injured its reputation elsewhere, that organization

[16] Winnipeg *Manitoba Weekly Free Press,* January 31, 1884.

[17] Winnipeg *Manitoba Weekly Free Press,* January 18, 31, February 28, 1884; J. W. Taylor to John Davis, January 18, 1884, Consular Despatches, Winnipeg, VI, 373.

[18] St. Paul *Pioneer Press,* February 18, 20, 27, 1884; Winnipeg *Manitoba Weekly Free Press,* February 21, 28, March 6, 1884; Toronto Globe, February 23, 1884. Both the Canadian and American governments took these rumors seriously. Diplomatic Notes, Great Britain, CX; Aitkins to Taylor, February 29, 1884, James W. Taylor Papers.

[19] St. Paul *Pioneer Press,* March 7, 1884; Toronto *Globe,* March 7, 1884.

completed a full day's work by shattering the solid block of support which it had enjoyed at home. It did this by unwisely and unanimously resolving that immigrants could not be advised to come to Manitoba as long as the burdens imposed on it precluded profitable agriculture.[20] This action was an incredible blunder in a province which was bending every effort to attract settlers. Many who had loyally supported the union repudiated its leadership after this misstep.[21] By discrediting the province outside, the union had discredited itself in Manitoba.

While the farmers' organization was busily digging its own grave, the government in Ottawa was trying to formulate a policy which would appease the province. Macdonald was painfully impaled on a dilemma. He wanted Manitoba's votes, but the price might be concessions which would endanger the completion and operation of the Canadian Pacific, a *sine qua non* of his National Policy. He attempted to buy his way off this comfortless perch by offering financial favors, while refusing to alter the railroad, land, and tariff policies. He cannily insisted that acceptance of this tender must constitute a quitclaim against the right to agitate for further concessions. Norquay refused the offer, as he had to do if he wished to survive politically in Manitoba.

Thus the Farmers' Union had failed to secure redress of a single important grievance, had lost the support of many Manitobans, and had made its loyalty questionable. This suspicion of its intent grew rapidly during the spring and summer of 1884. The annexationists in the organization busied themselves in a variety of mysterious and alarming activities. They tried, without outstanding success, to gain more support in the province and to extend their activities across the border. A number of ephemeral and secret societies for the promotion of annexation

[20] Toronto *Globe*, March 7, 1884.

[21] The people of Winnipeg were particularly incensed by this action. Begg, *North-West*, III, 89-90; Morton, *Manitoba*, 212-13.

sprang up in the United States and in Manitoba, and news and rumors of the plots being hatched leaked out and spread as far as Ottawa.[22] An intercepted letter to the president of the union, George Purvis, revealed that a few desperate adventurers contemplated seizing stores of arms and trying to involve the organization in an armed revolt.[23] One of their leaders, A. E. C. Pew, an American railroad promoter, commuted between Winnipeg and Washington in the hope of enlisting American aid.[24] He had been delegated by one of the protest meetings to go to the American capital "and see on what terms the Province could be admitted to the Union." Here he was squired about by Senator Henry Payne of Ohio and introduced to several officials, one of whom suggested that the proper procedure would be for Manitoba to secede, declare its independence, establish a republican form of government, then proceed to negotiate with the United States.

These suggestions pointed the way to action. The first concern of the Manitoban annexationists was to borrow $150,000 to further their plans. For this purpose, they conceived an amazing plot and one richly promising to the prospective lenders whom they hoped to uncover in the United States. Part of the money would be used to buy the three newspapers in Winnipeg, and the rest "to secure the cooperation and assistance of some public men who have offered under certain circumstances to aid . . . by their influence and political possitions [*sic*] to bring about the state of things set forth." Prominent Liberal leaders such as Sir Richard Cartwright had promised their help, the plotters averred, and Norquay had interviewed Bishop Taché, who was dissatisfied with existing conditions and particularly the pre-

[22] Toronto *Globe*, February 23, 1884; New York *Times*, February 23, 1884.

[23] Creighton, *Macdonald*, 385.

[24] William McDougall to Macdonald, August 14, 1884, Macdonald Papers, General Letters, August, 1884; Macdonald to Erastus Wiman, September 11, 1884, Macdonald Papers, Macdonald Letter Books, XXIII.

dominance of Orangemen in local offices. On or about November 1, when the western winter clamped its icy grip on communications with Canada, Norquay would proclaim practical independence, a convention would be held, and officers elected for the new republic. It would issue thirty million dollars in bonds, most of which a prominent "Romish religious order," under Taché's influence, would buy. Negotiations would then be opened with Washington for annexation, and the American government would be persuaded to guarantee the interest on the newly issued bonds, bringing them to par. Those who advanced the initial $150,000 would then receive their reward in the form of five million dollars' worth of the new bonds.[25]

This proposal was a fantastic, not to say libelous, document, but it alarmed Macdonald thoroughly. He condemned the Farmers' Union as mass madness; he urged Norquay to keep a close watch on its leaders; and he privately confessed that he feared a revolt in the province.[26]

Perhaps influenced by this fear and by the knowledge that the union had lost ground, Macdonald repeated his offer of better terms to the province and added new concessions.[27] Though he still refused to grant the major demands on the railroads and the tariff, he apparently allowed the rumor to circulate

[25] This plot is outlined in a long, rambling, undated, and unsigned document entitled, partly, "Memorandum of the Present Condition of feeling in the Canadian Northwest owing to the dissatisfaction growing out of the Manner in which the Dominion has treated the Province of Manitoba," in Macdonald Papers, Northwest Rebellion, 1885, I. The author was probably Pew, who later became president of the Toronto, Hamilton, & Buffalo Railroad. E. Wiman to Macdonald, September 6, 1884, in Joseph Pope, *Correspondence of Sir John Macdonald* (Toronto, 1921), 322-23.

[26] Macdonald to Norquay, July 1, 1884, Macdonald to Aitkins, July 28, 1884, Macdonald Papers, Macdonald Letter Books, XXIII.

[27] The province would receive $100,000 a year in lieu of the control of its public lands, an increased subsidy, and other lesser concessions. Begg, *North-West*, III, 118-19; St. Paul *Pioneer Press*, February 24, 1885.

that the monopoly clause of the Canadian Pacific charter would be repealed as soon as the road was completed and in operation.

The Farmers' Union denounced these terms because they did not cut the taproots of Manitoba's problems. But Norquay dared their wrath and accepted the proffer, emboldened by his understanding that the monopoly would soon be ended and by the fact that the power of the union was waning. The provincial legislature later endorsed his action.[28]

Norquay's decision aroused great popular resentment, and disloyal elements sought to exploit it and gain control of the Farmers' Union in a forthcoming convention called for March, 1885, to insist that the legislature repudiate Norquay and reject Macdonald's proposals. The several annexationists among the delegates assayed local feeling. They called a public meeting to form a secession league which would agitate for the withdrawal of Manitoba from the Dominion as a step toward union with the United States. It was an absurd fiasco. The chairman presented a secession resolution only to discover that he alone dared to favor it. He left the scene in haste, bearing on his person portions of eggs and well-matured vegetables presented to him in recognition of his sentiments.[29]

The fact that the meeting was held, despite its outcome, resulted in deepening the suspicion with which the Farmers' Union was now viewed throughout the Dominion. This regard proved deadly, because the punishment for its annexationists was soon visited upon the entire organization. Shortly after the convention, the second Riel rebellion broke out in the Northwest. This uprising was confined to the métis and Indians and had no apparent connection with the union. The interests which opposed and feared that organization, however, knew opportunity when they heard her knock. They cried out that the union had amply demonstrated its disloyalty in the past and

[28] Begg, *North-West*, III, 130. [29] Begg, III, 122-23.

was obviously behind this revolt. The accusation was unjust, and the leaders of the organization indignantly denied it. But it was useless, for the taint of disloyalty imparted by the annexationist fringe had poisoned the minds of many Canadians against the entire organization. So, despite its protests, that organization was tried and condemned by public opinion. It lingered on for a time, but almost devoid of influence or power.

Though the Farmers' Union had an untimely death, its enemies could not lay its ghost, and Manitoba continued to fight for the rights it had taught them to demand. The government of the province sent delegation after delegation to Ottawa seeking redress. Undismayed by federal disallowance, it chartered railroad after railroad to bring competition in transportation. Macdonald wearied under this close siege and capitulated in 1888, informing the provincial government that he would no longer disallow their charters.[30] A road was constructed to the American boundary, and the hated monopoly expired. As Macdonald had feared, the Northern Pacific soon had control of this line, but the Canadian Pacific was so well entrenched that it survived the assaults of its rival.

Though the Farmers' Union won its posthumous victory, its annexationist wing had suffered utter defeat. This is not difficult to understand. Few in the United States were interested in it, and so the movement received almost no support from outside. It had little strength of its own, and failing to take root, it quickly withered. The annexationists in Manitoba, being a small minority, could succeed only by exploiting anger and desperation. The willingness of the Dominion to grant concessions and the conviction that the transportation monopoly could be ended when the Canadian Pacific was completed

[30] Macdonald to Thomas Greenway, March 30, 1886, Macdonald Papers, Macdonald Letter Books, XXIV. The Canadian Pacific was compensated for its loss of the monopoly privilege. Governor-Generals' Correspondence and Files, 191, vol. I, 1884-1888 (Public Archives of Canada, Ottawa).

appeased Manitobans somewhat. Then, in 1884 and 1885, bumper crops were harvested and drained more anger from the protesting farmers.[31]

The attempts of the annexationists to infiltrate the Farmers' Union and use it as a vehicle to carry their cause was self-defeating. Far from profiting by using it, these jackdaws of treason killed it by their untimely and public shrilling. Their movement was almost hopeless from the start, and they ruined its infinitesimal chances by their blatant actions and words.

While the annexation movement was dying in Manitoba, it was reviving to the east. The prosperity which had smothered the agitation there early in the 1880's was merely a lull in the great depression. By 1884, Canada was again slowly sinking into an economic trough, while the United States climbed the road to recovery.[32] This had the usual effect of making the boundary appear to some Canadians to be the great barrier to their prosperity.

So economic distress, as always, was the primary cause for the return of annexationism in the mid-1880's, but other factors contributed. One was a lively debate over the anomalous political status of Canada. The country was not a colony, nor yet a sovereign state, but an indeterminate something between. The Macdonald ministry seemed to wander haphazardly through a maze of constitutional questions, handling each pragmatically as it arose. This apparent lack of definition distressed many Canadians who knew where they had been and wanted to know where they were and whither bound. Others resented the fact that their government was still subordinate to that of Great Britain, which, they contended, gave little in compensation for their devotion. The present constitution of the Empire was unsatisfactory to many, but how should it be changed?

[31] Macdonald to Aitkins, July 28, 1884, Macdonald Papers, Macdonald Letter Books, XXIII.

[32] *Canada Year Book*, pp. 125-26; Creighton, *Macdonald*, 352-54.

Some found their answer to this question in the Imperial Federation League, which was formed in England in 1884 and attracted Canadian supporters, including Sir Charles Tupper and the perennial premier of Ontario, Oliver Mowat.[33] Spurred by the irrepressible Joseph Chamberlain, the movement proceeded from the realm of pleasant and abstract discussion to action. When the first Colonial Conference was called in 1887, Canadians found themselves facing a fact and a decision. Most of them, including Macdonald, did not like Imperial federation. There were practical difficulties of geography, but beyond that, the proposal represented a retreat toward colonialism. The slowly and arduously constructed edifice of Canadian autonomy might be torn down overnight.

Imperial federation could best be countered by alternative proposals rather than by vague and rootless criticism. Two such alternatives, independence and annexation, became the topics of discussion. A nationwide debate ensued in which the advantages and weaknesses of each was aired. On the lofty plane of disinterested analysis, even the most loyal newspapers presented the arguments for, as well as the objections to, union with the United States. To some degree the venom was drawn from the word "annexation" and it became almost respectable as an article for discussion, if not for action. This emotional change may have strengthened the movement for continental union.

The discussion of Canada's future, and the possibilities of annexation, were also stimulated by a virulent revival of French-English strife beginning in the mid-1880's and rising in a steady crescendo into the following decade. This unfortunate development, which will be treated more fully below, began with the execution of Riel after the suppression of his second rebellion in 1885. Thus Ontario at last gained revenge for Scott at the

[33] A. L. Burt, *Imperial Architects* (Oxford, 1913), 147-95, describes the rise of this movement. See also Denison, *Imperial Unity*, 77-80.

cost of giving French Canada, in its turn, a martyr. A sequence of further events, including the Jesuit Estates Act and the Manitoba schools question, fanned the flame of animosity, exacerbated the friction arising from the Riel execution, and set English against French and Protestant against Catholic. The effects of these misfortunes were greatest in Quebec and raised a new crop of annexationists there. As in the 1860's, the English minority again learned to fear the French majority in the province, and the latter, in turn, were alarmed at what they regarded as the rising intolerance of the English-speaking majority in the Dominion as a whole.[34]

Another, and minor, noneconomic factor helped to promote annexationism in the 1880's. This was the continuing belief, which had emerged in 1849 and again after confederation, that the union of Canada and the United States would bring relief to the mother country. Britain supported Canada in her recurrent crises with the United States, thereby exposing herself to the danger of war and embarrassing her in the European transactions which were primary to her interests. Moreover, the necessity of defending Canada divided and weakened the Royal Navy and loaded the British taxpayer with a thankless burden. If annexation occurred, the principal cause of friction between the United States and Great Britain would disappear, to the relief of the Imperial government. Thus devotion to the mother country produced disloyalty to the empire in the small group which advanced this rarefied theory.[35]

The annexationists also shared with many of their fellow Canadians the belief that, like it or not, Canada was irretrievably destined to enter the United States. This sense of the inevitability of a natural process was widely held and frequently expressed on both sides of the boundary. Those who believed

[34] Toronto *Daily Mail,* undated, cited in *Senate Reports,* 51 Cong., 1 sess., no. 1530, pp. 1054-55.

[35] Detroit *Evening News,* August 26, 1887.

it were not always annexationists; in Canada they usually were not, and their conviction was as bitter as it was sincere. As the bonds of the Empire slackened and Canada became less British, they felt she would necessarily become more American. This tendency would reinforce the increasing economic dependence on the United States to pull Canada slowly, gently, and surely into the Republic. In short, these people believed that between British culture, economy, and nationality on the one side and American culture, economy, and nationality on the other, there was no room for a distinctive Canadian culture, economy, and nationality, connected with both, partaking of both, but fully possessed by neither. Such a concept, believed even by one who detested its conclusions, was dangerous, for it gnawed at Canadian resistance to absorption.

It should be added that occasionally, and unwittingly, the Liberal Party was an aid and comfort to the Canadian annexationists. Thrice since its victory in 1873 this party had assaulted the Conservatives in general elections and thrice had been hurled back, defeated, bruised, and bewildered. Liberal leaders, the dour Mackenzie and the brilliant but sometimes indecisive Edward Blake, were no match for the astute tactician Macdonald. Moreover, the Liberals had cultivated the natural disadvantages of an opposition party. They sank into a petulant negativism, croaking opposition to ministerial policies but almost sterile of constructive alternatives. And since they were criticizing the policy of nationalism, their opposition carried a faint—and unintended—flavor of disloyalty. They badly needed an issue, and by the mid-1880's they were almost frantic in searching for one. Desperation blunted discretion until many of them urged causes which squinted at political union, and a few finally came openly to accept annexation as their best possibility for an issue.

The sum of the following, then, produced the annexationism of the 1880's and early 1890's: despair at the economic distress in Canada and at the apparent failure of the National Policy, which had faded from bright hope to dreary burden; the revival of vicious English-French strife; the belief that annexation would benefit and not injure the mother country; the unconscious, or conscious, Liberal tendency to support measures which marched obliquely toward political union; and the melancholy conviction on the part of many that annexation was as inevitable as the climax of a Greek tragedy, twist, squirm, and resist as one might to escape the inexorable conclusion.

The movement produced by these forces entered where its predecessor had made its exit. Toward the end of the 1860's, as already noted, the annexationists had tried the efficacy of indirection and disguse, and had infiltrated the independence agitation, incidentally communicating an infection which killed it. Now, in the 1880's, they continued this strategy from the outset. Though they had no national and empowered leaders to make common plans for common action, they recognized and acted upon common assumptions. Individuals, who often made no skulking attempt to conceal their own beliefs, knew that a bold group appeal for their cause was useless. It was more practical to enter a popular movement which had no obvious taint and ride with it into power. From this advantageous situation, they could push Canada toward their real goal. If the agitation which served as their carrier also moved, innocently and obliquely, toward union with the United States, so much the better.

The movement for commercial union fulfilled these criteria. Though it blew up in mid-1887 with the speed, noise, and impact of a summer tornado, the idea was not new. It had been proposed in 1859 during the Reciprocity Treaty, but rejected as being inconsistent with the British connection.[36] The success of the German Zollverein revived the proposal, and desultory suggestions were made through the 1870's and in 1880 that Canada

[36] Charles C. Tansill, *Canadian-American Relations, 1875-1911* (New Haven, 1943), 374-75.

and the United States should apply in North America the plan which had succeeded so well in Europe.[37] These proposals aroused little interest and no support then. Why did the plan which met indifference in the previous decade threaten to rush Canada into an enthusiastic embrace in 1887? First, because the economic condition had deteriorated until it seemed to demand heroic remedies. Secondly, because the commercial union movement of 1887 had a well-organized and lavishly financed campaign which skillfully played upon the fears and frustrations of a wide audience.

The apparent leader of the movement was S. J. Ritchie, an Ohio capitalist who had mining properties about Sudbury and was president of the Central Ontario Railway.[38] In 1886 he besieged Canadian and American public men with his proposal and met a favorable response from Senator John Sherman and Representative Benjamin Butterworth, both also from Ohio.[39] In the same year the latter introduced a bill providing for the full admission of Canadian produce if the Dominion extended a like concession to American goods.[40] This motion did not come to a vote, but it did stir hope in Canada that the United States might be ready to grant trade concessions again. Other factors strengthened this expectation. The Democrats, traditional champions of a lower tariff, were in power in Washington, and President Grover Cleveland was taking his party's platform seriously. American denunciation of the fisheries agreement of the Treaty of Washington had restored to Canada's hand the trump card she had lost in 1871. She could exclude American

[37] Toronto *Bystander*, January, August, 1880; Toronto *Globe*, May 16, 21, June 8, 29, July 2, 1880.

[38] Tansill, *Canadian-American Relations*, 382-83.

[39] S. J. Ritchie to Macdonald, December 9, 1886, Macdonald Papers, Commercial Union, 1886-1887.

[40] Ritchie to Sherman, January 27, 1887, John Sherman Papers (Library of Congress, Washington).

fishermen from her territorial waters until the United States would purchase their readmission by commercial concessions. That time might be approaching. In the spring of 1887, Thomas F. Bayard, American secretary of state, invited either Macdonald or Tupper to discuss outstanding questions between the two countries. Tupper journeyed to Washington and reached an agreement to constitute another Joint High Commission for negotiating the disputes between the countries.[41]

Macdonald watched the commercial union movement and these overtures with mingled apprehension and hope. He knew the allure which the prospect of closer trade relations with the United States had for his people, tormented by depression and grasping for palliatives. Nor was he himself averse to a carefully contrived and bounded reciprocity treaty, confined largely to raw products.[42] But commercial union would never do. It would crash head on into the National Policy, kill the tender Canadian industries, and probably carry the Dominion into annexation. Clearly, he would have to pick his way carefully through this thicket of desire and danger to emerge with a reciprocity agreement which would satisfy his people without endangering his country. Or perhaps he should employ the tactics which had richly earned him the sobriquet of "Old Tomorrow"—to procrastinate, hoping that commercial union, like many another sudden storm, would soon blow itself out.[43]

Early in 1887 the latter alternative did not appear likely, for the commercial union movement seemed to be accumulating irresistible strength. As noted, it was promoted by able and purposeful men. The real leader emerged in the person of

[41] Creighton, *Macdonald*, 477, 479-80.

[42] Tansill, Canadian-American Relations, 385. He strongly favored a revival of the treaty of 1854. New York *Times*, June 4, 1887.

[43] He later stated that this had been his policy from the outset. Macdonald to Tupper, January 15, 1888, Macdonald Papers, Commercial Union, 1886-1887.

Erastus Wiman, a Canadian capitalist and citizen living in New York.[44] His lieutenants in the United States included Ritchie and Butterworth, and the Canadian leaders were Goldwin Smith, an English intellectual with an American background; Harry W. Darling, president of the Toronto Board of Trade; and Edward Farrer, perhaps the ablest journalist in Canada and an editor of the *Daily Mail*, the authoritative voice of Conservatism in Toronto. All except Farrer were men of wealth who dipped freely into ample resources to promote their cause.

The commercial union they proposed was modeled on the German Zollverein, whose name was often applied to it. Canada and the United States would have mutual free trade, behind the shelter of a common tariff to the outside world, and common internal taxes. The proceeds from the tariff and taxes would be divided between them in proportion to their respective populations.[45] The plan was practical; if it had worked with more than thirty German states and brought them prosperity, would it not repeat its success between two North American states?

During the spring and summer of 1887, speakers and literature advocating commercial union appeared throughout Canada, particularly in Ontario, where Wiman, Butterworth, Ritchie, and Goldwin Smith spoke to large and enthusiastic crowds. When many Liberal, and a few Conservative, newspapers embraced the cause, it received the publicity necessary to its growth. Both speakers and press used timely and persuasive arguments. Commercial union would increase Canada's lagging exports by opening wide the enormous markets of the United States; conversely, the free entry of cheaper and better American manufactures would decrease the cost of living.[46] Ontario farmers

[44] Tansill, *Canadian-American Relations*, 391-92.

[45] Goldwin Smith (ed.), *Handbook of Commercial Union* (Toronto, 1888). This pamphlet gives a complete description of the proposed organization.

[46] Wiman to Macdonald, July 28, 1887, Macdonald Papers, Commercial Union, 1886-1887.

gladly gave ear to a proposal to increase their dollars in number and in purchasing power. But commercial union promised something for everyone, even the manufacturer and his factory worker. The former would benefit from the enlargement of his market; the latter, from the increased demand for labor resulting from the erection of American-owned branch factories hard by the raw materials of the Dominion. Such plants would entice new capital and settlers to push up the demand for, and the value of, Canadian land.[47] The fallacies in these arguments were not apparent to people too eager for relief from the depression to be critically analytical. The movement swept through rural Ontario with the speed and irresistibility of a prairie fire. Forty farmers' institutes endorsed it within a few months, and some Liberal leaders of note succumbed easily and thought they had found here that dynamic issue which their party had needed so badly and so long.[48] It seemed in that summer and fall that Canada would soon be stampeded into economic amalgamation with the United States.

But Macdonald was not stampeded. Though the force and velocity of the movement gave him concern, he remained quiet. He could not support a project which would give the death sentence to his own central policy, but neither would he permit his party to attack it officially, lest he drive the Liberals to adopt it officially. This would set commercial union as part of the backdrop of Canadian politics rather than, as he hoped, a prop suddenly thrust on the stage, to vanish when the scene changed. Instead, he would allow the movement "to blaze, crackle and go

[47] Toronto *Globe*, May 24, July 23, September 10, 1887. Statistics of real estate transactions indicated that comparable lands were worth a third to a half more in the United States than in Canada.

[48] Sir Richard Cartwright, the party's financial expert, was the principal Liberal convert. Tansill, *Canadian-American Relations*, 398-99; A. Roberts to Department of State, June 27, 1887, Consular Despatches, Hamilton, VI, 66; W. Phelan to Department of State, November 16, 1887, Consular Despatches, Halifax, VI, 20.

out with a stink without giving it undue importance."[49] He anticipated that the warm enthusiasm of the Canadian people would cool when the defects and dangers of the plan showed through its temptations.

Macdonald would not lead the opposition to commercial union, for there were others who could and would do so. The project, which had charmed the farmers, was repulsive in several aspects to many others, and they attacked the proposed Zollverein from press and platform.[50] Those, for example, who had opposed the institution of a Canadian tariff because it would injure British commerce were outraged at a proposal to discriminate against the mother country in favor of the United States. Their feeling redoubled when Joseph Chamberlain, an authentic voice of the Empire, roundly denounced the plan in a speech at Toronto.[51] Other attacks came from the interests which Macdonald had fathered with his National Policy. For years he had fought for them; now they fought for him. Most Canadian industrialists carried on a merciless war against a proposal which would denude them of necessary protection in their home, and often only, market against the invasion of mass-producing and lower-cost American competitors.[52] The Canadian Pacific Railroad natur-

[49] Macdonald to Tupper, January 15, 1888, Macdonald Papers, Commercial Union, 1886-1887. Macdonald was cautious in his reactions. In an interview, he stated his opposition to commercial union but contrived to create the impression that its greatest enemy was the American government. New York *Times*, June 4, 1887.

[50] Denison, *Imperial Unity*, 85-94, describes the campaign against commercial union, which was joined by nearly all the Conservative and some Liberal papers.

[51] Tansill, *Canadian-American Relations*, 403-404.

[52] John Maclean to Macdonald, January 27, 1887, Macdonald Papers, Commercial Union, 1886-1887. Enclosed is a copy of the Toronto *Canadian Manufacturer and Industrial World*, April 15, 1887. The New York *Times* undertook a survey of Canadian opinion on the issue and discovered that the manufacturers, jobbers, and bankers were largely opposed to it, though there were some exceptions. New York *Times*, May 30, June 1, 13, 14, 1887.

ally fought a policy which would tempt American railroad barons such as James J. Hill to thrust branch lines north of the boundary and redirect the growing east-west trade of the national economy back into the old north-south channels of the continental economy.

Canadian supporters of commercial union had expected this opposition, but they were surprised and disheartened by the chilly reception which their plan encountered in the United States. Bayard's cordial invitation to negotiate seemed to foretell an American welcome for Zollverein, but events belied the hope. Bayard shortly informed the new Joint High Commission that the United States would negotiate on disputed points related to the fisheries, but not on more liberal trade policies.[53] The contrast between his warm proposal to parley and the niggardly haggling which ensued probably traced to his fear of Congress. The resistance of its protectionist bloc to any concessions on tariff was strengthened by American ill will against Canada arising from friction over the fisheries and the seizure of American ships. With an election looming, Bayard recognized that it was hopeless, and politically dangerous, to submit a general and fair treaty with Canada to the Senate.[54]

The soundness of his judgment was soon made clear by the bootless efforts of a few proponents of closer relations with Canada. When Congress convened, Wiman's allies set to work. In February, 1888, Butterworth introduced a motion for complete reciprocity with Canada, but it vanished in the Committee on Ways and Means.[55] The following month, Robert R. Hitt,

[53] Creighton, *Macdonald*, 490-91; Tansill, *Canadian-American Relations*, 402-403. Bayard told the commission privately that commercial union and unrestricted reciprocity were dead so far as the United States was concerned.

[54] Even the narrow Chamberlain-Bayard fisheries agreement was defeated in the Senate on August 21, 1888, by a vote of 27 to 30. Allan Nevins, *Grover Cleveland: A Study in Courage* (New York, 1933), 406-10, 412; Tansill, *Canadian-American Relations*, 60-86.

[55] *Congressional Record*, 50 Cong., 1 sess., 984.

Republican of Illinois and chairman of the House Committee on Foreign Affairs, submitted a resolution endorsing commercial union. Though his committee reported it out with a favorable recommendation, it never achieved the dignity of either a debate or a vote.[56] In fact, the real temper of Congress had been displayed the previous year by an act authorizing President Cleveland to exclude Canadian trade from the United States if Canada persisted in unfriendly treatment of American fishermen. This retaliatory act showed that Congress was ready to club Canada, not to woo her. Although Cleveland and his successors made no attempt to brandish the weapon, its existence chilled the ardor of Canadian advocates of commercial union.[57] Why should they labor to convert their fellow citizens to the cause if the United States would reject it out of hand?

The rapid decline and fall of the commercial union agitation came from the hostility of vested interests in the Dominion, from the rancorous attitude of the United States, and from a growing Canadian consciousness of its political dangers. Increasingly, commercial union loomed as a stalking horse for annexation. How could Canada keep its political independence after it had thrown away its economic independence? By a threat to terminate the Zollverein, the Republic could force the Dominion into political union; even if the United States refrained from cracking this whip, tightening economic ties would slowly draw the two countries together.[58] This is what the earlier Zollverein had done to the states of Germany. Many of the supporters of

[56] *House Reports,* 50 Cong., 1 sess., no. 1183.

[57] The act was intended as a lever to pry concessions from Canada. It was sectional in character and Cleveland disliked it, though he had signed it. Nevins, *Grover Cleveland,* 410-13; Tansill, *Canadian-American Relations,* 390.

[58] New York *Herald,* January 19, 1887; Governor General Henry Petty Fitzmaurice, Marquis of Lansdowne to Sir Robert Holland, October 31, 1887, Macdonald Papers, Commercial Union, 1886-1887.

commercial union recognized this danger, but their desperation made them willing to run the risks to gain the benefits.[59] If some Canadians were reckless of the hazards of annexation, others grew to desire it as the certain and permanent way of gaining the benefits of commercial union. As one of them declared, "Why make two bites of the cherry?"[60]

This attitude, the obvious fact that commercial union and political union were two points on a common continuum, and the support of Zollverein by known annexationists brought the movement into disrepute and armed its opponents. Their attacks increasingly were concentrated upon the issue of loyalty and with increasing effect.[61] Supporters of the movement shrank back from their earlier enthusiastic commitments. As the movement lost its dash and momentum, its heartened opponents redoubled their efforts.[62] In vain the promoters of commercial union turned from celebrating the virtues of their proposal to arguing that it would prevent rather than promote annexation. Their shift from the offensive to the defensive was the subtle harbinger of failure.

By the winter of 1887-1888 the movement was deflating as rapidly as it had distended earlier in the year.[63] This trend brought a final and mortal defeat to commercial union. The Liberals, consistent advocates of closer trade relations with the United States, had flirted with commercial union at first, hoping that it was their long-sought winning issue. When Sir Richard Cartwright, John Charlton, and other prominent members openly endorsed it, it appeared to be on the road to early

[59] Statement by John Charlton, Ontario Liberal. *Canadian Commons Debates, 1889*, p. 492.

[60] Edward Farrer to Erastus Wiman, April 22, 1889, printed in Toronto *Empire*, February 24, 1891.

[61] New York *Times*, May 28, June 4, 5, 1887.

[62] Creighton, *Macdonald*, 494-95.

[63] Creighton, *Macdonald*, 488-89, 494-95.

adoption as the official policy of the party.[64] But Wilfred Laurier, who had succeeded Edward Blake as the Liberal leader, was a protectionist at heart. He would not spurn a winning issue, but he doubted that Zollverein was that issue and refused to be hustled into giving it the cachet of his approval. Instead, he consulted the Liberal members of the federal Parliament.[65] They were divided in their opinions, but most of them urged caution because the dubious associations of the movement were bringing it into ill repute.[66] Since this coincided with his own inclination, Laurier kept silent on the issue, and the Liberals who had been supporting it slowly drifted away. The failure to secure endorsement completed the defeat of commercial union; by May, 1888, the movement was impotent in the Dominion. As Macdonald had hoped, Zollverein was a passing fancy, quick to arise and quick to fall.

Commercial union was killed by many enemies, and of these the greatest was the loyalty issue. The cry of disloyalty was an abused cliche of Canadian politics in the same manner as the "bloody shirt" and "twisting the lion's tail" were often the resort of the American politician who suspected that defeat lurked in his path. Its validity in any given case was, therefore, suspect. Was the commercial union movement an authentic threat to Canada's separate existence or, in Lord Elgin's philosophy, would closer trade relations with the United States have strengthened the political resistance of the Dominion? The

[64] Tansill, *Canadian-American Relations,* 398-99; New York *Times,* July 30, October 15, 1887.

[65] Form letter from Laurier to Liberal members of Parliament, July 11, 1887, Sir Wilfred Laurier Papers, D, 1887 (Public Archives of Canada, Ottawa).

[66] There were a number of letters opposing commercial union. The most interesting of these were A. Fisher to Laurier, August 11, 1887, and J. Edgar to Laurier, August 18, 1887. The only two strongly in favor of the proposal were Sir Richard Cartwright to Laurier, July 8, 1887, and John Charlton to Laurier, December 17, 1887. Laurier Papers, C, 1887.

question cannot be answered certainly, since Zollverein remained a proposal, not a policy. But available evidence testified that it contained the seeds of political union. These tendencies arose in part from the character of commercial union. Inevitably it would cut down part of the barrier between Canada and the United States and draw them closer commercially; the line which divides the political from the economic is thin and wavering. It would certainly blight the nascent economic nationalism, planted so carefully and nurtured so vigilantly by Macdonald.

These tendencies were in the nature of the thing; beyond them was the intent of man. There is no doubt that some, both Canadian and American, would use commercial union as a foot-in-the-door for annexation. Though the advocates of political union were fairly numerous in Canada in 1887, they were still a minority and the word "annexationist" remained a term of opprobrium. A man who admitted his desire for continental union might pay dearly for his candor.[67] Many who were annexationists at heart would never join an organization publicly dedicated to that proposition. Moreover, such an organization would be self-defeating by presenting an open and fair target for the loyal. Frontal assault would be fatal. The annexationists preferred to use sapping operations, hoping that by concealing their real objectives, they could gain help from unsuspecting allies. The commercial union movement offered ideal cover for this work. By infiltrating this agitation, the advocates of political union exploited the strength of the loyal majority. If Wiman's campaign succeeded, his annexationist followers would share power in Ottawa with the opportunity to hasten the amalgamation of the two countries. Of course, not all advocates of commercial union were annexationists, but nearly all annexationists must have been advocates of commercial union. They

[67] Denison, *Imperial Unity*, 123; P. Carroll to Department of State, May 6, 1880, Consular Despatches, Port Stanley and St. Thomas, I.

zealously supported that movement, trying to conceal their real purpose from their associates.[68]

Thus the wolves donned sheep's clothing and fared forth with innocent mien to labor for commercial union. Their imposture did not deceive many for long; incautious movements and speech frequently exposed the fangs under the innocuous disguise. And some, in their boldness, made little pretense of their belief and intent. It became apparent that there were advocates of political union in most of the towns and counties east of Lake Superior and in some to the west. It would be important to assay the strength and distribution of the movement at this point.

Ontario was the hive of annexationism in 1887 and the years following. The advocates of political union were quite numerous there in such commercial cities as Toronto, and in the railroad towns of the southern and central sections of the peninsula, including Woodstock, London, and Brantford.[69] Here prosperity varied with the fortunes of the roads which served them. Annexation would divert American traffic to Canadian railroads to shorten the long haul from the west by routing traffic through southern Ontario to Buffalo.[70] Cities which were the junctions of lines running through Canada and those from the United States saw additional advantages in annexation, which would enhance the value of their strategic locations. Hamilton was an example. A Canadian observer reported that a fair—and secret—

[68] This plan of action was later revealed in a letter from Edward Farrer to Robert Hitt, April 22, 1889, Macdonald Papers, General Elections, IV, 1891. Wiman also admitted that this campaign was intended to lead to annexation. Denison, *Imperial Unity*, 102-103. See also Sam Hughes to Macdonald, May 25, 1887, Macdonald Papers, Commercial Union, 1886-1887.

[69] Toronto *Globe*, March 9, 1887.

[70] American traffic generally avoided this shorter route because of the complicated bonding regulations. It is significant that some officials of the Grand Trunk Railroad, which operated the short line, were annexationists. Macdonald Papers, General Elections, IV, 1891.

ballot there would return a majority for annexation. This city was also a rapidly developing industrial center whose manufacturers, unlike most of their Canadian colleagues, feared American competition less than they desired access to the American market.[71]

As in the 1860's, the movement was strong in the corners of the Ontario peninsula adjacent to the international boundary. There the vaulting tariff excluded producers from the American markets, where prices, after 1885, were generally higher than in Canada.[72] The southwest section of the peninsula was a notable hotbed of annexationism.[73] This area was naturally tributary to Detroit, but the tariff forced it to seek the Toronto market, over two hundred miles distant and governed by lower prices. The frustration of being within sight but beyond reach of a tempting market overtested the loyalty of many. Their lamentations were loud and prolonged, and their desire to join the United States became an open political issue, an exceptional circumstance even at the height of the annexation movement.

The Niagara counties in the southeastern corner offered a parallel situation. Here Buffalo was the same magnet that Detroit was to the southwest, and the American tariff an equal frustration. The economic distress in Canada and the higher prices for real estate just across the river increased the attractions of political union.[74] In one county, real estate was mortgaged to 60 percent of its assessed value. The county's inhabitants paid, in Dominion and local taxes, interest on mortgages, and duties

[71] New York *Times,* May 31, 1887; Detroit *Evening News,* July 18, August 1, 1887; Chicago *Tribune,* August 19, 1887.

[72] From a comparison of market reports in Toronto *Globe,* Detroit *Evening News,* and Chicago *Tribune* after 1885.

[73] Dr. J. D. O'Brien to Laurier, August 2, 1887, Laurier Papers, D, 1887.

[74] New York *Times,* May 31, 1887; Detroit *Evening News,* July 25, 28, August 3, 1887. Real estate values were 25 to 75 percent higher in the United States than in Canada for comparable properties.

on goods imported from the United States, a total of $678,000 a year, or $28 per capita "a burden utterly beyond the capacity of our people to bear." The annexationist author of this remark estimated that union with the United States would save the people of his county $300,000 a year.[75]

Annexationism was thus dangerously prevalent in Ontario in the 1880's in rural and urban regions, in the east and in the west. Here was its citadel, but it had outposts elsewhere. The province of Quebec contained more annexationists than ever before, partly because of the depression. The loyalty of many commercial men in Montreal and Quebec was as unstable as it had been under earlier stress, and for the same reasons.[76] Railroad centers and junctions, such as Sherbrooke, were eager for the energizing effects which political union would have for their trade. Of the rural areas, the Eastern Townships were again receptive to the lure of annexation. Like the corners of Ontario, they were near American markets, and many of their American-born inhabitants cherished a primary allegiance to their land of birth rather than to their land of adoption.

The annexationists described above were confined almost entirely to those English-speaking groups which had formerly been susceptible to the lure of American trade and markets. But now, for the first time, political union began to make significant penetration into the hitherto impermeable French majority. Not materialism but conflict with the English fissured this wall of loyalty. Nationalist tensions and antipathies broke through the surface of polite suppression when a series of events sent emotions up in a rapid crescendo. These episodes began with a smallpox epidemic which broke out in Montreal and its environs late in the summer of 1885. Some of the French

[75] Toronto *Mail,* undated, quoted in New York *Times,* November 8, 1886.

[76] *Senate Documents,* 51 Cong., 1 sess., no. 1530, pp. 454, 477; New York *Times,* December 16, 1888.

combated the disease with piety rather than medical precautions.[77] But piety did not produce enough antibodies, and the epidemic spread, taking a number of lives. The distress in the city, arising from coincident physical and financial hardship, shortened tempers and judgment. The English condemned the French as a superstitious and ignorant folk whose careless attitude endangered the lives of all. They were answered in kind and with heat. Emotions flared up, and the minority, threatened with disease and burdened by depression, began to look south for relief from an increasingly difficult situation.

The two peoples were wound up to high tension when a second episode made its unwelcome intrusion—the execution of Louis Riel. This métis leader had, during the Red River rebellion, caused the death of Thomas Scott, Orangeman of Ontario. Protestants of that province called the deed murder, and were sworn to vengeance. Riel had prudently sought refuge in exile, a move which smacked of persecution and made him a hero to the métis of the West and a symbol of French nationalité in the entire Dominion.

In 1885, Riel led his second rebellion against the Canadian government, which had again allowed grievances to develop among the halfbreeds, this time on the Saskatchewan River. The rebellion failed, and the unlucky Riel was captured and condemned to death for treason, despite evidence of megalomania. Though they were certain that his sentence would be commuted, the French growled at its injustice. Ontario, on the other hand, cried out for his blood to atone for that of Scott.[78] Between this controversy and the still warm reaction to the smallpox scare, the two peoples were almost ready to fight when the day appointed for the execution of Riel arrived. Up to the very moment the trap was sprung, that unfortunate man and

[77] New York *Sun*, September 27, 1885.

[78] The reaction of the two provinces is carefully traced in Lamb, *Thunder in the North*, 201-22, 239-72.

nearly all of French Canada expected Macdonald to reprieve him.

The Prime Minister was in the unhappy position of having to choose between politically dangerous alternatives. Commutation might cost him Ontario, and execution would endanger his grip on Quebec. Either decision would damage the growing, but still tender, nationalism. Macdonald made his choice, and Riel died. Historians still cannot agree whether this was a political decision based on Macdonald's hope that the friendly Roman Catholic hierarchy of Quebec could hold their flock in the Conservative fold, or whether he considered that Riel was mentally responsible and must die as an example to all potential rebels and traitors.[79]

There was no uncertainty on two points: Riel had been hanged, and Quebec was on fire. Meetings of violent protest were held throughout that province.[80] The French bitterly cursed the Protestants of Ontario who had hounded Riel to his inglorious death and gloried in doing it, and the Conservative government which had supinely yielded to the blood lust of the Orangemen. The hanging of the métis leader gave a new force and direction to the nationalité of many of the French. They had been opposed to annexation because, they believed, Canada guaranteed the preservation of their way of life, as the United States would not do. This conviction was now badly shaken. Many felt they could no longer expect justice from the English Canadians who would use their votes and power to trample the rights of the minority. The execution of Riel had opened a breach in the wall of French loyalty to the Dominion.[81]

[79] The two points of view reappear in recent books. Lamb, *Thunder in the North*, 229-39, asserts that the execution was primarily political; Creighton, *Macdonald*, 432, 434-37, leans to the other interpretation.

[80] Quebec's reaction is best described in Lamb, *Thunder in the North*, 301-308, 313-14.

[81] Toronto *Globe*, November 18, 1885.

Thus annexationism began to make inroads in Quebec as well as in Ontario in 1887. In the vicious turmoil of rival peoples, the local English minority feared the vengeance of the local French majority just as the latter were alarmed at the rising intolerance among the English-speaking majority in the Dominion as a whole.[82] Each group was most concerned to gain security for its own way of life, and annexation seemed to some the best escape from an increasingly dangerous situation.

Though there were certainly many more annexationists among the French than there had been in 1849-1850 and after confederation, the desire to join the United States was by no means universal among that people in 1887. It was still the desperate reaction of an alarmed minority afflicted with nightmares of the intentions of the English Protestant majority. They formed the Club National to elect members to Parliament who would fight to the last ditch for French rights. This organization included some who despaired of a battle already lost in Canada; only radical change could preserve nationalité. Though the presence of such opinion was apparent in 1887, it had not been spoken often and loudly. Its voice would soon ring out more frequently and stridently as the crisis deepened.

If Quebec and Ontario were rather thickly dotted with annexationists in 1887, the other provinces seem to have had relatively few of them. Manitoba and the western territories, still in an ugly humor over the railroad and other unresolved grievances, had some political unionists who dared to speak their thoughts.[83] But the bitter experiences of the Riel rebellion and the untimely demise of the Farmers' Union had dampened disloyal tendencies there.

[82] Statement from Toronto *Daily Mail,* undated, in *Senate Reports,* 51 Cong., 1 sess., no. 1530, pp. 1054-55.

[83] New York *Times,* August 24, 30, 1887, February 13, 1888; Charles Mair to George Denison, November 6, 1888, George Denison Papers, IV, 1663 (Public Archives of Canada, Ottawa).

The Maritime Provinces were also surprisingly indifferent to annexationism in view of their outspoken earlier support of it. There were advocates of political union in the St. Croix and St. John valleys in New Brunswick, mostly lumbermen who had come from the United States, and in the commercial classes of St. John, once a bustling city now complacently dying on its feet. The local leader was said to be the influential John Ellis, editor of the St. John *Globe* and a member of the federal Parliament.[84]

In Nova Scotia, only Pictou County harbored any notable number of annexationists. Here the coal operators and miners still looked longingly at the American markets because cheaper British and German fuels precluded exportation to Europe and Ontario sought its supplies in Pennsylvania. The representative of this county in the provincial assembly, John McColl, boldly advocated annexation from the outset of the session of 1887. In April he presented a resolution calling for economy and reform of the local government. If this could not be obtained, there should be a popular referendum on the question of "a repeal of the union . . . as a first step to asking the Government of the United States to admit us as a State of the Union, which is no doubt our ultimate commercial destination."[85] The resolution never came to a vote. Other evidence also demonstrates the indifference of the province to the proposition. An American magazine polled its readers in Nova Scotia on the question of annexation; it reported that 620 were opposed to the proposition and only 65 favored it.[86]

Such an attitude is surprising in an area smitten by depression

[84] New York *Times*, August 8, 1887, December 16, 1888.

[85] Halifax *Morning Chronicle*, April 22, 28, 1887; New York *Times*, April 22, 1887.

[86] Toronto *Globe*, July 18, 1884; Halifax *Morning Chronicle*, January 4, September 15, 1887; Springfield (Massachusetts) *Farm and Home*, undated, quoted in Halifax *Morning Chronicle*, August 17, 1887.

and notoriously disloyal in a similar situation two decades earlier, but there was reason for the change. Nova Scotians were diverted from annexationism by a revival of the secession movement about 1880. The new repeal movement acted as a safety valve, enabling the people to vent their feelings against the Dominion short of ultimate proposals. W. S. Fielding, the Liberal premier of the province and leader of the new antis, kept a tighter grip on his followers than Howe had done. Moreover, the movement in the 1880's never reached the stage of an appeal to the Imperial government for secession.[87] It was the rejection of such petitions which had turned the earlier antis down the path to annexationism.

Geographically, the agitation of the 1880's was less dispersed than its immediate predecessor. Inhabitants of the peripheral provinces—the Maritimes and British Columbia—seem to have lost interest in annexation, leaving central Canada as the citadel of disloyalty. In terms of economic classes, it is more difficult to delimit the agitation because the division on political union cut across occupational groups. Only the commercial class seems, almost everywhere, to have harbored some annexationists. This is readily understandable, for this class would profit most, and most immediately, from the increased trade which would follow political union. On the other hand, it was equally natural for merchants involved in European trade to oppose annexation, for an increase in commerce with the United States might be at their expense.

The farmers were badly divided on the question. Those who lived near the border often favored it, while those who lived in interior districts usually did not. Annexation also found favor with some producers of raw and semifinished goods whose access to European markets was obstructed by high freight rates

[87] Phelan to Department of State, March 6, 1887, Consular Despatches, Halifax, XV, 225; Yarmouth *Herald*, April 25, 1887.

and cheap competition. They included the coal operators of Nova Scotia and lumbermen and quarriers of several provinces. Even Canadian industrialists were divided, though they were all supposedly inflexibly opposed to annexation which would expose them to the fatal competition of mass-producing and lower-cost American industry. The minority of Canadian manufacturers who favored joining the United States were those who had little to fear from mass production because they relied on skilled craftsmanship or nearness to raw materials for their protection rather than upon a tariff. Expansion and higher prices would reward their entry into the American market. Examples of such industrialists were those producing stoves, locomotives, steam engines, some types of hardware, and products of turned wood.[88]

As always, the economic magnet was the primal attraction drawing Canadians toward the United States. Longing for higher prices, wider markets, and increased trade explain the origin and strength of the movement in the 1880's. The expansion of American industry, the increase of its trade, and the general hustle and bustle of economic life in the United States seemed in sharp contrast to stagnation in Canada.[89] Many who had no more specific reason felt that annexation would bring American energy and capital to stir up Canadian lethargy.

The movement in Canada had little counterpart in the United States. Americans seemed as indifferent to annexation as they had been to commercial union. In January, 1888, Senator Eugene Hale of Maine introduced a bill for the incorporation of Canada into the United States, but it was not reported out

[88] Detroit *Evening News*, August 1, 10, 15, 22, September 26, 1887. This paper sent a reporter through the eastern provinces to investigate the causes and strength of the movement. See also Toronto *Globe*, June 4, 1887.

[89] This general sentiment was voiced in a number of letters printed in the Toronto *Globe*, October, 1888. The traveling reporter of the Detroit *Evening News* found many who voiced like sentiments.

of committee.[90] The debates on Cleveland's proposal for retaliation provoked desultory mentions of annexation, both favorable and unfavorable, but most congressmen did not consider the acquisition of the Dominion a practical question, and the debate soon died of inanition.[91] The plain fact was that few Americans were interested in either economic or political approaches to Canada, and most of those who were felt that the Dominion should make the first moves. The handful who actively promoted annexation—the merchants and railroadmen of the border states and capitalists with large investments in the Dominion—aroused little public interest or favor.

Thus 1887 passed and Canada's status was untouched by the movements for commercial and political union. But could the Dominion continue to resist the mounting economic and political pressures being placed upon her by the circumstances of the times?

[90] *Congressional Record,* 50 Cong., 1 sess., 474.
[91] *Congressional Record,* 50 Cong., 1 sess., 8275, 8439, 8670-71.

CHAPTER SEVEN

The Climax and Collapse of the Movement

The Canadian annexationist at the outset of 1888 had reasons both for hope and for misgiving. On the one hand, the movement was strongest where strength counted, in the central provinces whose weight swung the pendulum of Canadian policy, and the conditions which had created it there persisted. The political unionists had succeeded to some degree in infiltrating the Liberal Party and in pushing it to the verge of endorsing commercial union, the halfway house to their goal. These things were pleasant to contemplate, but there were clouds on the horizon. The Liberals had drawn back from the Zollverein movement at the crucial moment, and it had collapsed. Incautious actions and utterances of known political unionists, by tinging the minds of many Canadians with suspicion toward the movement for closer commercial relations with the United States and toward the Liberal Party, had compromised the strategy of indirect approach to political union.

To succeed, the movement must grow. Though virile in some places, it was weak in the peripheral provinces and in much of Ontario and Quebec. Specifically, the agitation must become strong enough to be the fulcrum of an early Liberal victory. If it did not, it would continue to beat itself futilely and fatally against the stanch and alert loyalty of Macdonald while he remained in power.

Did annexationism grow between 1887 and the general election of 1891? Since North America did not then rejoice in public opinion polls, this cannot be even imprecisely determined.

The evidence suggests that the movement advanced where it was already strong, and at least marked time elsewhere. It is significant that advocates of political union in sections of Ontario increasingly flaunted their views with a contempt for concealment which attests local acceptance. In October, 1888, the Toronto *Globe* opened its columns to expressions of opinion on the future of Canada. Loyalists were shocked when twenty-five of the seventy-five respondents not only endorsed annexation but had the audacity to sign their letters.[1] Characteristically, all but two grounded their opinions on economic desires.

If this result dismayed some, it did not surprise others. One Toronto Liberal informed his leader, "There is a strong, outspoken sentiment on this question [annexation] such as I never heard expressed before." Perhaps he was thinking of the fact that the Young Liberal Club of Toronto had openly debated, and endorsed, political union at one of its meetings.[2]

While loyal Toronto gave appalling evidence of sliding from grace, the western counties continued to be the conspicuous center of annexationist sentiment. Between 1887 and 1891 the movement there grew increasingly blatant. At the local election of 1889 in Windsor, three of the four candidates for mayor, including the victor, were avowed annexationists and together polled 950 of the 1,300 votes cast. One of them was Solomon White, veteran leader of the Conservatives of the western marches. Eight of the twelve city councilors chosen were of the same persuasion. The Windsor *Clarion* replied defiantly to the horrified comments of newspapers elsewhere: "Windsor is

[1] These letters were printed in Toronto *Globe*, October 5, 6, 11, 13, 17, 20, 26, 27, 1888. In addition to the twenty-five who favored annexation, twenty-seven preferred independence, sixteen were satisfied with the *status quo*, six were for imperial fedration, and one "individualist" was undecided.

[2] H. H. Cook to Wilfred Laurier, December 29, 1888, Laurier Papers, Correspondence, 1870-1891, pp. 927-29; Toronto *Daily Mail*, January 28, 1889.

alleged to be filled with . . . annexationists. This is true. . . . The people here have every opportunity of seeing how injuriously the tariff between the United States and Canada affects them. . . . They know that in many lines the prices in Detroit are lower by just the amount of the tariff. They see a city of one quarter of a million on one bank of a river while on the other bank . . . the population is less than ten thousand. These are reasons why Windsor is largely composed of political unionists."[3]

This election inspired the local annexationists to greater efforts. Meetings were held and continental union clubs formed in North Essex and other parts of the area. This work won early rewards. The following year, White was elected by acclamation as mayor of Windsor. When informed that Macdonald was surprised at this result, White replied: "Sir John is perfectly aware of the growing sentiment in favor of annexation in this section of Ontario." A few months later, White was returned to the provincial legislature on an annexationist platform, and by a substantial majority, though the Liberals carried the province as a whole.[4] It was obvious that support of continental union was more a gate than a barrier to a political career in western Ontario.

Disloyal tendencies in Ontario might have attracted more attention if the crescendo of English-French antipathy had not commanded the notice of most Canadians. The storm of anger raised by Riel's execution was scarcely subsiding when the Jesuit Estates Act of 1888 blew it up again. In character and background, this measure was peculiarly offensive to English Protes-

[3] Windsor *Clarion*, undated, quoted in Toronto *Daily Mail*, January 3, 1889. For the Windsor elections, see also Detroit *Evening News*, January 1, 8, 1889; Toronto *Globe*, January 8, 1889; Toronto *Daily Mail*, January 11, 1889.

[4] Interview with White published in Detroit *Evening News*, January 3, 1890. See also Toronto *Daily Mail*, January 10, February 1, 1889, November 13, 1890; New York *Herald*, May 5, 1890.

tants.[5] The Jesuits had received valuable tracts of land from the Crown and other sources during the days of New France. In 1773, Pope Clement XIV had dissolved the order, and upon the death of its last survivor in Canada, the British government had confiscated the estates. They were converted into an endowment for education in Quebec and placed under the control of the provincial government. Later, when Pope Pius VII restored the order in 1814, the Jesuits clamored for the return of their former Canadian properties. The question was complicated by conflicting claims from the Quebec hierarchy and from Laval University.

Political considerations made settlement of the issue expedient. For years the Roman Catholic Church had glowered upon the Rouge-Liberal Party with undisguised detestation, associating the liberalism of North America with that of Europe, which was belligerently anticlerical. After the declaration of papal infallibility in 1870 and the triumph of ultramontanism in the church, the Quebec hierarchy moved eagerly to the kill. The clergy used every pressure to proscribe the Liberals, even to declaring it a sin to vote for them. In time, the Vatican put a gentle hand of restraint on its zealot subordinates in Quebec, but the damage had been done. The Rouge-Liberal Party was reduced to a shattered and embattled remnant, supported by a last-ditch clutch of voters.

Slowly the party pulled itself from the abyss under the careful guidance of its young leader, Wilfred Laurier, who sought to disinfect the virus of radicalism implanted by the Rouge faction. Good fortune aided good tactics in this revival. Heretofore the French had earned the derisive title of *moutons* by their automatic voting for the party of Macdonald. But the execution of Riel shook this supposedly indestructible alliance

[5] The background of this question is given succinctly in Creighton, *Macdonald,* 514-15.

between church and Conservatives to its deepest roots.[6] The Liberals arose to the opportunity and shrewdly prodded the incipient rebellion in Quebec. They were not certain that Laurier had the superlative qualities of successful parliamentary leadership, but they were sure that he was a French Canadian and that his people's vote teetered in the balance. In 1887 they selected him as the national leader of the party to succeed Blake, a supreme compliment to Quebec, which now began to move toward the Liberals in the beginning of a landslide which would soon revolutionize Canadian politics.

The first tremors of this convulsion had already been registered. In the provincial elections of 1886 the Liberals donned a transparent disguise by calling themselves Nationalists. They invoked French pride in a campaign which accused the Conservatives of responsibility for the execution of Riel. The result was a striking success, as the Nationalists-Liberals swept into control of the provincial legislature. The architect of this cunning campaign was Honoré Mercier, a wily pragmatist with a dash of the demagog. Mercier rejoiced in office but realized that his power rested on a shaky foundation. The *moutons* had broken from the control of their clerical shepherds, who still regarded Liberals, by whatever name, with aversion. But these fickle sheep might return to the fold as rapidly as they had deserted it. The clergy too must be converted to clinch the Liberal gains.

The Jesuit Estates Act was Mercier's overture for the gratitude and trust of his church. The lands could not be returned without entangling complications, but cash would be a welcome substitute. This raised the awkward question, cash to whom? The Jesuits claimed it, but so did the formidable hierarchy and scholarly Laval University. It would be a poor political act which

[6] This change is described in detail in Lamb, *Thunder in the North*, 305-16.

made one friend and two enemies. But this problem was not beyond the wit of Mercier, who found a key to unlock the riddle. He would have the pope apportion the money.

So the Liberals offered the church an olive branch in the form of the Jesuit Estates Act which authorized the payment of $400,000 to extinguish the troublesome claims. The settlement was contingent upon ratification by the pope, who would determine how the money should be divided among the claimants. To protect his other flank, Mercier included a grant of $60,000 to compensate Protestants' schools which had shared the revenues of the estates. This was the complete answer and a master political stroke.

The act passed and Quebec quietly accepted this solution of its ancient and thorny problem. But by a natural law of reciprocal action, what pleases Quebec often angers Ontario. In wrath that province called the act infamous. Its opposition had several bases. Ontarians flatly rejected the idea of compensation to any section of the Roman Catholic Church in this matter. Should the new Jesuit order receive property which had belonged to the old simply because of the identity of name? Canada had discarded the policy of government aid to religious institutions at the earlier settlement of the clergy reserves question. Was it wise to reopen that explosive issue by endowing a single church?[7]

A further isue was charged with emotion. A Canadian legislature had invited the papacy to meddle in the internal affairs of the Dominion. Nothing was better calculated to fan the embers of religious antagonisms into flame again. The Orange order furiously demanded that Macdonald disallow this detestable act, and a new and fiercely intolerant organization, the Protestant Rights Association, was established to fight Catholic aggression. Like many other vicious diseases, this one was highly contagious. The English minority in Quebec had first accepted the settle-

[7] Creighton, *Macdonald*, 515.

ment. When their dislike of the French, ever near the surface, was stirred by their Ontario compatriots, they suddenly saw that the act was big with hitherto unsuspected consequences. The legislation was a precedent for Catholic dictation in provincial affairs and a symbol of French domination. If the French ruled Quebec, the pope would rule the French and smother English and Protestant rights.

The passage of the Jesuit Estates Act thus revived the old English nightmare of French domination. Fear fed upon itself and distended. The threat to their way of life, added to the economic depression, which had tried them sorely, unbalanced the judgment of the frightened minority. In Montreal, in Quebec, and in the Eastern Townships, they cried out for annexation. One of their papers, the Quebec *Telegraph,* which posed as the voice of English Quebec, demanded annexation because the American government would expunge the privileges of the Roman Catholic hierarchy; moreover, the change would benefit the province economically.[8]

Incongruously, the Jesuit Estates Act also stirred annexation talk among the French. When the militant Protestants of Ontario pushed beyond protests to demands for the Anglicizing of the French, at the point of the bayonet if necessary, the people thus attacked responded in kind. *La Patrie,* Nationalist organ in Montreal, remarked that "if the fanatics of Ontario continue to persecute us, remember that we can find shelter under the be-starred flag of the United States."[9] The Riel execution and threatened persecution were undermining the faith of French Canada in the efficacy of the British North America Act to protect their rights. Though they realized that they would become politically insignificant in the American

[8] Quebec Telegraph, undated, quoted in Halifax *Morning Chronicle,* September 29, 1890; Detroit *Evening News,* October 25, 1890; *Senate Reports,* 51 Cong., 1 sess., no. 1530, p. 755.

[9] Montreal *Patrie,* June 27, 1889. Montreal *Presse* spoke in the same vein.

population, many of the French felt that their religion, language, and laws would be safer in the more tolerant atmosphere of the Republic. Part of the Nationalists had already identified themselves with annexationism, and loyal leaders and Roman Catholic clergy, who had spent a lifetime combating the movement, were deeply disturbed.[10] The Club National endorsed resolutions for political union and important leaders of the organization openly favored this proposal. Even Mercier was suspect and, as later events would indicate, with some reason.[11] Still another segment of the French, mostly remnants of the anticlerical Rouge, saw the Jesuit Estates Act as further church encroachment on secular ground. They too pronounced for annexation as they had done earlier, hoping that the American government would rein in the wide-ranging Catholic hierarchy if Quebec became part of the United States.[12]

Thus the reactions to the Jesuit Estates Act made Quebec an emotional maelstrom of irrationality which cast the most diverse of malcontents into annexationism. To add the final absurdity to this catalog of paradox, some of the anti-Catholic elements in Ontario also called for union with the United States! In a letter to the Bowmanville *West Durham News,* a writer warned his compatriots that the Roman Catholic Church intended to take over Canada and threatened: "If Confederation is to bring us under Jesuit rule . . . and there are some who are willing to submit to a yoke which has blighted and blasted every country on which it has been imposed, there are others, and it may be a majority, who will say give us annexation and the rule

[10] Toronto *Daily Mail,* June 20, 1889, March 1, 3, 1890; *Senate Reports,* 51 Cong., 1 sess., no. 1530, pp. 1054-55.

[11] W. Kirby to Denison, January 5, 1889, Denison Papers, IV, 1867; New York *Herald,* November 12, 1889; Toronto *Daily Mail,* November 12, 1889; Quebec *Canadien,* undated, quoted in Detroit *Evening News,* January 5, 1890.

[12] *Senate Reports,* 51 Cong., 1 sess., no. 1530, pp. 1054-55; Toronto *Daily Mail,* March 3, 1890.

of the President of the United States rather than the rule of an Italian priest."[13]

The ease with which all groups of angry men shifted into talk of political union does not testify to their sincerity. On the other hand, the situation was ominous and bluster could become fact. Macdonald set about trying to calm the storm. Unfortunately, the zealots of both faiths and provinces were at white heat, and it was obvious that neither would accept as final any adverse decision. The Prime Minister discovered this when he refused to disallow the Jesuit Estates Act lest doing so destroy all hope of accommodation. But his decision goaded the extreme Protestants to take the offensive and carry the question over his head. They introduced a motion calling upon Parliament to overrule Macdonald by favoring the disallowance he had refused. This resolution received only thirteen votes, and the law officers of the Crown closed another gate to the opposition by ruling that the Jesuit Estates Act was constitutional.[14]

When even this double defeat did not halt the extremists, the exasperated Macdonald could remark with justice, "One of those insane crazes has taken possession of the ultra Protestants."[15] But if they were insane, they still had the wit not to try his resolution and that of the House of Commons again. Instead, they devised a flexible strategy of probing, with constant pressure, for a weak point. They shifted their attack to an appeal to the country, their actions to the West, and their issue from the power of the hierarchy to the question of education. Elusive success at last began to smile upon them.

The Manitoba Act of 1870 had provided for the right of separate Catholic and Protestant schools, supported by public funds, and had established French as a legal language. These

[13] Bowmanville *West Durham News*, undated, quoted in Toronto *Daily Mail*, February 19, 1889. Similar letters are found in other Ontario papers of the day, such as those quoted in Toronto *Daily Mail*, February 26, March 2, June 20, 1889.

[14] Creighton, *Macdonald*, 516-17, 520.

[15] Creighton, 518.

provisions were inserted at Riel's insistence and with an eye to the future. They would support French hopes and plans to make Manitoba a second Quebec. But if English and Protestant settlers flooded the West, the Catholics would have built-in defenses against the day when they were a minority. That day had long since come, and the French were heavily outnumbered in the Northwest.

The leader of the Protestant extremists, who bore the unlikely name of Dalton McCarthy, saw that Canadian Catholicism was sensitive and vulnerable in the West. Here he might strike it the blows which Macdonald had warded off in the East. Accordingly, he went to the West in the summer of 1890 and began a strong attack upon the privileges of the minority. They were, he contended, frustrating Canadian nationalism by encouraging French nationalité, and impairing educational opportunities by maintaining two substandard sets of schools in a region which could barely afford one strong system.

These sentiments won a warm welcome. First, the Northwest Territories asked and obtained the repeal of special privileges for the French language. In Manitoba the provincial government persuaded the legislature to do away with the guarantees of language and separate schools.[16] Now it was the turn of the French to call upon Macdonald for disallowance. But having accepted the Jesuit Estates Act, he could hardly cut down the Manitoba school legislation, and he refused to do so. Rebuffed politically, the French appealed to the courts to declare the offensive legislation *ultra vires*.

When the courts validated the school legislation, the frenzy rose to new heights and talk of annexation swelled. The Quebec *Canadien* expressed a typical point of view. The French had been loyal to British rule, it said, not from love or economic advantage but from expectation that the British would honor the constitutional claim, and the right, of the minority to its

[16] Background for Manitoba schools question in Creighton, 529, 543.

religion, language, and schools. Now, it was evident that the English-speaking majority intended to cancel this tacit bargain and to crush the minority. This would rupture the only tie which bound French Canada to the British Empire. Annexation was inevitable if these outrages continued, for having lost their nationalité anyhow, the French might better join the United States to gain the material benefits of such a union.[17] Other Catholics also saw the shadow of impending trouble. Though often at odds with the French, the Irish of Canada were one with them against Protestant intolerance. "One of two things must come—this war of Protestant against Catholic, race against race must soon come to a close or otherwise annexation."[18]

So the staccato beat of incidents, each overlapping its predecessor, shook the stolid loyalty of the French habitant. Laurier, who understood his people well, was clearly worried when he wrote a friend: "The movement for political union which now manifests itself in certain counties is not yet a serious one but might very soon become so, if a prominent man were to place himself at the head of it."[19]

The growth of the annexation movement in Quebec was demonstrated a year later at a meeting held in Montreal to consider the future of the Dominion. Ballots were passed to the 5,000 present, mostly French Canadians, and each was asked to indicate his choice. Of the 2,999 who responded, 364 preferred the existing situation, 29 wanted imperial federation, 1,614 desired independence, and 992 hoped for annexation. This formerly loyal province decidedly could not longer be taken for granted.[20]

[17] Quebec *Canadien,* undated, quoted in New York *Times,* August 2, 1892.

[18] Ottawa *United Canada,* undated, quoted in New York *Times,* August 5, 1892. This was the principal Irish-Canadian organ.

[19] Laurier to W. D. Gregory, October 26, 1891, Laurier Papers, V, 1891, p. 1913.

[20] New York *Times,* November 29, 1892.

The turbulence of Quebec was in sharp contrast to the placid loyalty of the eastern and western provinces. The latter continued to show little interest in annexation, and the movement marked time in the Maritimes, where it remained localized in St. John, New Brunswick, and in the coal regions of Nova Scotia.[21] The American consul at Pictou reported that many people thereabouts were still annexationists. He vainly urged his government to give financial aid to the Liberal Party, some of whose local leaders were favorably disposed to continental union.[22] As an example, Judge J. W. Longley, second to W. S. Fielding among Nova Scotian Liberals, when accused of advocating such a change, replied cryptically: "I have never declared for annexation . . . for the simple reason that I have never been able to reach a conclusion" on the subject.[23]

Despite the growth of the agitation in Quebec and Ontario and the maintenance of its strength elsewhere, annexationists were clearly a minority throughout the Dominion. Individuals were increasingly more outspoken, but the movement as a whole declined to challenge destiny by forming an organization. Despite their failure to ride into power on the coattails of Wiman, the annexationists continued to seek their goal indirectly when another opportunity to do so presented itself. The Liberals had attributed the failure of the commercial union movement to its sinister political implications which had neutralized its undoubted economic appeal. If the former could be discarded and the latter retained, they might have a winning issue. The answer, they thought, was unrestricted reciprocity which would bring free trade with the Republic but avoid the obnoxious aspects of Zollverein—a single tariff and battery of excise taxes for the two countries. The annexationists eagerly,

[21] The New Glasgow *Chronicle*, formerly the *Eastern Chronicle*, advocated annexation as it had done in the postconfederation period.

[22] George Tanner to Department of State, March 24, July 9, 1890, Consular Despatches, Pictou, X.

[23] Yarmouth *Herald*, December 5, 1888.

but quietly, supported this issue, still hoping to smuggle themselves into power under the Liberal cloak. They were certain that complete reciprocity would evolve into complete union, though more slowly than commercial union would have done.

The Liberals unveiled their new policy on March 14, 1888, when Sir Richard Cartwright offered a motion that Canada should seek the largest possible freedom of trade with the United States. Well aware of the popularity of reciprocity, the Conservatives avoided head-on opposition. George E. Foster, soon to become minister of finance, offered an amendment to the effect that the government seek a commercial agreement which would not violate the National Policy. Specifically, this meant free trade in raw materials.

In the ensuing debate the Liberals stressed the contrast between American prosperity and Canadian depression. They anticipated the standard Conservative argument by denying beforehand that reciprocity was disloyal. As in 1854, it would still rather than stimulate annexationism. This disclaimer did not disarm government speakers. Admitting that limited reciprocity might be beneficial, they contended that free trade would dislocate the Canadian economy by destroying its industry and, with it, the National Policy. Since it would increase the already dangerous forces for political union, those who advocated unrestricted reciprocity were little better than traitors. To this the opposition offered the obvious retort that the Conservatives were the real annexationists because they opposed the best remedy for depression and discontent. The divisions on the Cartwright motion and the Foster amendment followed party lines to their foreseeable conclusion. The former was defeated 67 to 124, and the latter carried by the same vote.[24]

[24] Motion, amendment, and debate in *Canadian Commons Debates, 1888*, pp. 144-77, 218, 240-42, 321, 380, 414-15, 646. Four Conservatives, all from Quebec, voted with the Liberals, and two Liberals and one Independent supported the government. J. A. Gemmill, *The Canadian Parliamentary Companion* (Ottawa, 1889), 95-183.

Defeat did not discourage the Liberals, for they had expected no other result. The Cartwright motion was intended to introduce and to publicize a new policy, and it achieved its purpose. It also put the Conservatives on the defensive, and in an awkward posture. To denounce reciprocity was dangerous. In the eyes of Canadians, the legendary golden years of the treaty of 1854 shone more brightly than ever in contrast to the drab conditions of the 1880's. The Conservative contention that some reciprocity was efficacious, but more reciprocity was dangerous, smacked of logical inconsistency. Where, on this continuum, did one draw the precise line which separated good from evil? Such delicate distinctions might not impress the Canadian voter. It appeared that the Liberals had at last uncovered an exit from the unprofitable cul-de-sac of carping negativism in which they had been trapped so long.

Events in the American Congress also encouraged the Liberals. Representative Robert R. Hitt of Illinois introduced a commercial union bill which passed the House after a debate singularly lacking in the usual annexationist effusions. Hitt set this mood by stating at the outset that his bill was entirely economic in purpose and content; few Americans now wanted to acquire any more territory or population. Only two representatives tried to intrude political union into the debate, and the House refused to follow them down this bypath. In the Senate, the Committee on Foreign Relations reported the Hitt bill favorably, but on the floor, Senator Henry W. Blair of New Hampshire objected and the measure never came to a vote.[25]

These events heartened the Liberals. Reciprocity would be an abortive issue in Canada unless American acceptance seemed possible. The passage of the Hitt bill in the House indicated that the cause of free trade was not lost.

[25] The Hitt bill was printed as *House Reports*, 50 Cong., 2 sess., no. 1870. Debates on the measure are found in *Congressional Record*, 50 Cong., 2 sess., 121, 211-14, 272, 2511, 2539, 2583, 4172, and Appendix, 125-27.

Before they pushed further down this promising path, the opposition party had to close up its ranks. The commercial union bill had aroused some annexation talk in the United States which seemed to sustain the Conservative contention that closer economic connections would incite American lust for Canada. Timid Liberals, including Blake, took fright and were skeptical of the pious disclaimers accompanying the Hitt bill. They urged Laurier to drop the issue quickly, because the same Americans now advocating free trade had earlier "avowed themselves as simply for annexation."[26]

New and uncertain in his leadership, Laurier wavered under this pressure and seemed inclined to yield to it. But his aggressive followers refused to permit abandonment of a promising issue which could win the next general election for them. They remonstrated to their vacillating chief that the party was almost solidly behind reciprocity. The Conservative cry of treason had grown stale and few Canadians took it seriously.[27] Laurier capitulated to these arguments, but it was evident that he had no great enthusiasm for reciprocity.

Having patched over their intramural rift, the Liberals renewed the debate on reciprocity in Parliament. On March 7, 1889, Cartwright moved that the passage of the Hitt bill in the lower house of Congress made it imperative that the Canadian cabinet discover the terms upon which the American government would negotiate a commercial agreement.[28] Each party then donned its threadbare arguments to do battle. The Liberals deplored, and exaggerated, the wretched economic conditions from which

[26] J. Edgar to Laurier, January 6, December 16, 1889, O. Weldon to Laurier, January 15, 1889, Laurier Papers, F, H, 1889; Frank H. Underhill, "Laurier and Blake, 1882-1891," *Canadian Historical Review*, XX (December, 1939), 403-404.

[27] D. B. Meigs to Laurier, December 16, 1888, W. C. Edward to Laurier, January 1, 1889, Laurier Papers, H, 1889.

[28] *Canadian Commons Debates, 1889*, pp. 704-705.

reciprocity alone could rescue Canada and cited Hitt's declaration against annexation as proof of the noble intent of the American government.

Macdonald and his cohorts hooted derisively at the gullibility of the opposition. Against the pious assurances of Hitt they weighed numerous earlier political union motions in Congress and quoted from the American press and politicians to show that reciprocity was merely the breaking plow to raise a crop of annexationists. No less a person than James G. Blaine had stated that Canada could not have both its independence and trade concessions from the United States; the New York *World* was printing maps that showed the Dominion as part of the Republic.[29] Here, said the Conservatives, the real American intent stood revealed.

The result of the vote on the second Cartwright motion was as inevitable as that on the first, and showed little numerical change.[30] Again the Liberals accepted defeat cheerfully, confident that the widely publicized debates were accumulating popular support for them in the next election. In 1890 the same issue was renewed, and the debate moved automatically into its well-worn groove. To lend variety, and to authenticate their protested loyalty, the Liberals introduced a resolution of loyalty to the Queen, which passed unanimously.[31] They restrained themselves, however, from submitting a similar motion endorsing the Deity.

In view of their protestations to the contrary, it is interesting to note that some Liberals in their private correspondence agreed with the Conservative contention that the United States intended to gobble up the Dominion if it could, and despite solemn disclaimers. Were these suspicions well founded?

[29] *Canadian Commons Debates, 1889*, pp. 713, 721.
[30] The vote in 1889 was 77 for the motion and 121 opposed.
[31] British Parliament, *Accounts and Papers, 1890*, XLIX.

The evidence points to apparently contradictory conclusions. The active annexationists in the United States seemed too few to threaten Canada's integrity, but they included such leaders as Blaine and Sherman who were determined to acquire the Dominion, preferably by cunning indirection. These actions, so far as they were visible, would get little active support from most Americans, some of whom were indifferent to annexation, some opposed, and others willing to accept Canada if the initiative came from the Dominion. Few American newspapers clamored for Canada, and Goldwin Smith, who knew the United States well, asserted that its citizens were almost completely indifferent to the Dominion. The Detroit *Evening News,* a rabid annexationist sheet, agreed with him.[32] The weak American movement was limited to the tier of states along the border. Even there, its support came largely from businessmen who had direct interests in, or connections with, Canada. In short, the desire for annexation came, as usual, from those who had a material stake in it.[33] The old fear of the Dominion as a British base menacing the United States was fading, and the expansionist impulse was shifting to the vast reaches of the Pacific. The depression in Canada, the fear of competition with its raw material producers, and the ugly outbursts of

[32] Interview with Goldwin Smith in Toronto *Globe,* September 24, 1890; Detroit *Evening News,* July 27, 1889. Of the influential American papers, only the New York *Herald* and the Detroit *Evening News* consistently advocated annexation. The New York *Sun* and the Chicago *Tribune* showed occasional interest, but general hostility. Such papers as the New York *Times,* the Boston *Daily Advertiser,* and the Cincinnati *Commercial* consistently opposed continental union.

[33] Based on a mass of testimony submitted by businessmen to a Senate Committee on Canadian-American Relations. This committee was established to take evidence on the state of trade between the countries, the terms of agreements between them, and the extent to which the Dominion might have violated such pacts. Senator George F. Hoar of Massachusetts was the chairman. *Senate Reports,* 51 Cong., 1 sess., no. 1530.

English-French hatred made the Dominion unattractive to most Americans.

Their representatives in Congress generally reflected this opinion. From 1888 to 1891, only three motions for annexation were presented to Congress, and none of them emerged from committee or was discussed on the floor. The few random mentions of political union occurred during debates on commercial measures.[34] Only ten members of Congress, representing the border states of Maine, New Hampshire, New York, Ohio, and Michigan, showed favorable interest in the subject.[35]

But it would be wrong to assume that Canada was at last completely safe from the United States. As noted, some American leaders desired to acquire the Dominion, whether public opinion supported them or not. They intended to keep constant economic pressure on Canada to drive her to political union for relief from coercion. Under Cleveland, the retaliation act was an ugly, if unused, threat. The Harrison administration was definitely menacing. The secretary of state was the powerful James G. Blaine, implacable foe of all that bore the name British. His animus arose from his Irish descent and from the fact that, in Congress, he had long represented Maine, a state which still felt the wounds of the boundary dispute and whose fishermen were usually at swords' points with Dominion authorities.[36] He, and others, consistently displayed a cold contempt

[34] *Congressional Record,* 50 Cong., 2 sess., Appendix, 125-27. The only mention of Manifest Destiny was made by Senator John Sherman, who was rebuked by his colleagues for his attitude. *Congressional Record,* 50 Cong., 1 sess., 8670-71.

[35] The ten were Senators John Sherman and Henry Payne of Ohio, Henry W. Blair and Jacob H. Gallinger of New Hampshire, and Eugene Hale of Maine, supported in the House of Representatives by C. S. Baker and Amos Cummings of New York, Benjamin Butterworth and George E. Seney of Ohio, and John L. Chipman of Michigan. All but Payne, Seney, and Chipman were Republicans.

[36] Alice F. Tyler, *The Foreign Policy of James G. Blaine* (Minneapolis, 1927), 318 n32.

for Canada and a delight in affronting her. Blaine believed that a negative policy of refusing to deal with, or grant concessions to, Canada would ultimately force her into continental union, while overt actions would be self-defeating. On one occasion he stated that "Canada is like an apple on a tree just beyond our reach. We may strive to grasp it, but the bough recedes from our hold just in proportion to our effort to catch it. Let it alone, and in due time it will fall into our hands."[37] Keeping pressure on Canada would have an inevitable effect: "The fact is we do not want any intercourse with Canada except through the medium of a tariff, and she will find she has a hard row to hoe and will ultimately, I believe, seek admission to the Union."[38]

President Benjamin Harrison was sympathetic to this policy, and Canadians were convinced that others, in addition to the ten congressmen mentioned above, were giving the secretary bipartisan support. They included the influential Republican Senators George Hoar of Massachusetts and John C. Spooner of Wisconsin and the prominent Democrat, A. G. Thurman of Ohio, Cleveland's running mate in the campaign of 1888.[39]

Blaine was consistent to his policy. The fur seal negotiations were conducted with maximum acrimony, but the McKinley tariff exceeded it in arousing Canadian resentments and fears. Many in the Dominion did not doubt that its real purpose was to drive them into the United States. One of England's great

[37] Toronto *Daily Mail*, February 13, 1889.

[38] James G. Blaine to Benjamin Harrison, September 23, 1891, in Albert T. Volwiler (ed.), *The Correspondence between Benjamin Harrison and James G. Blaine* (Philadelphia, 1940), 193-94.

[39] Toronto *Daily Mail*, July 26, 1888, September 20, 1890; W. Kirby to G. Denison, December 9, 1890, Denison Papers, IV. It is unlikely that Hoar, later the outspoken enemy of imperialism, and Spooner were annexationists. Canadians probably identified their support of economic retaliation against the Dominion with a desire for continental union.

foreign ministers agreed with this judgment: "I have no doubt that the McKinley Bill was passed by Blaine and the Republicans with the main intention, if not the sole intention, of provoking a political crisis in Canada."[40]

This was not the final irritation. Canada began to refund Welland Canal fees to ships, principally Canadian, carrying grain to St. Lawrence ports for export; the government in Washington naturally charged a violation of the treaty of 1871, which had granted American vessels use of Canadian canals on equal terms. When the Ottawa government continued its policy unperturbed, Harrison ordered heavy tolls levied on ships of the Dominion using the Sault Ste. Marie Canal. To prevent the ruin of her trade on the upper lakes, Canada yielded, her people furious at what they interpreted as further evidence of American hostility.[41]

Anger became revulsion when many Canadians began to divine that some of their own might be implicated in the American policy. A few Liberal leaders were trekking south for unknown and suspect purposes. Farrer of the Toronto *Daily Mail* was accused of informing the Senate Committee on Canadian-American Relations that it would be possible for the United States to coerce Canada into annexation; one member of the committee admitted the substantial truth of this charge.[42] Sir Richard Cartwright came to New York, thence secretly to a rendezvous with American leaders in Washington. The substance of the interview is unknown, but these transactions were so furtive that an important employee of the Toronto *Globe*, which often spoke for Cartwright, resigned because the Liberal

[40] Sir Alexander Galt to William Gladstone, February 26, 1891, Galt Papers; Robert Gascoyne-Cecil, Marquis of Salisbury, to G. Denison, March 21, 1891, Denison Papers, IV, 1975-77.

[41] New York *Times*, August 23, 1892; Tyler, *Blaine*, 357-59.

[42] New York *Times*, January 23, 1890.

knight was involved in "political intrigue" of a nature "extremely discreditable and dubious."[43]

Mystery implied sinister intent. That they had treasonable purposes is by no means certain, but skulking interviews with men planning to force Canada into annexation were, at the least, injudicious. It is small wonder that those intent on preserving their country's identity watched with foreboding.

In 1890-1891, then, a tense and contradictory situation prevailed, ruffled and roiled by crosscurrents. While the mass of the American people ignored Canada, a coterie of their leaders intended to acquire her, not by direct aggression, but by coercion or stealthy intrigue. In spite of this, the Liberals were gambling their political future on reciprocity, which demanded just those concessions Blaine and his group were bound to refuse. The opposition party asserted that freer trade would exorcise both the depression and annexationism. Yet some of its members, not all obscure, were suspect of having a hand on the helm of the American policy of coercion. Nor did the ministerial party, on its side, exhibit a nice consistency. Loudly though they bewailed the disloyalty of reciprocity, they were trying to get it![44] This contradiction was dismissed with the ingenuous explanation that a Conservative reciprocity would be safe and a Liberal reciprocity would be dangerous.

In this welter of confusion, Macdonald called for a general election in 1891. Unrestricted reciprocity was the issue in the ensuing campaign; fundamentally, the fate of the National Policy was at stake. From the outset, Macdonald left no doubt of his strategy by his famous pronouncement: "A British subject

[43] E. Wiman to E. Thomsen, February 15, 1890, Wiman to H. P. Dwight, Jr., March 7, 1890, Thomsen to Robert Jaffray, March 22, 1890, Denison Papers, IV, 1774, 1775-77, 1780.

[44] For several years there had been persistent "feelers" and attempts to obtain reciprocity. This complicated story is skillfully unraveled in Tansill, *Canadian-American Relations,* 412-41.

I was born—a British subject I will die. With my utmost effort, with my latest breath will I oppose the 'veiled treason' which attempts by sordid means and mercenary proffers to lure our people from their allegiance."[45] Like an ancient tweed coat, this sentiment was well worn but had always been serviceable. Yet the old appeal had waned, and early Conservative attempts to impugn the loyalty of the Liberals aroused little reaction. The out-and-out annexationists, having learned a lesson in the commercial union campaign, supported unrestricted reciprocity inconspicuously. The rumors of Liberal intrigues with American leaders were not widely known and were discounted as Conservative political mouthings. Unrestricted reciprocity was not obviously dangerous. At most, it meant a rapprochement which might ultimately, but only after a long time, lead toward political union. Because reciprocity balanced immediate gain against remote danger, many hard-pressed Canadians wavered in their allegiance to the program of economic nationalism.[46] The Conservative campaign was going badly.

There was another reason for this. Macdonald had been caught in what the opposition gleefully called a typical sample of his political chicanery. It happened this way. Shortly before calling the general election, the Prime Minister had played what he thought to be the ace of trumps. This was an announcement by the Toronto *Empire* that the government of the United States had approached Macdonald seeking a reciprocity agreement.[47] If true, this would pull the platform from under the Liberals, leaving them dangling in midair with an election impending. Laurier and his cohorts were frantic at the theft

[45] Quoted in Creighton, *Macdonald*, 553.

[46] The desertion of many Conservatives to reciprocity was notable as early as 1889. W. Preston to Laurier, August 20, 1889, Laurier Papers, H, 1889.

[47] John S. Willison, *Sir Wilfred Laurier and the Liberal Party; A Political History* (Toronto, 1903), II, 151.

of their key issue, but possessed the presence of mind to check Macdonald's claim.[48] They discovered that the American government had been negotiating a trade agreement with Newfoundland when Great Britain, prompted by Canada, insisted that the Dominion be included in any treaty.[49] Macdonald then proposed a revival of the treaty of 1854, the most extensive agreement which his convictions and consistency would permit —and one certain to be refused.[50]

Blaine rejected this proposal but agreed, perhaps reluctantly, to private talks, after March 4, with an unofficial delegation. He also specified that the conversations must be kept secret.[51] Macdonald pledged silence, and then apparently violated this promise in the *Empire* article.[52] Historians disagree on the reasons and motives for this revelation, but there can be no doubt that it would help the Conservatives and damage the Liberals.[53] Blaine was outraged, or pretended to be, at this breach of faith and soon found his revenge in a flat denial of the existence of negotiations for reciprocity.[54]

If Macdonald had hoped to smite the Liberals with their own

[48] Tyler, *Blaine*, 352-53.

[49] Robert Bond to James G. Blaine, December 3, 1890, Diplomatic Notes, Great Britain, CXVIII.

[50] Tyler, *Blaine*, 353.

[51] Blaine to Bond, December 20, 1890, Diplomatic Notes, Great Britain, CXVIII.

[52] He claimed that it was his understanding that the proceedings of the conference were to remain secret but not the fact of its existence. Creighton, *Macdonald*, 550.

[53] There is much disagreement in the interpretation of this episode. American writers and Canadian Liberals generally maintain that Macdonald had initiated the negotiations and committed a willful breach of faith to gain political advantage. Apologists for Macdonald say that Blaine indicated willingness to negotiate, that Macdonald mistrusted the whole affair from the outset, and that newspapers published rumors regarding the negotiations, virtually forcing Macdonald to clear the air by his announcement. See Creighton, 548-52.

[54] Willison, *Laurier*, II, 158.

weapon, it had proved to be a boomerang. To all appearances, Blaine and the Liberals had exposed him in a bald lie and backed him into a corner. Could he now denounce reciprocity as disloyal when he had been seeking it? The transaction seemed to rob him of the means either to attack or to defend.

In this winter of adversity, fate delivered the Liberals and the election into his hands. As already noted, Edward Farrer, the Liberal journalist and now of the Toronto *Globe,* had drawn questioning attention to himself by his comings and goings to and from Washington. From indiscretion he now proceeded to folly. He allowed a friend to persuade him to prepare a pamphlet for private circulation. This booklet, purportedly written from the American point of view, contained a short section describing coercions by which the United States could dragoon Canada into continental union, including the termination of the bonding privilege and the placing of prohibitive tariffs on Canada's key exports and tonnage duties on her shipping. The pamphlet was set up by Hunter, Rose & Company in the greatest secrecy, but the stealthy proceedings piqued the curiosity of an employee of the firm, who ran off a proof of part of it. When he realized what he had, he either gave or sold his copy to the Conservatives.[55]

Here was what Macdonald needed. He had long suspected that some of the Liberals were in touch with American annexationists through the liaison of Farrer. Now he had evidence to impugn the loyalty of the journalist and of his associates in the Liberal Party. With this deadly weapon in his armory, he called for the dissolution of Parliament, February 3, 1891.

Through the early stages of the campaign which followed, Macdonald persistently hinted that great revelations would soon be unfolded. With interest and attention at a peak, he delivered

[55] Affidavit of Christopher Clark, January 30, 1891, and the proof copy in Macdonald Papers, General Elections, IV, 1891; Toronto *Daily Mail,* February 18, 1891.

his major speech on February 17 at Toronto, laying bare the infamy of Farrer and the Liberals. His proposition was simple, direct, and usefully exaggerated. Farrer was a traitor who would deliver Canada to the United States. Since he was the hireling of certain Liberal leaders and their messenger to American expansionists, part of the opposition were annexationists in disguise, the rest accessories or dupes, who would use reciprocity as the wedge to force the gates of annexation. Loyal Canadians must entrust their future, and negotiations with the United States, to the safe party, the Conservatives.[56]

This sudden turn electrified the public. Hitherto vague suspicions and formless accusations assumed shape. If Farrer were an annexationist, what about Cartwright, what about Charlton —could one be sure even of Laurier?[57]

The Liberals were equally shocked. Confidently reaching for the gonfalon of victory, they were rudely dumped into this pit of treason. Stunned and befuddled, they fought back as best they could. With enthusiastic unanimity and illogic, they simultaneously disowned Farrer and protested that the fatal pamphlet was not really disloyal.[58] The unhappy cause of this sensation, forgetting that silence is usually the better part of dubious explanation, assured all that the pamphlet did not state his own beliefs, not at all, not a bit of it. He was merely writing from the American point of view, outlining the policy of coercion that an American might try to activate. Stony disbelief greeted this protestation.

[56] Willison, *Laurier*, II, 164-71; Oscar D. Skelton, *The Life and Letters of Sir Wilfred Laurier* (Toronto, 1921), I, 413-17. Even the Governor General considered the Farrer pamphlet thin evidence for the indictment of an entire party, and told Macdonald so. Lord Frederick A. Stanley to Macdonald, January 31, 1891, Macdonald Papers, Governor-Generals' Correspondence, XVII.

[57] W. Kirby to Denison, February 21, 1891, C. Mair to Denison, February 23, 1891, Denison to Marquis of Salisbury, March 7, 1891, Denison Papers, V, 1936, 1940-41, 1959-60.

[58] Toronto *Globe*, February 19, 26, 1891.

After the first shock had worn off, the opposition began to recover its aplomb and even sought to regain the initiative by scolding the Conservatives for the soiled ethics of campaigning on stolen documents![59] But worse was pending. Sir Charles Tupper took his turn to publish a batch of letters, these stolen from Erastus Wiman and proving that Farrer and others desired a Liberal victory and unrestricted reciprocity primarily to hasten annexation.[60] This was the final blow to the hopes of defeating Macdonald. In the eyes of most voters, the Conservatives had amply documented their contention that the election presented a clear-cut issue between annexation and loyalty.[61]

With these developments, the election of 1891 became the closest approach to a plebiscite on annexation in Canada's history. Not all, probably not even most, who voted Liberal were annexationists, but many were and others were willing to run the risks of political union to get the benefits of reciprocity. Though Macdonald won, the results were neither crushing to the annexationists nor exhilarating to the loyalists. The margin of victory was narrow, and the Conservatives and attendant interests had to wage a grueling campaign to gain it even after the Macdonald-Tupper exposés had discredited the Liberals. It is significant that the Conservatives lost the annexationist areas described above, and particularly the border regions, by considerable margins.[62]

Though they had come close to victory, the Liberals read a conclusion in the results. They had journeyed into a far country, and they must return. Unrestricted reciprocity was a good issue, but it was tainted with treason and must be removed. The

[59] Toronto *Daily Mail*, February 18, 20, 1891.

[60] Macdonald Papers, General Elections, IV, 1891; Toronto *Daily Mail*, February 26, 1891.

[61] Macdonald to W. F. Roome, January 31, 1891, Macdonald to L. McCallum, February 21, 1891, Macdonald Papers, Macdonald Letter Books, XXVII.

[62] G. Denison to Marquis of Salisbury, March 7, 1891, Denison Papers, V, 1959-60.

amputation was performed at a party convention in 1893. In its stead the Liberals substituted a cautiously defined demand for reciprocity in raw materials with the addition of a "well-considered" list of manufactures.[63]

The annexationists also stood at a fork in their road. The defeat of 1891 had killed any hope of achieving victory by indirection and gaining power under the cloak of another and apparently innocuous issue. They were too well known longer to disguise their intent, and a change in tactics was clearly necessary.

Despite this, their cause was not lost. The election had been close enough to indicate that they had gained, and might hope to gain more. Besides, an amazing pronouncement by Edward Blake cheered them. This unpredictable man was a sore trial to his associates. Perhaps he regretted his sudden retirement as leader in 1887 and resented Laurier's disinclination to step aside so that he might resume the mantle. In any event, he bitterly opposed unrestricted reciprocity, and the Liberals barely restrained him from blurting open denunciation during the campaign.[64] With the polling completed, he could no longer be contained, and he burst forth with a public letter to the voters of his old Ontario riding, West Durham. This "Address" was so cryptic that it still occasions conflicting interpretations among historians. Undeniably, it gave aid and comfort to the annexationist. The National Policy, Blake declared, was driving Canada into bankruptcy. The only escape from this fate was commercial union, but "assuming that absolute free trade with the United States may and ought to come, I believe that it can and should come only as an incident or at any rate a well understood precursor of political union."[65]

[63] New York *Times*, June 22, 1893.

[64] Underhill, "Laurier and Blake," 404-408; Blake to Laurier, March 4, 1891, Laurier Papers, L, 1891.

[65] Letter printed in Toronto *Globe*, March 6, 1891.

The continental unionists were heartened by this statement from the most brilliant, if not the most stable, mind in Canadian politics, who seemed to be saying that annexation was inevitable. Some of them, including Goldwin Smith, thought that the West Durham address was Blake's apologia for his conversion to their cause. They toyed with the idea of launching an annexation party led by the former Liberal great.[66] This notion soon died, perhaps at the hands of Blake, and the continental unionists turned instead to a dual plan. They redoubled their activities at the grassroots level, organizing public meetings openly dedicated to annexation and in the areas most likely to respond favorably, in hope of creating the impression of great and growing strength. This would advance the second phase of their plan, which was nothing less than the subversion of the Liberal Party to a thoroughgoing annexation organization through the conversion of its prominent leaders.

The press and private correspondence of the years following the election of 1891 testify to the vigor and success with which the annexationists pressed this dual plan. Numerous public meetings were held for the open discussion of continental union. Most of them were in the deeply disaffected counties of southwestern Ontario, but others occurred in communities farther east, including Shelburne, Simcoe, and Toronto. These gatherings followed a common course, indicating central planning and direction. All began with addresses celebrating the obvious virtues of annexation and generally delivered by the same orators. When the speakers had practiced their persuasions on the audience, the chairman would propose resolutions endorsing union with the United States. These usually carried, in one instance by a recorded vote of 413 to 36.[67] If the margin of

[66] W. D. Gregory to Laurier, October 21, 1891, Laurier Papers, N, 1891.

[67] New York *Times*, February 6, 1892. The meeting was held in Windsor.

victory were gratifying, an attempt would be made to organize an annexation club to advance the cause locally.[68]

A series of incidents, each minor in itself but collectively ominous, soon attested the effects of this activity. A number of civil servants, including a Crown attorney, became notorious supporters of the movement and had to be discharged to root treason out of the very organ it was intended to subvert.[69] One of them remarked that if the government fired all of the annexationists in its employ, it could no longer function. A county Liberal Association debated continental union openly and endorsed it almost unanimously. The Dominion Trades and Labor Congress circularized its local chapters, urging them to discuss the possibilities of independence and annexation and to report the prevalent opinions at the next annual meeting.[70]

In all such episodes it was apparent that most of the known annexationists were also Liberals, since such persons would naturally gravitate to the party which favored closer connections with the United States. Such easy rationalization was no consolation to the veteran Ontario leader, Oliver Mowat. This doughty loyalist had long and sorely smitten the local Conservatives, and had jousted over provincial rights with the great Sir John and unhorsed him, no common feat. The threat to his beloved party stimulated the old warrior's abundant combative instincts, and he prepared to do battle.

Though he lightly dismissed the dangers of annexationism in early public pronouncements, his private correspondence told a

[68] This composite description is derived from numerous references, including the following: C. Mair to Denison, October 28, 1891, Denison to Marquis of Salisbury, December 19, 1891, October 22, 1892, Denison Papers, V, 2048-51, 2078-80, 2230-31; G. Smith to Laurier, November 27, 1891, June 1, 1892, Laurier Papers, V, VI; New York *Times*, November 29, 1892, April 5, 1893.

[69] Denison to Marquis of Salisbury, October 22, 1892, Denison Papers, V, 2230-31; New York *Times*, February 9, 1893.

[70] New York *Times*, November 29, 1892, February 9, 1893.

different story.[71] He saw political union as a looming menace and proposed to fight it at the risk of dignifying, even enhancing, the movement by open opposition. Mowat first made his position and intent unmistakably clear in a public letter ostensibly addressed to Alexander Mackenzie, former Liberal Prime Minister. Herein he followed Blake's address in lamenting the sorry plight of Canada, resulting, of course, from the benighted National Policy. But annexation was too dear a price for relief. The Dominion had its destiny to fulfill, and coercion could not drive, nor temptation seduce, it into the United States. Mowat roundly cursed the Ontario annexationists as traitors, and read them out of his party.[72]

Having uttered his strident battle cry, Mowat carried the fight to the enemy on their own terrain. He mustered loyal followers through members of the provincial parliament and urged them to go, with disruptive intent, to the public meetings of the annexationists. Soon these gatherings were no longer pursuing, unvexed, their smooth course. Speakers were interrupted and challenged, and resolutions endorsing annexation were contested and defeated. Goldwin Smith was presently complaining that Mowat was packing his meetings; the agitation for continental union began to lose its momentum.[73]

Mowat had other work. He seemed to doubt the disposition and intent of Wilfred Laurier, new national leader of the Liberals. Did this French Canadian understand the situation in Ontario, the inroads which the continental union doctrine had made there in the ranks of the party? Did this remote, but courtly and gracious, man have the requisite of leadership?

[71] Interview with Oliver Mowat in New York *Times*, November 27, 1891.

[72] O. Mowat to Alexander Mackenzie, December 12, 1891, later issued as a pamphlet, *The Reform Party and Canada's Future* (Toronto, 1891).

[73] G. Smith to Laurier, November 27, 1891, Laurier Papers, V, 1891; Denison to Marquis of Salisbury, December 19, 1891, Denison Papers, V, 2078-80.

Under the shell of urbanity was there the bit of steel which would hold him resolute to the right even at the cost of political division and personal quarrel? Mowat did not know, but he wrote a blunt letter to his leader to discover him as well as to inform him. "The [Toronto] *Globe*," he told Laurier, "is creating an annexationist party out of the members of the Reform party and has accomplished more in that direction than I was aware of." Laurier must make "a very distinct declaration, so clear and emphatic that there can be no cavil as to its meaning, against political union. . . . If nothing can be done, an open division of the party is inevitable. . . . Whether a strong annexation party can be created from its ruins I do not know, but I should hope not."[74]

Mowat might have been spared his concern over the presumed ignorance of Laurier, who actually knew more about the activities of the political unionists than did the Ontario leader. Laurier's information was source material emanating directly from the leader of the movement, Goldwin Smith. The purpose of the public meetings, as noted above, had been to impress and convert Liberal leaders. Laurier was the most desirable prospective proselyte. It must have been ironic and disconcerting to one who had stated that the annexation movement would become a menace if it discovered an able leader to find himself singled out for that role by the skillful advocate and tempter, Goldwin Smith. The latter was an interesting and important personality. English by birth and training and a former professor of history at Oxford, he had come to America as one of the original faculty at Cornell University. He then removed to Toronto, which welcomed this intellectual emigrant from the motherland. A man of independent means, he indulged a taste for political journalism and displayed a remarkable affinity for liberal, and lost, causes. Smith was a unique specimen in the Canadian continental union movement. He had no material interest or

[74] Mowat to Laurier, December 26, 1891, Laurier Papers, V, 1891.

racial antipathy to serve but was, rather, an intellectual annexationist who felt that union with the United States was the only logical destiny for Canada. The Dominion could not remain a colony, for imperialism was detrimental alike to mother country and dependency. Sprawling size, formidable geographic barriers, and a small, fragmented population made nationhood an absurd illusion. Canadians were rational beings who needed only to have these cold facts explained to realize that annexation was their clear and certain destiny.[75] Smith expended much oxygen and ink to illumine such self-evident truths, but most of his auditors continued to display invincible ignorance. He now turned his persuasive powers upon Laurier, whom he impeached of failing to keep up with his fast-paced party. Smith stressed particularly "the continental character of the Liberal party here [Toronto?] . . . the Canadians who are likely to follow you as leader are by this time fully up to the mark, whilst some of them, and an increasing number, are daily advancing beyond it." If people uttered what was in their hearts, the great strides which annexationism had made would be obvious. This was the clear opportunity for the Liberal Party, which eventually must come to political union as its issue because destiny strode that way and because the Conservatives had already staked out their claim to the issue of loyalty.[76]

In the spring and early summer of 1892, Smith concentrated his fire on Laurier. He informed the latter of the movement, its organization, its well-attended and successful meetings in Ontario towns, and its plan to gain control of the provincial legislature at the next election. The spectacular conversion of a respected leader would embolden the timid and galvanize the hesitant. If Laurier declared for annexation, Ontario, already on

[75] There is brief mention of Smith's annexationist proclivities in Elisabeth Wallace, *Goldwin Smith: Victorian Liberal* (Toronto, 1957), 253, 265.

[76] Smith to Laurier, November 19, 27, 1891, Laurier Papers, V, 1891.

the verge, would plunge in, Quebec would follow its favorite son, and the thing would be done.[77]

Had Laurier capitulated to this siege, it is barely possible that Canada might have been swept into the United States. Macdonald, great captain of the loyalists, was dead, his party wracked with internecine strife and mutiny, and the country adrift economically without a strong, sure hand at the helm. In this strait the dramatic conversion of a prominent figure to annexation might have been the critical event for Canada's future. But Laurier's loyalty was impregnable to all the weapons in Smith's armory—facts, arguments, and half-veiled threats—and he blandly but firmly repulsed the advances of the political unionists. Goldwin Smith had failed in his great test.

Similar attempts with lesser Liberals had greater success. Such local Ontario leaders as E. A. Macdonald, W. D. Gregory, Elgin Myers, and Peter Ryan joined the annexationists. The last of these vigorously seconded Smith's attempt to bring Laurier around. He assured his leader that the desire for political union was growing in Canada and that the Liberals could profit from this because "the flour barrel will beat the old flag any day, and barley will be more potential as an argument than so-called loyal guff."[78] But Laurier resisted his colleague as obdurately as he had Goldwin Smith.

Evidence suggests, however, that two important Ontario Liberals, John Charlton and Sir Richard Cartwright, may have been won over, at least for a time and surreptitiously. Charlton was an American-born, wealthy lumberman whose equivocal behavior aroused the mistrust of loyalists and annexationists alike. The former unhesitatingly catalogued him as a continental unionist, while an American annexationist denounced him as a turncoat whose loyalty varied inversely with the American duty

[77] These ideas are expressed in letters from Smith to Laurier, June 1, 25, July 10, 26, 1892, Laurier Papers, VI, 1892.

[78] Peter Ryan to Laurier, November 2, 1891, Laurier Papers, V, 1891.

on his product. "When he [Charlton] met his revenue reform friends there [in Washington, D.C.] he sang their Hymn tunes, and when he crossed over to call on his Continental Union friends, he whistled a Continental Union Pslam [*sic*]. He was seeking funds to help Sir Oliver [Mowat] and to elect Mr. Laurier. He called upon the friends of Continental Union to supply them." Meanwhile, the Wilson-Gorman tariff had put lumber on the free list but "a duty of two dollars per 1000 feet upon pine boards will make him an active Continental Unionist again."[79] Evidently Charlton was not mulish in his convictions.

There was also reason to look askance at Sir Richard Cartwright. He had supported commercial union and gone to Washington for clandestine meetings with American expansionists. This and similar activities aroused suspicion. When the Liberals adopted unrestricted reciprocity, he warned Laurier that Macdonald would raise the old cry that this would lead to independence. Cartwright suggested that this was true, should be admitted, and made a virtue and a campaign issue. The Liberal Party should advance beyond reciprocity and make its stand on independence.[80] The affinity between that issue and annexation made this suggestion a dubious testimonial of Sir Richard's devotion to Dominion and Empire.

Such tendencies disturbed some of his colleagues, including Mowat, who commented with typical bluntness: "I should gather from it [a Cartwright address] that he is contemplating and desiring political union."[81] His imprudent speech also shocked the poet Charles Mair: "the Grits really mean annexa-

[79] Quotation from F. W. Glen to editor of New York *Press*, March 26, 1894, and to editor of Toronto *Empire*, March 27, 1894, in Denison Papers, V, 2533-35, 2537; see also W. Kirby to Denison, February 21, 1891, Denison to Marquis of Salisbury, December 19, 1891, Denison Papers, V, 1936, 2078-80; New York *Times*, February 8, 1893.

[80] Cartwright to Laurier, January 12, 1889, Laurier Papers, Correspondence, 1870-1891, pp. 950-51.

[81] Mowat to Laurier, December 31, 1891, Laurier Papers, V.

tion. . . . Sir Richard Cartwright was in the Pullman coming up. . . . He let himself out to Gault about annexation without reserve, so you see you are strictly right in your conclusions."[82] All of this convinced a Niagara editor that, as Mowat had warned Laurier, the Liberals were split into the loyal party of Blake and Mackenzie "and the rebel Reform party of Cartwright—Charlton—Goldwin Smith and their like."[83]

Quebec Liberals did not escape the taint, though it touched them more lightly. Mercier was affected, and P. A. Choquette, Liberal member of the Canadian Parliament and close friend of Laurier, exposed some remarkable sentiments in his paper, *Le Sentinelle.* Commenting upon Conservative charges that unrestricted reciprocity would lead to annexation, Choquette replied: "Well, what if it does. We shall certainly have no objection to that. It must come sooner or later, and it will be better to annex us *en bloc* than one by one, as is the case by immigration. If reciprocity brings about annexation, this will be of more use to us than the British flag."[84]

By 1892 it was thus evident that annexationism had invaded the Liberal machine, particularly in Ontario, and had penetrated to high places. But it was also evident that few leaders of that party would make an unequivocal public commitment favoring the issue. Perhaps for this reason the political unionists reverted, as a last resort, to the policy they had anxiously avoided—that of standing alone and seeking their objective openly and directly rather than through other issues and organizations. In 1892 they established the Continental Union League, an international body with its principal stations in New York and Toronto.[85] The

[82] C. Mair to Denison, February 23, 1891, Denison Papers, V, 1940-41.

[83] W. Kirby to Denison, February 21, 1891, Denison Papers, V, 1936.

[84] Montmagny *Sentinelle,* undated, quoted in New York *Times,* November 30, 1891.

[85] This organization was known as the "association" in Canada and the "league" in the United States. Wallace, *Goldwin Smith,* 277. To avoid confusion, the term "league" will be used here.

former boasted an impressive membership roll, including John Hay, Theodore Roosevelt, Andrew Carnegie, Charles A. Dana, and Elihu Root. Dana was its sponsor and strategist, while the day-to-day work was carried on by the remarkable Francis Wayland Glen. Born in the United States, Glen had emigrated to Canada, entered politics, and represented an Ontario riding in the federal Parliament for nine years. Almost from the day of his arrival in the Dominion, he was convinced that annexation was that country's best and inevitable destiny and that the desire for it was steadily increasing. Upon his return to the United States, he joined the league and had much to offer it. Able and devoted, he had an intimate and useful knowledge of Canadian politics and its practitioners, and could direct the funds and activities of the league into the most promising channels. He also presented some serious personal defects. Irascible and unpredictable, he was contemptuous of Canadian politicians who sought annexationist aid and money but refused to pronounce for the movement. On occasion he even tried to betray them to their fellow Canadians as hypocritical opportunists. Such candor did not assist the work of the league in Canada.

The American branch of the organization devoted itself to raising funds for promoting by constitutional means the union with Canada which "will deliver the continent from any possible complications [with Great Britain] and add enormously to the power, influence and prestige of North America. It would securely dedicate the continent to peaceful industry and progress."[86] The sums raised were devoted to the publication of pamphlets and to aid for the Canadian organization and deserving politicians in the Dominion. The Canadian wing, centered in Toronto, principally occupied itself with publicity, establishment of local branches, and designation of Canadians worthy of

[86] Circular letter soliciting funds and signed by Dana and Carnegie, November 6, 1893, Denison Papers, V, 2462. This letter brought contributions of $3,120.

financial assistance.[87] This organization was headed by John Morison, an obscure Ontario politician, with Goldwin Smith as honorary president. Its membership included Farrer, Elgin Myers, E. A. Macdonald, and Solomon White, the veteran Conservative annexationist; Charlton was also strongly suspected of having been a member.[88]

Although the league was strongest in Ontario, Quebec politicians were most assiduous in seeking its funds. At various times such provincial leaders as C. A. Pelletier, J. E. Robidoux, Royal Mercier, and Israel Tarte made their way to New York, stalking the organization's cashbox.[89] The most importunate supplicant was Honoré Mercier. This fascinating demagog had fallen upon evil and desperate days. His clever exploitation of the Jesuit Estates Act and the Ontario Orangemen's bitter hostility to it seemed to have entrenched him impregnably in the premiership of Quebec. But fate was fickle. His administration was exposed in outrageous corruption and was summarily dismissed by the lieutenant governor. In the subsequent provincial election of 1892, Mercier recklessly campaigned on the issues of extreme French nationalité and Catholicism, only to be utterly routed, a result which damaged him and benefited the Dominion.

In 1893 he tried to repair his shattered fortunes by a speaking tour of eastern Canada, ostensibly to promote a movement for independence. His speeches contained some incongruities. He would devote a considerable portion of them to exulting the

[87] A pamphlet, *Continental Union, A Short Study of the Economic Side*, was distributed in Canada. W. Kirby to Denison, July 21, 1893, Denison Papers, V, 2403-404. For other league activities, see Denison to Marquis of Salisbury, October 22, 1892, Denison Papers, V, 2230-31; New York *Times*, April 5, 1893; G. Smith to Laurier, July 10, 1892, Laurier Papers, VI, 1892.

[88] Denison, *Imperial Unity*, 108. Macdonald was prominent in Toronto and later became its mayor. Charlton was a member of the federal Parliament.

[89] Various notes in Denison Papers, VI, 2540-51.

virtues of union with the United States, abruptly state a personal distaste for annexation, briefly damn independence with faint praise, and slyly suggest that it was the easiest avenue to political union![90]

Those who troubled to follow these meanderings would not have been surprised to learn that Mercier was in close touch with the Continental Union League, from which he derived intellectual and material sustenance. "As the matter placed before me concerns chifley [*sic*] the American side of our common cause, I thought better to have your views first and be guided by you. . . . My trip to the East has been a success & will bring out a strong and very important move in favor of Canadian Independence. . . . Allow me to bring your attention to my state of poverty & to ask you if our New-York friends could not come to my rescue in order that I might continue the work."[91]

Despite its influence on a few leaders and despite the notice which it received, the league evidently did not increase the political union movement to any extent. Some local chapters were formed, but the passion of most Canadian annexationists for anonymity prohibited widespread organization. Though the loyal Liberals continued to worry about their annexationist faction, it is significant that they were readily able to contain and silence it at their party convention.[92] As the movement declined elsewhere, it continued active in Toronto, where a real estate "boom" collapsed with disastrous effects. Part of the business community saw annexation as the remedy for their distress and sent representatives to Washington to confer with

[90] A typical speech reported in New York *Times*, April 5, 1893.

[91] Mercier to Dana, August 9, 1893, Denison Papers, V, 2417-18. He evidently got the cash he requested. Dana to James Morison, August 12, 1893, Denison Papers, V, 2416.

[92] J. S. Willison to Laurier, July 14, 1892, Laurier Papers, VI, 1892; Denison to Marquis of Salisbury, August 12, 1893, Denison Papers, V, 2419-21.

sympathizers there. A farce ensued and further discredited the cause. The Toronto delegates spent most of their time—and all of their money—in sociological inspections of the fleshpots in the American capital and had to borrow railroad fare to return home![93]

Such buffoonery and other setbacks led prominent members to desert the league, until Goldwin Smith remained almost its only important supporter. The decline of the league is also apparent from the attitude of the Dominion government toward it. For some time an informant in the confidence of the continental union group had fed intelligence to the government in Ottawa. To enable him to devote his time to this activity, he had been given a sinecure in the customs service. Though his information proved to be consistently reliable, he was suddenly discharged in 1894—not the action, surely, of a worried government. They knew that the movement was moribund.

It had, in fact, probably been declining since the election of 1891, when many abandoned it as a lost cause. Subsequent reverses progressively thinned its ranks until the already tottering organization received its coup de grace from the financial crash which shook the United States in 1893. This spectacular smash dropped the Republic into a terrible depression. As in 1873, the United States on its way down passed the Dominion, which was beginning its long climb back to prosperity. Canadian envy of the United States, rankling for a decade, disappeared and carried with it the desire for annexation. The scattered embers which remained were extinguished in 1895-1896 by the Venezuela boundary dispute. The menacing truculence brandished against the motherland by Cleveland and Richard Olney penetrated to the deeply buried British sentiments of even the annexationists. A former vice president of the Continental Union League, editor Daniel McGillicuddy of the Goderich

[93] Hector Charlesworth, *Candid Chronicles* (Toronto, 1925), 167-68.

Huron Signal, abandoning his prior convictions, stated that he and the remnants of his group would fight and die for Empire and homeland, singing "The Maple Leaf Forever."[94] Fortunately, this extreme sacrifice proved unnecessary, but there is no doubt that the lingering traces of annexationism vanished in the crisis.

What caused the failure of this, the last, the longest, and the strongest of the annexation movements? Probably the reason was that its appeal was essentially ephemeral and material. Though it came too close to success in the 1880's and 1890's for the comfort of its enemies, it lacked stamina and the touch of sentiment which so often rules the lives of men, and broke itself on the rugged loyalty of most Canadians, a "loyalty" which had several meanings among the components of Canada's population.

The French Canadian's loyalty, as always, was to his way of life—language, church, and folkways. This attachment led a significant minority of the French to annexationism because they feared the intolerance of English Canada. But the same nationalité, in curious contradiction, caused most of the French to oppose political union. Joining the Republic would strip them of their main lines of defense, political power, and constitutional guarantees. If English threats remained verbal, they were tolerable. Most of the French would endorse annexation only when talk shifted to action. In the meantime, they felt safer as they were. Extreme nationalité, blown to white heat, soon burned itself out. Besides, Mercier had so thoroughly identified himself with it that his defeat was also its disgrace.

English-Canadian loyalty, on the other hand, was tripartite. The first aspect, like the French, was to a way of life. When the French of Quebec threatened to tyrannize its English minority,

[94] Denison to Marquis of Salisbury, January 20, 1896, Denison Papers, VII, 2984-85.

the latter espoused annexation to protect their own institutions by drowning the French in an Anglo-Saxon flood. But the great majority of the English, and especially those outside the province of Quebec, did not see political union as the salvation of their way of life but its assassin. They were restrained from supporting it by something fundamental which distinguished their society from that of the American. It was their form of government. They were bred under a constitution which focused responsibility on a single point, the cabinet, and regarded the American government as chaotic, inefficient, and even undemocratic.

The English-Canadian loyalty had two other facets, sentimental attachment to Dominion and to Empire. The spirit of Canadian nationalism, deliberately cultivated as a prophylactic against annexationism, powerfully reinforced the continuing devotion to Britain. In other parts of the Empire, nationalism and imperialism often worked at cross-purposes; the shadow of annexation, always lying across Canada, eased this tension in the Dominion. Here the annexationists faced barriers too high to hurdle and too deep to undermine.

The attitude of Americans toward annexation was no great assistance to it in the 1880's and 1890's, for most of them were indifferent or opposed. Congressional attempts to promote commercial and political union in the 1880's had failed, and the failures continued in the 1890's. On February 2, 1893, Representative Amos Cummings of New York introduced a bill to promote the amalgamation of the two countries, but it never emerged from the House Committee on Foreign Affairs.[95] The following year, Senator Jacob Gallinger of Vermont moved that because annexation would establish peace and promote trade and commerce between the two countries, the Canadian people should be invited "to cast in their lot with their own continent

[95] *Congressional Record,* 52 Cong., 1 sess., 1270. Cummings reintroduced the motion later, and it again met the same fate.

and we assure them they shall have all the continent can give them." The motion was printed, but never debated.[96] Thereafter, the name of annexation was silent in the halls of Congress for nearly two decades.

The few Americans who sought political union included some, such as Blaine and Sherman, powerful enough to persuade their apathetic countrymen to accept annexation or to dare to present them with a *fait accompli*. But they defeated their purposes by their methods of coercion and intimidation which hardened the resistance of Canadian opponents of political union and incensed the undecided. Further, the collection of money in the United States by the Continental Union League to influence or to corrupt leaders in the Dominion was an affront to all Canadians. In short, the annexationists in the United States were something less than an asset to their Canadian counterparts.

The movement of the 1880's and 1890's was at once the climax and finale of annexation as a serious question. Shortly after its collapse, the western world, including Canada, entered a period of prosperity, promoted by the discovery of new goldfields and of the cyanide process. The production and supply of gold expanded sharply, and world prices shot up in response. Canada rejoiced in special, and particularly favorable, circumstances at this time. The North American frontier disappeared from the United States as the supply of good land there began to run out, and reappeared on the almost unbroken sea of fertile soil in the Canadian West. Migration from the Dominion to the Republic, which had delayed recovery in the former and hastened it in the latter during the 1880's, ceased and then reversed itself. Settlers flooded onto the Canadian prairies and stimulated an extra-

[96] *Senate Miscellaneous Documents*, 53 Cong., 3 sess., no. 30. Goldwin Smith wrote the resolution for Gallinger. Denison, *Imperial Unity*, 112-13.

ordinary expansion in all fields: railroad building, industry, and agriculture.

Under these happy circumstances, the movement for continental union vanished, never to reappear as a genuine agitation. It is true that annexation was widely mentioned in the United States in connection with the congressional debates on the passage of the reciprocity agreement of 1911. It is equally true that this was not an authentic agitation. The opponents of reciprocity had learned well the lessons of Canadian history. Knowing that they could not defeat the agreement in Washington, they sought to kill it in Ottawa by stirring up Canadian antipathy with the old bogey of political union. These congressmen loudly trumpeted their conviction that closer economic connections would bring political amalgamation. They succeeded well in their purpose, and talk of annexation contributed to the surprising defeat of the agreement in Canada.[97] This was, perhaps, the most obviously spurious of all the "annexation movements."

The Canadian election of 1911, fought on the issue of reciprocity, demonstrated that nationalism had become a major force in Canada, despite the fact that its power had been employed against a strawman and not a real threat. Canada was at the height of prosperity, and there was no cogent reason to wish or fear annexation. There were, as there always have been, a handful on both sides of the line who hankered to make one country out of the two, but they were infinitesimal in numbers and influence. The real meaning of the election of 1911 was not the repulse of a dire threat but a demonstration of the power of Canadian nationalism, and another illustration

[97] For typical expressions of "annexation" opinion and the Canadian reactions, see *Congressional Record*, 61 Cong., 3 sess., 2436, 2451, 2520-21; *Canadian Commons Debates, 1910-1911*, p. 8305. See also the definitive work on the agreement, L. Ethan Ellis, *Reciprocity, 1911* (New Haven, 1939), 96, 109, 114, 133, 158-59, 166, 173, 178-79, 181-85.

of the effect which fear of the United States has had upon Canadians and their history.

After 1911, talk of annexation was silent, and the World War pushed it further into the background. Canada's splendid record in that conflict indicated that she had become a nation in fact, if not in law. Concurrently, relations with the United States were acerbated because many Canadians could not understand American reluctance to enter a war as vital to their security as to Canada's. After the war, the refusal of the United States to join the League of Nations distressed them, and the rapid American retreat into isolationism, except for petulant outbursts on the war debts question, disgusted them. So the rise of Canadian nationalism and aversion to the United States prepared stony ground for the cultivation of annexationism.

The great depression of the 1930's again set the scene for an encore of the movement, but no one appeared to act out the drama. A few murmurs from the distressed Prairie Provinces joined the mutterings of a handful of the English minority in Quebec, still grumbling over its inferior position in relation to the French majority. These groups were lost in the whole of the Canadian population, which regarded annexation with aversion—if they happened to think of it. In the United States there was an equally profound silence on the subject, broken occasionally by the shrill piping of some supernationalistic newspaper publishing its annual annexation editorial, evidently intended more to vex Canadians than to convince Americans.

By the example of history, the decade of the 1930's should have produced the greatest political union movement of all, for it suffered from the greatest depression of all. But annexation was dead indeed. Canada had become a nation, despite some quibblings over her precise status, and her people had grown to the full-blown pride of nationhood. One could as well ask an American if he wished to be annexed to Canada as to ask a Canadian if he wished to be joined to the United States. Moreover, the depression confirmed the suspicions of many Canadians that the vaunted and wealthy economy of the United States had grave weaknesses.

The outbreak of World War II, and particularly the fall of France, temporarily aroused talk of political union when some argued that a Nazi conquest of Great Britain would expose Canada and force her to join the United States in self-defense. They overlooked the fact that the Republic must defend Canada as she defends her own soil and, in self-interest, could no more tolerate aggression against Canada than aggression against California, Texas, or New York.

During the war, a survey of opinion published by *Fortune* indicated that relations between the two peoples were unusually cordial. Though more than half of the Canadians polled believed that their southern neighbors were more materialistic, but no more democratic, than themselves, they also agreed that Americans were "fine people" and generally did not assume an unwarranted air of superiority.[98] A surprising 23.3 percent of them favored annexation and an additional 62.7 percent, who did not want to join the United States, hoped that Canadian policies would show distinct favoritism to the Republic.

In the United States, the study showed that 24.4 percent of Americans desired annexation, including 28 percent of the businessmen but only 15 percent of the "intellectuals" polled. Another 28.2 percent would have liked to see Canada favored in American policies.[99]

These figures were consistent with the record of history, which

[98] Of those polled, 59.5 percent said that the United States was more materialistic and 51.2 percent considered Canada equally as democratic. On the other hand, 53.3 percent considered Americans fine people and 55.9 percent said Americans did not show an objectionable attitude of superiority.

[99] The results of the poll were published in *Fortune*, XXV (April, 1942), 112, (June), 6, 9, 14.

shows that annexationism has always been a minority movement in both countries. They also indicate that the Dominion showed a greater concern than did the United States over relations between them, and that Canadians had developed a remarkable tolerance of those American shortcomings which have been criticized so often and bitterly to the north.

CHAPTER EIGHT

Effects of the Continental Union Movement

The continental union movement had meandered through Canadian and American history for sixscore years. Like the rubbings of water and wind upon the rock, its immediate effects were small, its cumulative results impressive. But those results did not coincide with the purposes of its proponents.

First, it is important to consider the characteristics of the agitation itself—its origins, strengths, weaknesses, and failures. The repetitions in the descriptions of the three great outbursts of annexation sentiment indicate their fundamental identity. They have chanted their monotonous lines, then again and yet again, and shall have only a last brief encore here. At bottom, the annexation movement was the expression and intensification of basic forces ceaselessly and noiselessly drawing Canada and the United States together. One was the common origin and social heritage which created a strong bond between most Canadians and Americans. Geography also linked them. In settlement, Canada is in most places the northern fringe of the United States. The direction of the great physical barriers of North America has walled off the Canadian sections from each other, smoothed the paths of north-south trade, and cluttered the east-west aisles of commerce. Geography has also made a North American nation of Canada. Canadian life has hardened in a mold fashioned largely by the conditions peculiar to this continent. With the passage of time, the people of the Dominion have steadily become less like those of Great Britain and more like those of the United States in many ways. Thus ethnic and geographic backgrounds have constantly tended toward cultural, economic, and political assimilation. To create a separate and distinctive Canadian state and identity has meant to fight against the stream of nature's forces rather than to drift with their slow and gentle current into the oblivion of assimilation.

Geography has also given Canadians a box seat at the pageant of American progress. They could hardly avoid seeing, and contrasting, the relative developments of the United States and Canada. This observation has made many Canadians discontent with their lot, particularly when the United States was more prosperous than Canada—from 1847 to 1850, from 1867 to 1871, and from 1884 to 1893. The mainspring of the annexation agitation was always economic distress, coupled with the melancholy conviction that Canada lacked, and would never have, the ingredients of a viable national economy.

Cultural and religious factors were important but secondary causes of the movement. The English minority in Quebec frequently contributed to the agitation. Though they were normally vine-ripened Tories and aggressively devoted to the motherland, crisis proved that their first loyalty was to way of life. To escape the threat of French domination, they threatened to sever the beloved ties and join the United States, a country they normally held in contemptuous disdain. Other circumstances at times produced the same unlikely behavior among the Tories. When pending constitutional change threatened the old colonial system and their snug, favored position in it, their exaggerated loyalty could reverse into violent annexationism. Thus the Montreal Tories reacted in frenzy to Lord Elgin's quiet acquiescence to responsible government, and the Victoria Tories resisted the proposed change from colony to province. The threat of transformation from the understood, well-ordered, and socially graduated way to new and uncertain paths under the guidance of democracy seemed to make them desperate. To escape the British system, about to be polluted with self-government, they demanded union with the United States, epitome of that despised system! This was the action of men whose desperation had overridden their logic.

Annexationism thrust tender and easily withered roots among the French of Canada. Its most persistent advocate there was the small but boisterous Parti Rouge. The prime motive of this group, not always frankly exposited, was anticlericalism rather than materialism. The Rouge was convinced that the American government, dedicated to the separation of church from state, would prune the privileges enjoyed by the Roman Catholic hierarchy under British rule and emancipate French Canadians from the blight of clerical tutelage. Many of the Rouge were also doctrinaire republicans, eager to shed monarchic British institutions. They were, however, merely a fringe of the French, who as a whole opposed annexation, well aware that their balance-of-power political position in Canadian politics—forfeit if they joined the United States—was the surest guarantee of their way of life. Only in the 1880's and 1890's was this solid loyalty shaken, and then because of alarm over the rising tide of English and Protestant intolerance. When the French realized the exaggeration of their fears, the aberration soon disappeared.

Aside from such secondary causes, annexationism was, as stated, the product of economic forces, which also determined the distribution of its strength. Again the three movements showed basic similarities. Each tended to thrive in the commercial cities, where annexation would increase trade, and in the border areas, where the inhabitants were conscious of economic disparities between the two countries and were eager to invade nearby American markets.

As common factors gave birth to the three major movements, common factors killed them. One of these was the consistent opposition of Imperial authorities to continental union. The

British government, speaking through Lord Grey, denounced the agitation of 1849-1850 and appealed to the colonists to preserve their ties with the Empire. In the sixties, authorities in London hastened confederation as a bulwark against annexation, encouraged the Dominion to expand from sea to sea, and turned their backs upon those who petitioned to escape the new union. Thereafter, the British government consistently supported efforts to integrate the Dominion and frowned upon attempts to bring Canada closer economically or politically to the United States. It seems evident that the Imperial opposition to annexation grew more from a desire to contain the Republic than from efforts to retain Canada. British authorities frankly stated that Canadians were masters of their own destiny. If they chose to join the United States, no hindrance would be placed before them; if they chose not to join the United States, the British would resist, even to war, attempts to force them into such a union. In fact, the Imperial government anticipated the ultimate independence of Canada and sought primarily to bolster it against the pull toward the United States.

Economic and emotional factors were, however, more important than opposition from London in balking the annexation movement. The onset of depressions caused the aggitations, and the return of prosperity killed them. The depressions which produced the movements of 1849-1850 and of the post-confederation period were limited in extent and did not directly affect the majority of the people of British North America. The weakness in the vitals of the movement was its materialistic appeal and lack of sentimental counterweights to offset Canadian loyalty to country and Empire. This loyalty seemed greatest where economic distress rested lightly, but many who suffered from the depressions, ignoring self-interest, spurned annexation as a refuge only for mercenary traitors. Even ardent advocates of continental union slipped quietly back to loyalty when economic conditions returned to normal. The first two agitations vanished when British America was again prosperous, and the third disappeared when it became evident, after 1893, that Canadian conditions were better than those in the United States.

A corollary to Canadian devotion to the Dominion and Empire was a reciprocal, and often virulent, dislike which many harbored for the United States. This grew, and always will to some extent, partly from the inevitable fear and resentment of a smaller nation tucked against a great power. Beyond this, Canadians regarded the American form of government as inexplicable and inferior to their own. They watched with mixed wonder and disgust the workings of American republicanism with its frequent scandals, its embattled deadlocks between executive and legislature, and its flamboyant, brawling, national campaigns, so different from their own restrained canvasses. Since the years between the Civil War and 1900 represent a nadir in the quality and integrity of American political institutions and leadership, it is not surprising that many Canadians opposed annexation in revulsion at the thought of living under such a form of government.

The outward manifestations of American social change were also repellent. The Republic was undergoing basic revolutions —industrialization, urbanization, and attempts to digest swarms of immigrants. These processes engendered unattractive external convulsions—rising crime rates, altering moral standards, a growing class of rootless paupers, and the contrasting ostentatious antics of the parvenu. Canada, almost untouched by these developments and maladjustments, watched them with disgust and attributed them to inferior institutions and character which annexation would force them to share. To most in the Dominion, the presumed social and political degradation which union with the United States would bring more than outweighed its economic attractions.

Similarly, on the American side, indifference and even hostility was the general attitude toward annexation. Most Americans remained coolly indifferent to the agitations in the north and in their own country. The general fear of Canada as a British base threatening the United States had reached its climax during the War of 1812, flared up briefly during and after the Civil War, but generally declined. Before the middle of the nineteenth century, it was apparent that the interior provinces would be likely victims of the American army in the event of a war with Great Britain. Even confederation left Canada a British hostage, more than a British menace, to the United States. When the American drive to acquire the provinces as a measure of defense lost its validity, a basic cause of annexation became more a memory than a force. Even the call of Manifest Destiny to the north was heard only fitfully and weakly. In 1849, recent acquisitions from Mexico had stated the American appetite for territory and cooked up a surplus of domestic discord. In the postconfederation period the problems and strains of reconstruction occupied American energies. Then and thereafter, it was evident that annexation might be a prelude to conflict with Great Britain, and the United States had had its fill of war. In the 1880's and 1890's, most Americans felt that the Republic was already beset with too many problems. Why, then, double its size and troubles by the annexation of a depression-ridden country afflicted with thorny strife between French and English?

The American movement for political union was thus spotty and localized. It is obvious that the inhabitants of the southern states, remote from the colonies, had no interest in acquiring them, for they saw little to fear in a British Canada and little to gain from an American Canada. The single flash of interest in the western and mountain states was their brief desire to annex British Columbia after the Civil War. Only the eastern and midwestern states, bordering on or near Canada, showed consistent interest in the Dominion, or any part thereof. Even here it is possible to detect three distinct streams of opinion, with only a minority of active annexationists. Those who desired to acquire Canada were the men who profited from trade with the provinces and wanted to liberate it permanently from fettering tariffs. In addition, many American industrialists hoped to have free access to Canadian markets.

These annexationists had to contend not only with indifference but with an important opposition in their own country. Many Americans feared that Canadian producers would flood the markets of the United States with their cheaper raw materials and force prices down. The arguments used in support of annexation in Canada, and the occupations of those who supported it there, gave substance to this apprehension. Consequently, many farmers, dairymen, quarriers, and lumbermen—and even a few manufacturers—in the United States opposed continental union.

A third, and considerable, group in the eastern and midwestern states were passive annexationists. They favored continentalism, or considered it inevitable, but refused to commit the slightest motion to bring it about lest such action arouse Canadian anger and British resistance, even to the point of war. Inertia was the true policy, they believed, for destiny in good time would deliver the prize if man abstained from clumsy interference. The appeal of this doctrine is obvious. Though it entailed neither action nor risk, it promised great gain, truly something for nothing. There were, as always, skeptics who querulously wondered just what process in inactivity could produce this magnificent result. The impatient answer was an analogy. If one permitted fruit to ripen, it would fall from the tree. If this explanation did not satisfy all who heard it, it was nevertheless seldom challenged.

In summary, it can be said that mong the people of the United States an annexation "movement" in the strict sense of that word did not really exist. Most Americans were hostile or indifferent to the project; others favored it but waited complacently for some slow inscrutable process to drop an unresisting Canada into the embrace of the United States. The few who were active were not only a minority but generally an unorganized one. They found many reasons to plead for continental union, but few positive actions to take. Two exceptions should be recalled. The attempt to obtain the Red River region in 1869-1870 was organized, financed, and directed by Jay Cooke. This was undoubtedly the best led and articulated of the American movements. In the 1890's, prominent Americans joined the Continental Union League and financed its activities, but lost interest when the agitation made little headway.

The real threat to Canada was less in such feeble annexation efforts and outcries among the general populace than from the works of prominent American politicians. Fish, Grant, Blaine, and assorted congressmen wanted the Dominion and sought to obtain it on the diplomatic and political level. Grant and Fish repeatedly urged the Imperial government to surrender its North American prize, and Blaine used the pressure of coercion to persuade the Canadian people that their separate existence was unsupportable. Numerous bills were introduced in Congress to invite or facilitate annexation. These actions apparently grew in part from a desire to protect the United States and to injure Great Britain by foreclosing her North American holdings and partly from a desire for personal fame and historical prestige. Certainly, he who doubled the area of the United States and pruned the British Empire of its finest colony at a single stroke would have a deathless name in the annals of the Republic. And the American people would probably accept such an act as a *fait accompli.* But the efforts of these leaders, except Blaine, were subject to early and easy discouragement. Blaine worked with cold and relentless persistence, but his fall from power abruptly terminated his fruitless venture.

Thus the movement failed because it could not command the support of a majority, or anything like a majority, of the people on either side of the line. Furthermore, the nature of the agitation prevented its reaching its summit simultaneously in both countries. Economic distress brought annexationism to its peak in Canada but, at the same time, made it unattractive to the United States as a material asset. Since annexationism lacked the majority to become a reality through the democratic process, American conquest of the Dominion remained as the only certain method of uniting the countries. After the War of 1812, this idea was repugnant to the great majority of Americans, who had little desire to gain Canada by any means. Even the ardent annexationists in the United States shrank back from the use of force; only an unscrupulous and foolhardy handful of them favored aggression to gain their ends. This was most clearly evident at the end of the Civil War when, although the Republic had a large army and navy and an accumulation of grievances against Canada and Britain, those who urged an attack upon the provinces were an insignificant minority. Obviously, if the annexationists could not win the support of a popular majority and refused to employ naked force to gain their goal, the failure of their movement was foreordained.

What effects did the annexation movement, despite its repeated failures, have upon the two countries? Relatively, American history has been less influenced by the agitation than Canadian history. Here, it was a component of Manifest Destiny, a basic factor in American development. But the drive to the north was less important, and much less successful, than the drive to the west and southwest, where expansion did not confront a major and menacing power. The annexation movement in the United States was also a thread in the complex pattern of struggle over commercial policy. Both the advocates of a high tariff and economic nationalism and the supporters of low tariff and internationalism contended that their particular policy would promote annexation. This was a minor factor in the outcome of policy determination, however, since it had no important audience or appeal.

In the case of Canada, on the other hand, the annexation movement had been a major dynamic in historical development. For one thing, it profoundly affected the relationship between Britain and her North American colonies. It is no accident that Canada has been the bellwether leading the way up the slow and tortuous path to dominion status and practical independence for a large section of the British Empire. The presence of the United States gave Canada a potential alternative to British rule and curbed any inclination of Imperial officials to deal brusquely with their American dependencies. The memory of the American Revolution and the threat of continental union hung darkly over their councils and decisions and generally impelled them ultimately, and often reluctantly, to yield concessions on which Canada insisted. Among other things, these included the grant of responsible government and of commercial autonomy. The individual provinces and interest groups, in their turn, found this efficacious weapon too good to ignore and used it against the Dominion. In this way, Manitoba secured provincial rather than territorial status, and Nova Scotia and British Columbia gained better financial and other terms. Those with grievances were often not slow to imply that lack of redress by Canada would impel them to look toward the United States. Perhaps most of these "annexation movements" were counterfeit, but authorities could never be quite certain of this and often attempted to allay the grievances which had caused them. Nor could they forget that the political union outcries of the Nova Scotian antis, spurious at first, became genuine when their demands were repulsed. The ugly word "annexation" did not have to be uttered in situations of tension; its presence was implicit.

The influence of the annexation movement on developments in Canada has been as great as its effects upon Empire-Dominion and federal-provincial relations. The people of British America have always been aware of the forces, human and natural, ceaselessly at work to pull their country closer to the United

States. Their conscious efforts to counteract these forces have been at least partly responsible for the enactment of many of the great policies of Canadian history such as the treaty of 1854, the formation of the Dominion and its transcontinental expansion, the building of the Intercolonial and Canadian Pacific railroads, the adoption of the National Policy, and the careful cultivation and development of nationalism. The effects linger even today, when anxiety at the growth of American investment in the Dominion has made Canadians apprehensive that economic penetration will lead to economic control and ultimately produce political penetration and control. These alarms, incidents, and policies have been the cordillera of Canadian history, the upthrust of deeper strata. Fear of annexation has been a dominant factor in the psychology of politically alert and concerned Canadians and, consciously or subconsciously, has led them to weigh proposed policies, in any way connected with the United States, in light of their possible relationship to annexation.

Bibliographical Essay

Inquiry into the subject of annexation presents several knotty problems. The most daunting of these, the questions of the motivation of men and the reliability of materials, have already been described in the preface. Another difficulty was the great variety of possible sources of information and the relatively sparse and widely scattered facts to be found in any one of them, with a few exceptions to be noted below. Understandably, annexation was not a popular topic nor a frequently mentioned one in Canada. The author has combed the likely, and a good many of the unlikely, sources. The law of diminishing returns and the restrictions of time have necessarily limited the search. Doubtless, other newspapers and collections of correspondence would have yielded some additional data, but a considerable amount of panning would be necessary for every nugget washed out, and in all probability, these would do no more than add confirmatory detail to the narrative already established. Even in the most fruitful sources, there are many arid stretches of six, eight, even twelve months when letter files or newspaper volumes do not yield a single item of applicable information.

Within the bounds of these qualifications, certain materials may be identified as the essential bases for this study, and the most important of these are the manuscript sources, particularly the ones to be found in the Public Archives of Canada. Here the enormous, but carefully divided, collection of Sir John A. Macdonald Papers was indispensable. There is at least some information in many of its numerous volumes, but the most important were those on Nova Scotia Affairs, Governor-Generals' Correspondence, Commercial Union, General Elections, and the Letter Books for the years 1867 to 1871 and 1887 to 1891.

The correspondence of Sir John's associates, Sir Charles Tupper and Joseph Howe, furnished the basis of the story of annexationism in Nova Scotia. The Sir Wilfred Laurier Papers, and particularly those for 1890-1893, were a mine of information on party politics, commercial union, unrestricted reciprocity, and annexationism within the Liberal Party. Equally valuable for approximately the same period were the George Denison Papers. Denison was a superpatriot who ardently pursued information about the disloyal and the suspect, and corresponded voluminously with others of like interest. Less important except for an occasional item were the Sir Alexander T. Galt Papers and the "G" series, the correspondence of the Governors General. In the latter set, volume G 573 A, Secret and Confidential Despatches, 1867-1869, was very useful.

American manuscript materials, found largely in the National Archives, were generally less helpful than those in Canada. The Consular Despatches to the Department of State, coming from cities all over Canada, were principally commercial in content but often had political material. A number of consuls were interested in the agitation for continental union, and those in Winnipeg, Montreal, and Toronto were particularly faithful in reporting its progress to their superiors in Washington. The official correspondence contained in the Diplomatic Despatches, Great Britain; Diplomatic Instructions, Great Britain; and Diplomatic Notes, Great Britain, had some references to annexation, particularly in the post confederation period. The volumes of Miscellaneous Letters to the Department of State were a mine of material, containing letters and petitions from Canadian and American advocates of annexation.

In addition to the above, the Foreign Office, Great Britain, Series 5, comprising the correspondence between the British minister at Washington and the Foreign Office, was valuable in its revelation of the attitudes of British officials toward annexation. Photostats of this collection are in the Library of Congress.

The Minnesota Historical Society has two collections of great value in tracing the story of the annexation movement which accompanied the Riel rebellion. They are the Alexander Ramsey Papers and the James W. Taylor Papers, documents left by two of the principal American actors in that drama.

A number of printed American official sources yielded information of considerable significance. The *Congressional Globe* was valuable for the period from 1865 to 1871, particularly the debates of the 41st Congress, 2nd session. The *Congressional Record,* on the other hand, had only scattered references to annexation, since motions to consummate it did not come up for debate after the 1860's. Of the congressional documents, only the Senate and House reports yielded important data. *Senate Reports,* 51 Cong., 1 sess., no. 1530, should be mentioned for its considerable volume of information on all aspects of Canadian-American relations, including the movement for annexation.

On the Imperial side, the *Debates of the House of Commons* of the Canadian Parliament had many references to annexation, especially for the sessions of 1887, 1888, and 1889. However, the Canadian *Sessional Papers* and the British sources such as Hansard's *Parliamentary Debates* and the British parliamentary papers had very few mentions of continental union, though they were useful for background material, especially on reciprocity and economic conditions.

Of the nonofficial printed sources, *The Elgin-Grey Papers, 1846-1852,* 4 vols. (Ottawa, 1937), edited by Sir Arthur Doughty, were indispensable for the annexation movement of 1849-1850. They contain correspondence between the Governor General and the colonial secretary, to which the editor has added excellent commentary, some additional dispatches, and many of the enclosures contained in the original communications. A few of the autobiographies, memoirs, and reminiscences consulted added some information, the most useful being Sir Joseph Pope, *The Memoirs of the Right Honorable Sir John Alexander Macdonald,* 2 vols. (London, 1894).

Of the considerable number of secondary works consulted, both books and periodicals, only a few can be mentioned here. These fall into two groups: some were useful for background material, but were not used in the book in the sense of being cited; others were both useful and used. The appropriate volumes of the Carnegie series on the relations of Canada and the United States are good examples of the second category. Those most important to this study were Lester B. Shippee, *Canadian-American Relations, 1849-1874* (New Haven, 1939); Charles C. Tansill, *Canadian-American Relations, 1875-1911* (New Haven, 1943); and Frederic W. Howay, Walter N. Sage, and Henry F. Angus, *British Columbia and the United States* (Toronto, 1942). These volumes span the entire period of the annexation agitation, as does James M. Callahan, *American Foreign Policy in Canadian Relations* (New York, 1937), which is useful but is also exasperating because of its organization and method of citation.

For the movement of 1849-1850, the one important secondary work directly on the topic is the comprehensive volume by Cephas D. Allin and George M. Jones, *Annexation, Preferential* Trade and Reciprocity (Toronto, 1912). The economic background of the period, including the treaty of 1854, is well described in Donald G. Creighton, *The Commercial Empire of the St. Lawrence* (Toronto, 1937), also in the Carnegie series; Gilbert N. Tucker, *The Canadian Commercial Revolution, 1845-1851* (New Haven, 1936); Donald C. Masters, *The Reciprocity Treaty of 1854* (London, 1937); and Charles C. Tansill, *The Canadian Reciprocity Treaty of 1854* (Baltimore, 1922).

Material for the postconfederation period is much more abundant. The superb political biography by Donald G. Creighton, *John A. Macdonald: The Old Chieftain* (Boston, 1956), is indispensable for the years to 1891 and demonstrates the influence which fear of the United States had upon the thinking and policies of Macdonald. Allan Nevins, *Hamilton Fish: The Inner History of the Grant Administration* (New York, 1936), describes the attempt to use the *Alabama* claims as a means of acquiring Canada, and contains some information on annexationism in the Dominion. Also on the American side of the movement, Joe Patterson Smith, *Republican Expansionists of the Early Reconstruction Era* (Chicago, 1933), shows that the Radical Republicans used expansionist doctrines to garner votes rather than to gain Canada. Also useful was Reginald G. Trotter, *Canadian Federation, Its Origins and Achievements* (Toronto, 1924). It is the standard work on the subject and includes information on the extension of the Dominion from sea to sea.

A considerable and excellent literature on the first Riel rebellion was important to the study of annexation. The classic accounts, Alexander Begg, *History of the North-West*, 3 vols. (Toronto, 1894-1895), and Arthur S. Morton, *A History of the Canadian West to 1870-1871* (London, 1939), were supplemented by George F. G. Stanley, *The Birth of Western Canada* (London, 1936); William L. Morton, *Manitoba: A History* (Toronto, 1957), a model for local histories; and Robert E. Lamb, *Thunder in the North* (New York, 1957), a study of the effects of both Riel rebellions on the relations between English and French Canadians. Also useful was George Bryce, *The Remarkable History of the Hudson's Bay Company* (Toronto, 1910).

Secondary works dealing with the final movement, 1880-1893, were principally biographical in nature. There was much background material on economic and political developments, but almost nothing directly on annexation in Sir John S. Willison, *Sir Wilfred Laurier and the Liberal Party*, 2 vols. (Toronto,

1903); Oscar D. Skelton, *The Life and Letters of Sir Wilfred Laurier* (New York, 1922); and the acutely perceptive John W. Dafoe, *Laurier* (Toronto, 1922). Elisabeth Wallace, *Goldwin Smith: Victorian Liberal* (Toronto, 1957), has brief mention of its subject's annexationist leanings, while George T. Denison, *The Struggle for Imperial Unity* (London, 1909), has a great deal of important data on the movement in the 1890's. On the American side, Alice F. Tyler, *The Foreign Policy of James G. Blaine* (Minneapolis, 1927), was valuable, with modifications in light of the Volwiler article listed below.

Periodical materials used for this study fall into two categories. The first group is articles of opinion contemporary to the annexation movement and advocating its success or failure. Such materials were abundant in the 1880's, though rare earlier, and the articles cited here are samples of a considerable literature. Paul Bender, "A Canadian View of Annexation," *North American Review*, CXXXIV (April, 1883), expresses the view of an advocate of continental union in the Dominion who predicts the ultimate success of the movement for economic reasons, though admitting the strong resistance to it in his country. On the other hand, Frederic G. Mather, "Obstacles to Annexation," *North American Review*, CXXXIII (August, 1881), forecast the failure of the agitation and also because of economic factors. Perhaps the most penetrating of contemporary articles is Joseph Cook, "Political Union with Canada," *Our Day*, IV (August, 1889). The author presents arguments both for and against continental union, leaving the reader to make his own choice.

The second type of periodical material on annexation is the group of recent and historical studies of the movement or of the conditions which produced it. Again, there are too many to be cited *in toto*, and the listing here is confined to some of the important examples. Most of these were found in the *Canadian Historical Review*, the principal ones being Arthur Penny, "The Annexation Movement of 1849," V (1924), which consists largely of correspondence between advocates of political union; John P. Pritchett, "The Origins of the So-Called Fenian Raid on Manitoba in 1871," X (1929); Frank H. Underhill, "Laurier and Blake, 1882-1891," XX (1939); and Alvin C. Gluek, Jr., "The Riel Rebellion and Canadian-American Relations," XXXVI (1955). Several articles in other publications contributed significantly; for example, Theodore C. Blegen, "A Plan for the Union of British North America and the United States, 1866," *Mississippi Valley Historical Review,* IV (1918). Walter N. Sage, "The Annexation Movement in British Columbia," Royal Society of Canada, *Transactions,* 3d ser. XXI (1927), gives a succinct account of the economic background in British Columbia, and the struggle between the annexationists and the confederationists. Some new insights on the policy of the Harrison administration are given in Albert T. Volwiler, "Harrison, Blaine, and American Foreign Policy, 1889-1893," American Philosophical Society, *Proceedings,* LXXIX (1938).

The final important source for the study of annexationism was the newspapers. Some thirty papers were used, selected for geographic coverage and representation of the various points of view in the two countries. Their value and reliability varied greatly. For Canadian news and opinion in general, the Toronto *Globe* was useful, while the Halifax *Morning Chronicle* and the Winnipeg *Manitoba Free Press* gave thorough regional coverage for the Maritimes and the West respectively. The Yarmouth *Herald,* St. John *Morning Freeman,* and New Glasgow *Eastern Chronicle* were authentic voices of Canadian annexationism. The Quebec *Morning Chronicle* spoke for the minority in its province and gave some general coverage, while the Montreal *Pays* and *Patrie* represented French-Canadian opinion. The Victoria *Daily British Colonist and Chronicle* was indispensable for information about the movement in British Columbia.

In the United States, the New York *Times,* at most a passive annexationist journal, was by far the most valuable for its wide coverage and the restraint with which it handled the news. The annexationist papers consulted included the Chicago *Tribune,* St. Paul *Daily Press,* New York *Herald,* and Detroit *Evening News.* The last was exceptionally useful, for it sent writers into the Dominion to report the movement there at first hand. Though it was a strong advocate of annexation, its reports were uniformly reliable insofar as it was possible to check them against independent sources.

Index

DATE DUE
APR 24 1990
MAY 28 2002
JUN 28 1971
JAN 26 1976
NOV 27 1989